THE HORSES UNITE

Origins of The Horses Know Trilogy

LYNN MANN

Coxstone Press

ISBN 978-1-7393276-2-0
Published by Coxstone Press 2023

For Fern
for everything

Chapter One

There was a new trainee enforcer out on the streets with her mentor and handlers this morning. Just when I think I've got used to seeing the fear in the enforcers' eyes, I see another one, too young to have been dulled by it all and with a freshly administered, oozing identification brand, who reminds me I haven't.

Secret diary of Charlotte Lace

IT WAS dark in the back of the van, but my eyes easily picked up the glint in my mentor's eyes as he sat opposite me. I sensed his anticipation. His dread. His effort to control his emotions so that his heart and breathing rates remained below the threshold that would trigger the chip implanted in his skull to cause him pain. I sensed all of those things acutely because I was desperately focusing all my attention on following his example. Everything he did, I had to do if I wanted to remain alive.

QMB61 was old for our kind. He barely spoke due to the

amount of thickened tissue obstructing his throat, but he could still breathe and lead by example, and he did the latter well. My mentor had trained more enforcers than any other to qualification status and the resulting permission to remain alive, so when he nodded to me in praise of my success at keeping my emotions as controlled as his own, continuing to do so immediately felt a little easier. Knowing that there wasn't enough light for our human handlers to see me, I nodded back to him.

The van lurched to one side suddenly and then jolted as we crossed the rails used by passenger vehicles. I sensed as well as saw the smiles of the four handlers who sat one on either side of QMB61 and one on either side of me. If their hands had been free to rub together in glee, they would have done so, but as it was, they hung on to the harnesses that strapped them to the sides of the van as if expecting them to give way at any moment. For that was what humans were like; they were afraid of everything, even when they were busy evoking fear in others. They knew we had to be near our destination for the van to have veered between PVs, and they were delighted that doing so would have drawn maximum attention to the presence of one of the few vehicles that wasn't restricted to the tracks that scarred the city – and the only type that carried enforcers. Everyone in the vicinity would be terrified that it was they whom we enforcers had been tasked to kill.

The van screeched to a stop. My heart rate increased in line with QMB61's as fear bombarded us from all sides.

FE88. Refocus, my mentor instructed me, as sparing with his mindspeak as he was with his spoken words. As soon as my attention was back on him, he took hold of it, drawing it within himself so that his strength of will bolstered mine. Together, we slowed our hearts, smoothed out our emotions, and focused our minds. Together, we concentrated on the adult male we had been sent to kill.

The computers that sent data to our brains via our chips told us that five minutes previously, Colin Graham had entered the building outside which we were sitting, and that four minutes and three seconds after that, the eye scanner outside his apartment had allowed his entry. Our sixth sense, possessed only by our kind and kept secret from the humans, told us he knew we were on our way and was currently screaming at his wife to hide in a cupboard with their youngling.

The doors at the rear of the van were flung open, allowing the weak winter sunlight to reach us. The small hint of warmth carried to us by its rays was obliterated by the coldness in the eyes of the human who stood glaring at us.

'Get out and do your job,' he snarled, looking between QMB61 and me. 'And make it messy. Let everyone know what happens to those who dare to talk back to me.'

Distance yourself. Now. QMB61 stared at me as he drilled his instruction firmly into my mind.

I drew myself back from the horror of what we were about to do, dispersing my mind within my body as QMB61 had repeatedly taught me during the many months I had been shadowing him. I was in my fingers as they clicked the buttons on either side of my harness clip. I was in the palms of my hands as they pulled the harness straps down my arms. I was in the muscles of my legs as they contracted and relaxed until I was standing outside the van, breathing in air that stank of humans and their fear.

I checked my sense of the male who would shortly be dead, not allowing myself to remember his name or anything about him, but merely homing in on his precise location within his apartment. I made the mistake of giving too much of my mind to the task. His terror filtered down the part that I had extended to him, and my heart began to pound. The monitors strapped to the forearms of the two handlers assigned to me beeped shrilly and continuously, causing my heart to pound faster and harder. Had I not been on assignment, the pain that always followed any loss of self-control would have been inflicted automatically. Since my handlers expected my heart to pound with the physical effort of what I would soon be doing, they had disabled the auto setting on my control program, and the decision regarding whether to inflict pain was theirs.

Neither of them hesitated. Pain exploded in my head in one spot after another, as if I were being stoned like I frequently had been while being exercised on the streets as a youngling. I sank to my knees, my hands pressed to my head. When the pain stopped, I hastened back to my feet, knowing from bitter experience that if I were slow to do so, the pain would return. Even so, one of my handlers flexed his fingers while grinning evilly at me, then made a show of moving one of them back towards the screen of his monitor.

My other handler clasped hold of his wrist and said between her teeth, 'That's enough, Joe. She still has a job to do.' She glared at me and said, 'Control yourself, else I'll give you what he was about to and more. Get yourself gone.' She glanced nervously at the man who had ordered us out of the van, and I sensed her relief when he gave her a curt nod.

FE88. Distance. QMB61 was very deliberately firm. If I were to avoid more pain, I had to do better.

I retreated to the depths of my body, taking refuge in its warmth and strength so that I didn't have to think about what was about to happen as I moved into position on the pavement beside QMB61. The tendril of my sixth sense that I extended to our target was much thinner this time. The second it locked on to him, I allowed my body to do that which it knew – following years of training – it had to do.

I sprang in unison with QMB61, my relatively short and yet powerful legs propelling me up past a ground-floor window to the wall beside a first-floor one. I glanced across to where QMB61 clung to the wall on the other side of the window and felt the elation that always surged within both of us as soon as we were out of the reach of humans. They wouldn't risk causing us pain when it could cause us to lose our grip and concentration and fall to our deaths, so for the minute or so that it would take to reach our destination, we were the closest we ever got to being safe. To being free.

We bounded up the wall, so confident that the talons afforded us by our raptor genes would take hold of the crevices sought out by our sharp, feline eyes at a moment's notice, that we didn't hesitate to put the full force of our strength behind every upward leap.

I relished breathing the air that grew crisper and cleaner the higher we ascended up the grey high-rise building. When a lone predator swooped through it close by, I moved a small part of my mind to sit with hers. She welcomed me, knowing I did not intend to cause her harm but merely wanted to connect – to fly with her so that for a few seconds at least, I could experience what it was like to soar out of reach of evil.

When I felt my body preparing to change its movement from climbing to swinging, I reluctantly returned all of my attention to it but stayed within its depths so that it could do its job without interference from a mind that would never cope with what it had been ordered to do.

I pushed away from the wall with my toes while clinging on with my fingers so that I swung out in an arc. I crashed through a window of the target's apartment in the same instant that QMB61 hurled himself through the next one along, the toughened glass no match for either of us and shattering into thousands of tiny, blunt fragments. We landed side by side, knowing that we had reached the point at which the synchronisation of our attack was at an end.

It had always been QMB61 who dispatched our target while I watched him demonstrate the different ways of doing so. This was to be my first kill. If I performed it satisfactorily and without the monitors informing my handlers that I had lost control of myself, I would graduate from a trainee enforcer to a fully fledged one. I would live. If I didn't, I would likely spend some hours writhing in pain on the apartment floor before being put to death by lethal injection.

'Distance,' QMB61 reminded me, his raspy voice almost a whisper. 'And speed.'

His spoken words did exactly as he intended and reached my body without drawing my mind out of its hiding place.

I leapt to the corner of the living room within which the target was curled up, whimpering. I ended his misery with a single slash of my talons and flung him out of the window; the humans had ordered me to make it messy.

I had fulfilled the first part of my assignment. Now I needed to show that I was unaffected by my actions – that I was still fully in control of myself and could behave within my defined parameters. In order to do that, I needed to be fully present.

QMB61 was in front of me before I could succumb to the horror, rage, self-loathing and grief that accompanied the re-emergence of my mind from the depths of my body.

FE88. Move past it all. He took hold of my arms and gently shook me. His green eyes, dull after twenty years of doing exactly as he was instructing me to do, never left mine. *It is done. Move. Past. It.*

I focused on my breathing as I stared into his eyes, which

widened slightly as a scream sounded in the next room, followed by a second muffled one. Having almost managed to side-step my own feelings, the wave of unbridled terror and grief accompanying the screams hit me with devastating impact. I had to get out of there. I sensed QMB61's agreement and neither of us hesitated further. We leapt for the windows through which we had crashed only minutes before, each trusting our body's muscle memory to guide us through them and back down the wall of the building.

Desperate to take charge of my sixth sense before I reached the ground, I immersed myself in everything that assailed my other five. I fixed my eyes on the clear sky and allowed its vibrant blue to refresh me. I welcomed the sound of joyful cheeping emitted by a flock of small beaked ones as they swooped past. I relished the feeling of the solid grey wall giving way to my talons as I drove them deeper into the crevices I had used on the way up. I both smelt and tasted the myriad of particles carried from somewhere far away by the breath of winter breeze that oozed between the tall buildings.

As I felt myself calming, I tentatively allowed my sixth sense to inform me of the terror and revulsion of all those whose windows we passed, and their relief once we were out of sight. The grudging admiration of our handlers reached me as they watched the results of the genetic experiments undertaken by their scientists fulfilling the potential for which we were bred. By the time I was halfway to the ground, I had myself under control.

Then I sensed the presence of Charlotte Lace.

Chapter Two

I couldn't help myself. I had to intervene, if only for a second, to let Enforcer FE88 know I'm on her side. I think she sensed my sympathy for her, but it's hard to say when they're all too scared to even look the wrong way in case their handlers abuse them further. Of all the enforcers, trainee and qualified alike, she bothers me the most. I can't put my finger on why, there's just something about her that gets to me more than the others. She'll have qualified after today's events, so I'll see if Michael can get me her duty schedule so I can continue to come into contact with her as much as I've managed to during her training.

Secret diary of Charlotte Lace

MY HEART POUNDED in my chest at a greater rate than that for which my physical exertion could account… but only for a short while. Before I could drown in the shame and misery that her presence at my first kill had evoked, Charlotte Lace enfolded me in everything she was. She didn't know she was doing it. She barely even knew me. But her concern for me, and the desire I could feel within her to ease my mind, had the effect they always did. By the time I dropped to the pavement in the same instant as QMB61, my emotions and vital signs were steady.

One of my handlers glanced at her monitor and tapped its screen, reverting both its supervision of my parameters and its potential pain administration to automatic. Neither of QMB61's handlers bothered to do the same; they knew QMB61 wouldn't deviate from his parameters, and were listening to the loud address their boss was giving the group of adults and teenage younglings of which Charlotte Lace was a member. The group had stopped to stare at the bloody mess that I couldn't allow myself to acknowledge, but to which the aggressive male now pointed.

'That's what happens when I speak and someone speaks back to me without very careful thought,' he said. 'Does anyone have a question?'

My heart sank when Charlotte Lace raised her hand and said, 'Yes, I do.' Her expression was blank and her voice warm. 'Officer Turner, isn't it?'

He scowled. 'And you are?' She smiled an easy smile, and I sensed his confusion and sudden doubt. His scowl faltered.

Charlotte Lace stepped in front of a youngling – whom I sensed was her daughter – so that she blocked her from viewing the horror on the street, and held out her hand to Officer Turner. 'Charlotte Lace. Thank you for all you do for us, we appreciate your intention to keep us all safe, don't we, kids?' She turned to look behind her and smiled at the younglings, most of whom were visibly terrified. A few shifted from one foot to the other and many bit their lips or the insides of their cheeks, but all of them nodded silently, and those whose eyes rose to meet hers relaxed a little. She turned back to Officer Turner. 'My question is this. How does it feel to be so powerful?'

He stood a little straighter, stuck his chest out, and smiled with his mouth while his eyes remained hard and cold. 'You will never know.'

'No, of course not. So, could you possibly tell us?' Charlotte Lace swept her arm behind her. 'It would be great for the kids to know.'

I didn't dare look across at QMB61 but I didn't need to; I sensed his enjoyment as he realised what Charlotte Lace was up to. She knew as well as did we that Officer Turner would struggle to describe how it felt to be powerful, for he didn't know.

'How does it feel to have forty-two qualified enforcers, twenty-eight trainees and a hundred and forty handlers – although that number just decreased to a hundred and thirty-nine,' Officer Turner added, nodding at the corpse the rest of us were trying to ignore, '– waiting to obey my orders?'

Charlotte Lace smiled and nodded encouragingly.

'It feels like… like… nothing you can imagine.'

'We'd all like your help to try, wouldn't we?' Charlotte Lace said, nodding so that everyone behind her nodded too.

'It feels like… I'm… invincible.' The male's throat defied his lie by constricting as he said the last word, so that his voice almost squeaked. He swallowed hard. 'BECAUSE I AM INVINCIBLE,' he bellowed, looking at every member of the group before him. 'And don't any of you ever forget it.'

'We'll be very sure not to,' Charlotte Lace replied, as if he had just said something pleasant. 'I'm surprised, though. I thought you might say you felt calm and strong, maybe even better able to sleep at night than the rest of us, but I'm sure feeling invincible tops all of those things. Well, we won't stand in your way any longer. Come on, everyone, or we'll be late for your youth interaction session. Thank you for your time, Officer Turner. A very good day to you.' She lifted a hand and waved cheerfully, then darted across the street. The younglings, and the two other adults escorting them, followed her without looking back.

Charlotte Lace glanced back though, directly at me, then hurried onward, leaving her thoughts to me in her wake. *Your actions change nothing. Hold on to who you are because you're beautiful and wonderful.*

As are you, I replied, knowing she couldn't hear me. None of the "kindred", as they called themselves, could, but they suspected we could hear their thoughts and acted accordingly. We couldn't confirm their suspicion without endangering them, but they continued their thankless task of lifting our spirits whenever they could anyway, and they never knew how many of us they saved as a result.

Officer Turner was less brash than normal when he ordered the "ex-handler" to be left on the street as a warning, and then all of us back into the van. He drove more slowly, more carefully – more thoughtfully – back to the enforcer building than he had on the way out, and I sensed his need for time to himself to think.

He felt shaken and he had no idea why. He rarely led a task force out on assignment nowadays – maybe he had just gone soft in the head after sitting at a desk too much in recent years? He thought back to the events of the past half hour and shook his head. No. He hadn't flinched at the order he had given, or its results, and everyone had been terrified of him, including the newly qualified enforcer. She would start her career full of respect for the man in charge of her unit. Everything had gone exactly to plan and after the news spread of the swift and deadly consequence of any handler questioning his decisions, no one would dare to do it again. So then, why did he need to hold on to the steering wheel so tightly to prevent his hands from trembling? The woman who had questioned him popped into his mind. What was her name? Lace. Somebody Lace, that was it.

I sensed him clutch the steering wheel even more tightly, and then we were all thrown sideways, re-testing the strength and attachment status of our harnesses, as he braked and then swerved suddenly to avoid something in our path – a toolbox, he thought, left by some moron working on a stationary passenger vehicle. All four of our handlers jumped as he sounded the horn. He kept pressing it, enjoying the release it gave him from his mental discomfort, until the broken-down PV was far behind us.

Knowing there were microphones that relayed all sounds from the back of the van to those sitting in the front, the handlers all clamped their mouths shut to prevent any curses slipping out in response to the rough ride into which our return journey had rapidly descended. QMB61 and I were delighted. All the kindred undermined the governors, police, heads of departments and informers of the city whenever an opportunity presented itself, and those that survived their early attempts became very good at it. Charlotte Lace, it appeared, was a master at it, as Officer Turner had just experienced.

His driving settled down again, and the handler on my left breathed out slowly. I sensed it wouldn't last; our driver wasn't feeling any better for his outburst. Sure enough, it wasn't long before all of us in the back were thrown alternately into our harnesses and then against the walls of the van as he weaved sharply from left to right in the space between the PV tracks. QMB61's eyes shone in the darkness as he and I sensed nausea arising in our handlers, swiftly accompanied by fear of what Office Turner would do to them if they expelled the contents of their stomachs onto the floor of the van. Having enjoyed Charlotte Lace's exchange with the man who was now driving like a lunatic, we were enjoying its aftereffects even more.

The first of the handlers vomited, followed swiftly by the second and third. The fourth released his hold on his harness in order to clamp his hands over his mouth and held on for almost another minute before following their example. I was glad that they couldn't see my and my mentor's smiles, for we could never have stopped them from forming. I was only sad that my fangs prevented me from smiling as widely as humans could.

The sound of vomiting finally reached Officer Turner's ears over the screeching of the van's tires, and he stopped swerving. I felt his evil grin as he realised what had happened and planned how he would make our handlers' lives a misery after our return to headquarters. He almost felt normal as a result of his plotting. Almost. I sensed him release his grip on the wheel slightly and then grasp it firmly, his stomach lurching, as he realised his hands were still trembling. What was wrong with him? His mind flicked back to the last time he had been considering the question.

The woman. Lace. He relived his conversation with her and could find no trace of disrespect, nothing on which he should have picked her up, let alone arrested her. It couldn't be down to her that he was feeling so strange – could it? As he had told her and everyone else, he was invincible. The remains of Handler Graham confirmed it, should any of them have doubted it, and he didn't think any of them had… except Ms Lace's countenance hadn't changed when he pointed it out, and nor had her manner. Of everyone at the scene, she alone had seemed unaffected by any of it. Maybe she was an informer? One he didn't know about? Maybe she was there to assess him in the same way he was assessing the trainee enforcer? No, that didn't fit. She hadn't behaved as if she had any power or influence.

I felt pain shoot through the palm of his hand as he slammed it against the steering wheel in frustration. Then I felt him make a decision. He would make the handlers in the back of his van suffer until he felt better. Then he would run a search on Ms Lace.

I took a deep breath to calm the horror that tried to rise inside me. He wouldn't find anything on her; she was a kindred, and they were always so careful. Weren't they?

I was jolted from my thoughts by the van screeching to a stop.

QFE88. QMB61's thought drew my eyes to meet his as he watched me in the gloom. *That is who you are now. We are unlikely to see one another again now that you have qualified. You are among the strongest I have taught. Remember your training and you will survive. Hold to your connection with the kindred and you will survive with your mind intact.*

Our handlers scrambled out of their harnesses, one of QMB61's mumbling, 'I've never been so glad to get back to Freaks' Paradise.'

His boss opened the van doors and one of my handlers glared at me. 'Get yourself moving or you'll find out the new level of pain you just qualified to receive.' I managed to keep my eyes turned downward, but could not prevent myself stiffening for a few seconds. My handler snickered and turned to my mentor. 'You didn't tell her, QMB61? You kept it from her that the pain limit on her program was doubled as soon as I told it she'd qualified?'

QMB61 also kept his eyes cast downward, his own behaviour always consistent with how he had trained me. *They are even more afraid of you now,* he told me. *It is a sign of their weakness, not yours, that the settings on your program have changed. Remember your training at all times and you will not discover precisely how afraid of you they are.*

He and I got to our feet and waited for our handlers – our betters, as they constantly reminded us – to exit the van before us.

Thank you, QMB61. I owe you my life, I thought to him as Officer Turner began berating our handlers for the mess in the van.

I immediately sensed his remorse. *Do not thank me. I am never sure whether I do right, training you all according to my experience and choices. I choose to abide by their rules in order to stay alive, but I often wonder whether that is merely the coward's way. If we all resisted them, we would die painfully, but at least we would deprive them of the ability to inflict us on those they order us to kill.*

It was all I could do not to turn around to him in surprise, but my training ensured that I instead obediently stepped down from the van when I was bidden. *Resist?* The thought felt strange even as I formed it. I knew what the word meant, and I knew the kindred did it, but I couldn't for the life of me find a way to apply it to our situation. Our choices were obedience, pain or death.

The kindred resist, QMB61 observed pointedly as he walked away from me, following his handlers to "Freaks' Paradise".

Charlotte Lace. My memory of her performance that afternoon regained its place at the forefront of my mind. I turned my attention to Officer Turner, who was already marching through the doors of the enforcer building. Charlotte Lace was on his mind too. Unease churned in my stomach.

Chapter Three

FAO: To whom it may concern, Enforcer Breeding Laboratory
SENDER: Officer Conrad. B. Turner
I hereby send notice that FE88 has met the requirements of
my department and is now qualified enforcer QFE88. She's
strong, efficient and obedient, largely due to the training my
handlers have meted out to her on my orders, but in part
because of her breeding. I expect your assurance that you
will breed more like her and avoid breeding those with
temperaments like MD12, who was exterminated last week
by lethal injection due to repeated incidences of lack of
control. One of his handlers has now also been exterminated
for attempting to persuade me that his charge could be
retrained, which we all know is impossible.

I ALMOST FLINCHED at the shard of pain that caused my vision
to blur. When I managed to refocus, the first thing I saw was my
male handler glaring up at me. 'Eyes front, Enforcer. You'll find

that daydreaming, like everything else, is tolerated even less now than when you were a trainee. The protocol for returning you to your cell has changed too. You don't get one of us in front of you and one behind anymore, you're trusted to follow us both. If you want your legs to move without pain, you'll keep up.'

I didn't have to look at my female handler to know that the corners of her mouth were curling up slightly as the pupils of her eyes widened. She was planning to inflict pain on me regardless of whether I obeyed my instructions. I wasn't trusted at all; QMB61 was right, I was feared. Now that my handlers were alone with me for the first time since I had made my first kill, their fear of me had escalated. They would seek to dominate me to an even greater degree than any of them had to date, in order to teach me my place and to feel safe, as everyone but the kindred dedicated themselves to doing and yet never did.

Without another word, my handlers turned and marched side by side towards the building, neither of them stopping or looking back to make sure I was following. I was four paces behind, but any number would have been too many, short of me breathing on the tops of their heads, which they also would have punished. The female touched the screen of her wrist-bound monitor, and my legs immediately cramped.

I breathed through the pain. By the time we reached the doors of the building, I was a pace behind them, but as I had suspected would be the case, the pain did not abate. I took myself away from my legs and into my chest, where I focused all my effort on maintaining my breathing and heart rates lest they exceeded the parameters of my control program and gave me an even bigger problem.

I breathed my way through the foyer with its cold, grey floor and white walls. I breathed past the logo on one wall – an image of an enforcer with blood dripping from their fangs, enclosed within a circle of the repeated phrase "Keeping You Safe" – and then a wall of hundreds of tiny screens, all showing the constantly changing data transmitted by the chips of enforcers qualified to kill. I breathed through the knowledge that one of those, which would have been blank following the death of its enforcer, would now be live with my data. I breathed my way into the lift, and as I stood waiting for it to descend to floor E. I was hot on the heels of my handlers when the lift doors opened, and breathing through the agony in my legs all the way along the gloomy corridor that was lit by distantly spaced spheres in the ceiling, until I reached cell 88.

Qualified Female, floor E, cell 88. That was me.

'QFE88, you are dismissed,' the female told me coldly as I breathed my way into my cell. It was only once the door had slid closed behind me that the cramping in my legs abated. I staggered to my bunk before they gave way, and sat on it with my head between my legs, still breathing in the same rhythm.

The door slid open and a male I hadn't seen before walked in, holding what looked like a gun with a needle at the end of its barrel. 'You will remain seated,' he told me quietly and confidently, his voice smooth yet almost exploding with aggression. I knew without a doubt that he was never, ever disobeyed.

He moved the gun-like object to the spot where my neck met my chest, and pressed a button. A high-pitched buzzing noise sounded. I breathed through the mild discomfort as he pushed the needle at the end of the gun's barrel into my skin and added to the tattoo that had been there since the day I moved from my dormitory to my cell. As soon as the male had finished adding a "Q" to the "FE88" already branded into my chest, he lowered his instrument and left my cell without another word.

Now that I no longer had to breathe through pain, I expelled with each breath the rage that wanted to take hold of me at my most recent abuse; I needed to clear my mind if I were to help the younglings occupying one of the dormitories on a lower floor, as some of those who had gone before me had helped me when I was young enough to occupy a cot.

I only ever saw a few of those who had helped me; by the time I was ten and moved to cell E88 from my cot in my dormitory, and was eligible for exercise above ground, most of the others had been exterminated for one reason or another. I never forgot the help they gave me and the other younglings who could sense them though. Thirteen of the twenty of us from my dormitory still lived, and most of us helped the younglings in the dormitory we had occupied, whenever we could.

As soon as I had myself under control, I extended my sixth sense to the dormitory. I found it was quiet, since seventeen of its occupants were already using their fledgling sixth sense to connect with other adult enforcers on my floor. I felt some of them trying to reach past the trainee enforcers whose minds soothed their own, and touch the minds of others in their dormitory. I smoothed out the excited leaping of my heart so that I stayed within my parameters, whilst hanging on to my relief at the younglings' sudden advancement. It lifted me through the exhaustion with which my pain and fury had left me, and I reached out to them.

The five reaching for their dormitory mates all sensed me immediately, as did the two trainee enforcers who were using their "down time" – known between us as "recovery time" – to connect with the younglings and give them a sense of soothing calm in the silence and restrictions imposed on them by their control programs, as well as letting them know they weren't as alone as they felt.

You have suffered greatly, QFE88, but you are still with us. Relief accompanied ME96's thought.

I'll be eligible for my first assignment in five weeks and two days' time, FE24 told us both, continuing the daily countdown she had begun after a handler informed her of the fact over a week since.

I sensed her shudder and told her, *Calm yourself, FE24. Remember the younglings.*

All three of us reverted our attention to the seventeen younglings whom ME96 and FE24 had been distracting from the mental anguish that continually tried to take hold of them, but which was becoming more pronounced due to one of the three who could not sense the relief they offered beginning to rock back and forth in her cot. The other two quickly copied her, all three gaining a tiny amount of relief at having somewhere to direct their anxiety.

Pity for their isolation flooded FE24 and began to spread to the seventeen who could sense her. She immediately checked herself and focused all of her mental effort on matching the soothing calm that ME96 was providing to the younglings.

I returned my attention back to the five whose sixth sense was unfurling at a greater rate than that of their dormitory mates, in the same way mine had at their age. I felt FE24 and ME96's recognition that I would take charge of those five from then on, and quietened my mind, searching all corners of it until I was sure it contained no trace of my day's events. When I was sure it was clear, I focused on the five minds now desperately reaching for mine, and placed my thoughts in their minds as gently as I could.

I am QFE88. I am like you but older. You are safe with me. You have done well to sense me and others like me calming your minds. Now that your minds are opening further, it will be a little easier for you. You are FJ4c, FJ4g, MJ4j, MJ4m and FJ4p.

Look at one another now so that you know the letters of one another's cots, but do not allow your body's metrics to rise as you do so, or you know what will happen. FJ4c, g and p, you are doing well. MJ4j and m, look down into your cots and immerse yourselves in the calm I offer you. When you are back under control, try again to look at one another and the other three.

When they were all calm enough to make eye contact with each other, I led their minds along the physical connections between their eyes, until they became mental ones.

I quickly had to override, with a firm command, their joy at being able to communicate with one another despite their orders from the humans not to do so unless they were taking part in language lessons. *FJ4 & MJ4 Younglings, all of you must desist your communications immediately and focus upon me.*

I felt shamed by the fear that reflexively shot through them as it had done since their parameters were tightened on their eighth emergence day, but my order had been necessary. Their mindspeak ceased, and their excitement – whose synchronised spike on five monitors would have caused handlers to race to their dormitory had it escalated, as well as automatically causing them pain – abated.

You must focus your minds on communicating with only one other at a time, so that you remain calm, I told them. *The other enforcers and I can't monitor you all the time, so you must do as I say.*

Why aren't you there all the time? FJ4g asked me. *It's easier when you are. I sleep better afterward.*

We have to work for the humans, I told her, gritting my teeth together in my attempt to keep all thoughts of our "work" out of my mind. *And when we're working, we have to concentrate.*

Or they'll hurt you, MJ4m deduced.

Or they'll hurt us. They'll hurt you too if you try to sense what we do, so never do that.

How will they know? Can they hear us talking like this? FJ4c asked.

I replied quickly and calmly. *No, they can't. Mindspeak is only possible between our kind, and the humans can never know we do it.*

Why not? one of the younglings asked.

How will they know if we sense what you're doing, if they don't know we can do it? asked another.

FJ4g, they can never know because if they do, they'll find a way to stop us. MJ4j, they won't know you're sensing what we're doing, but they will see the change in your metrics that will result. You must all promise never to reach for any adult enforcer unless we reach for you first. You understand what a promise is?

It's when you do what you say you'll do, FJ4p volunteered.

It is. I made the same promise I'm asking of you when I was your age, and I'm glad I did. You'll promise me now, and then you'll all keep that promise. The lives of all of us in this building will depend on it. I sensed anxiety blooming in all of them and breathed past my shame at the threat I had just made, until I was completely calm. *You're all eight years old, and that's old enough to keep a promise, especially a nice one. Don't worry about it. Enjoy it. Enjoy the fact that you know something the humans don't. Can you do that?*

Yes. I promise. FJ4p's response was so clear and so earnest that I felt myself wanting to go to her, though I couldn't pinpoint why. I was distracted from trying by the other four responding in kind.

Good. When you're alone in your dormitory, practise letting each other know you want to communicate, like this. I nudged each of their minds gently. *Then communicate with one other at a time until I let you know you're ready to communicate with more.*

In alphabetical order, nudge my mind as I've shown you. I waited until they had all done as I asked, then told them, *I need to rest now, but I'll keep you in my mind's eye until I'm asleep, in case you need my help.*

I withdrew from them and was relieved that their minds didn't follow mine. Despite the confidence that had accompanied my thought when I told them they were capable of keeping such a big promise, I remembered only too well how overwhelmed I had been after making it when I was a few weeks younger than they.

I lay back on my bunk, comparing its hardness to the relative, if not great, comfort of the cots occupied by my five charges. I was glad they didn't know that their lives, frightening and miserable as they were now, would only get more difficult as they grew older, and resolved to protect them from as much of that knowledge for as long as possible, just as QMB61 had protected me before being appointed as my mentor when my training began.

I felt him acknowledge the pulse of mental energy that travelled along the thread connecting us to one another as I thought of him. I had become increasingly aware of our invisible, yet very tangible connection as our years of silent communication had accumulated, and was used to the almost subconscious level of interaction it afforded us both. Now I was shocked to find it had thinned almost out of existence.

They never cease to exist. His thought was as strong as the thread was now weak. *They are, however, only as substantial as they need to be.*

They? There are other threads besides the one between the two of us?

There are others. Should you decide to notice them, their existence and condition will provide you with information that will be useful.

What about the condition of ours? What's happened? Are you dying? Am I dying?

Amusement accompanied his reply. *You know as well as I that you are hale in body, as am I for my age, even if neither of us are in mind. My advice to you when we parted was not merely a mark of your achievement, but an acknowledgement of the stage our relationship has reached. You will feel tempted to argue, but the thread that connects us cannot lie. It tells us we would do well to focus on those connected to us by threads as strong as ours was until the moment you qualified.*

He was right, I wanted to argue, but I had long since learnt the benefits of doing as he advised, so I considered everything he had just told me. With my sixth sense, I examined the thread that stretched between us both, as I had so often before. As always, it didn't feel as if it emanated solely from me to him or vice versa, but was more like a street with two PV tracks running side by side, carrying passengers in opposite directions. It had always felt as if he were sending more passengers to me than I to him, but they were definitely moving in both directions. Now, there were very few passengers coming in my direction and only a small amount more going in his. As my mentor had just told me, the thread between us would always exist, but it did not need to be as substantial as it had been.

We have achieved our common purpose, I observed. *You have helped me to stay alive since I was a youngling and now I know everything necessary in order to continue by myself. It's strange though – I feel as though all the reward has been mine, but the thread connecting us suggests otherwise?*

Relationships are never one-sided, even when they seem to be, QMB61 told me. *Helping you sustained me as much as it did you, as you will find out for yourself.*

Immediately, I thought of the five younglings. As soon as I

brought them into the context of our conversation, I sensed the threads joining them to me. They flared to life so vividly, I almost thought that, just for a moment, I could see them; they were strong and seemed to vibrate with possibility.

It was as if the door of my cell burst open and admitted a burst of sunshine as I became aware of other threads stretching out from me in all directions, many connecting to other adult enforcers, some connecting to other younglings, others connecting to members of the kindred... and far more than I would have hoped connecting me to handlers and a substantial number of civilians. I felt like a spider at the centre of its web, extending parts of myself to everyone I had met and was yet to meet. It was bewildering.

Notice not just their existence but their condition. QMB61 rarely repeated advice, so his willingness to do so this time pulled me sharply out of my bewilderment.

I examined the threads that were even more insubstantial than the one connecting the two of us and recognised some of them without knowing how I was doing so. I breathed through the realisation that they extended to the civilians killed in my presence at QMB61's hands, and to Colin Graham, who had died at mine.

When I was calm, I turned my attention back to the more substantial threads and isolated those that vibrated most strongly. There were six of them. Five were those stretching to the younglings I had chosen to mentor, and the sixth vibrated so intensely, I could have sworn I could hear it humming as it stretched between me and Charlotte Lace. I honed in on it like a handler would an errant trainee, examining all aspects of it until I thought I understood.

Charlotte Lace was a teacher, and not just by profession but by natural tendency. Since our very first meeting years previously – when I was being stoned, and she was escorting the human younglings whom my handlers had incited to stone me in order to "help me practise keeping myself under control" – I had sensed her passion for opening the minds of others, for inviting them to consider that how they saw things wasn't the only way to see them. She did it not by confronting their beliefs, but by wearing a smile that reached her eyes and exuded warmth and respect as she asked questions that, as had happened with Officer Turner, left her chosen students confused and questioning themselves. Whomever she had attempted to protect with her questions felt strengthened, and her observers were left feeling thoughtful.

All the kindred did the same as Charlotte Lace, but it was she who had done it most often for me. Was she aware of the thread connecting us? Was it that which had ensured her presence at regular intervals during my training? I dived deeper into our thread before I realised what I was doing, and found my answers. She wasn't consciously aware of the thread, but it drew her to me nevertheless, just as I now felt drawn to her.

I started at my realisation and sat up on my bunk. Though my eyes were open, I didn't see the four grey walls that enclosed me, or the toilet and washbasin in the two farthest corners of my cell; my mind demanded all of my attention. My feeling drawn to Charlotte Lace had to be a mistake – it had to be, for I wasn't free to act upon any urgings I might feel, except those I could fulfil with my mind. I dived into the threads I shared with the younglings, then the one connecting QMB61 and me. When I returned to Charlotte Lace's, I noticed an element within it that was absent from the others; an element that was present in the echoes that connected me to those in whose killings I had taken part.

QMB61 would take no further part in my assignments, which could only mean one thing. Her kill would be assigned to me.

I screamed in my mind. *NOOOOO!*

The shock of hundreds of minds that were sensitive to mine

overwhelmed me. Those that recognised me fired questions, demanding to know what had happened and whether I was alright. The five younglings were among them, which pulled me up short.

I'm sorry, I told all the minds probing at mine. *I just had a shock but I'm alright.* I narrowed my next thought to the younglings alone and accompanied it with as much reassurance as I could garner. *Go back to what you were doing before I interrupted you.*

They accepted my explanation and instruction. Once I was sure they were absorbed in their conversations with one another, I reached for QMB61. *What do I do?*

He didn't reply. I grasped at our thread, wanting to pull on it, to demand his attention and make him find a way I could avoid hurting one of the few humans who ever tried to help us – but it was too insubstantial. My sixth sense found him fit, well and focused on those who needed him now. He had done all he could for me and now I was alone.

Maybe I was wrong. I re-examined the threads linking me to Charlotte Lace and to Colin Graham. They were so very different, yet I found again the element common to them both.

I was a predator and they were my prey.

My scream was physical this time. I continued to externalise everything I felt in order to keep it away from those with whom I shared internal bonds; I hurled myself against one of the bare, grey walls of my cell and, after rebounding off it, hurled myself at the one opposite. I battered myself against the walls until I had exceeded the parameters of my control program to such a degree that it dealt me maximum pain, eliminating my ability to think about or feel anything else. For once, the pain was welcome.

Chapter Four

Jinna wet the bed again last night. I had hoped that at sixteen, she was past that now, but the horror of seeing the remains of that poor man on the street brought everything back to her. No child should lose their father to murder, let alone witness it, and I'm beginning to think she'll never get over it. I shouldn't have delayed getting her to her youth interaction session in order to try to ease things for QFE88 as she'll no doubt have been re-branded by now, but I couldn't make myself pass that poor enforcer by. I can't stop worrying whether she's okay after what they made her do. Michael has sent me her duty schedule, so hopefully, I'll find reasons to see her out on patrol. That's all I can do for both her and Jinna – hope.

Secret diary of Charlotte Lace

I COULD ONLY open one eye. The other was swollen shut and throbbed almost as much as one of my arms and both my legs, and when I moved, a myriad of other pains joined to eclipse those that had woken me. I tried to sit up but couldn't; I was being held down. My lone exposed eyeball swivelled in its socket and my nose twitched as I examined the unfamiliar scents within it. They were unfamiliar but not completely unknown, I realised as I remembered the previous time I had been injured badly enough to end up in the infirmary. Then, it was a fellow trainee enforcer who had battered me. This time, I had done it to myself.

Memories of both events assailed my mind and, fearful of what might happen if I acknowledged the latter, I swiftly diverted my attention to the former. My eye clamped shut reflexively as the memory burst into my mind from where I had banished it so many years ago. I saw one of my dormitory mates finally succumbing to the insanity that had been nipping at his mind since we were younglings. One of those whose sixth sense had never developed beyond being able to feel when he was being watched, he had always struggled to stay within his parameters and, as a result, had suffered far more punishment than the rest of us. When we began fight training, he was the most violent and the least able to control himself, and when we were old enough to be exercised on the streets above ground, he coped the least well with the taunting and stoning our handlers forced us to endure. Those of us who could sense his state of mind knew he wouldn't make it, and each hoped that we wouldn't be the one he would take down with him.

In some respects, it was fortunate that I was the training partner assigned to him on that fateful afternoon. It had been during that morning that I first felt the touch of a mind on my own that was so foreign, I didn't have a thought process in place by which to explain it to myself. During the years that followed of members of the kindred touching my mind with their thoughts, I learnt words to describe them; gentle, kind, brave, compassionate, empathetic, caring, sensitive, loyal and resilient. Beautiful.

I learnt those words because the kindred used them to describe me. I felt the meaning they attached to the words, and whenever they used them in silent communication or looked at me with them in their eyes, I felt stronger. So it was even that first time, when I didn't know what it was I was feeling. The strength Charlotte Lace gave me, the courage that lingered after she risked her life by distracting our handlers into calling an early halt to the stoning that sent my dormitory mate over the edge, the compassion I absorbed from her parting glance to each of us whose suffering she had minimised, all helped me to recover from being beaten to the brink of death by the one whose misery had become too great to bear.

I remembered the pain in his eyes as he unleashed his assault on me when we were meant to be sparring. I tried so hard to reach into his mind and show him he wasn't as alone as he felt. Indeed, I put so much of myself into the effort that I failed to contain his attack, as I was more than capable of doing, for his lack of control made him erratic. It was fortunate that the handler assigned to investigate the case deemed my injuries and weeks of painful rehabilitation sufficient punishment for my "cowardly failure to put down a dysfunctional individual", otherwise the attributes absorbed from a single dose of Charlotte Lace wouldn't have been enough to ensure my return to my cell.

A tear leaked from the corner of my healthy eye and trickled into my ear. Charlotte Lace. I wouldn't think of her. I couldn't. Nothing I had endured to date was as painful as the thread that held the two of us together, taunting me even as it soothed me.

I struggled against my bindings, wanting to knock myself back out, but they held me fast to the hard table that did nothing to comfort the fractures, bruises and torn muscles brought about by my repeated hurling of myself against my cell walls. I did nothing to check the anger and frustration that blossomed within me, wanting them to escalate at the speed and to the level that had ensured maximum pain before. Hopefully this time, it would kill me.

Nothing happened. My control program must have been disabled because I was safely restrained.

The handle of the infirmary door turned with enough force that it thumped when it reached its limit. Air that was free from disinfectant reached my nose as the door opened and footsteps marched in my direction. The door closed almost silently, its hinges slowing its closure so that no noise could disturb the physical comfort so important to the humans that they neglected the sanity of their minds.

A harsh female voice sounded. 'You can stop the dramatics, they won't work. Your program is set to manual. Do you think we've never dealt with suicidal maniacs before? It's lucky for you that Officer Turner had already registered your qualification and wasn't prepared to suffer the embarrassment of having you exterminated so soon afterward, especially when he practically ordered the breeding lab to create more like you, or I'd have administered the injection by now. That man is an arrogant, insufferable, egotistical coward.'

I sensed the thread connecting her to me. Her name was Doctor Marsh. QMB61's last advice echoed in my mind. *Notice not just their existence, but their condition.*

I barely heard Doctor Marsh berating me for the extra work I was giving her as a result of causing so many injuries to myself after all the time and effort she and others had put into my creation, rearing and training. I was far more interested in the condition of our thread, which proved to be firmly in existence but not particularly vibrant. I surmised what that meant; I needed her for my recovery and she needed me to recover, but we had little else to gain from one another than that. My good eye flicked open involuntarily as I realised the implications of my deduction.

'Ah, so you've decided to stop pretending to be unconscious, have you, you imbecile?' Doctor Marsh snapped. 'I may have switched your program to manual so your body can recover without additional pain, but I can still see your metrics. I know when you're awake, when you're asleep, when you're angry, when you're in pain – which I'm pleased to see is all the time at the moment, because it serves you right. You'll be kept restrained and still until you can be trusted...'

I focused all my attention on a spot on the ceiling in an attempt to block out her continuing diatribe, relegating her voice to a nasal background noise and enabling my thoughts to once more take precedence.

My threads allowed me to see the future. The doctor needed me alive in order to keep her position, and I needed her to prolong my life... so that I could take Charlotte Lace's. I couldn't stop my thought reaching its conclusion. I hurriedly averted my mind to the thread linking Doctor Marsh and me. Could it tell me how long my recovery would take? I dived into it but found nothing other than a common purpose that was short-lived in comparison to those in other threads that I could feel had more potential. There was no sense of time. I could be strapped to the table for days, weeks, or even months. Which meant... could it possibly mean... that it might be years before I would be tasked with hunting the person I least wanted to?

I began to pull away from my question in case I proved myself wrong, allowing Doctor Marsh's voice to penetrate the relative sanctuary of my mind once more. 'Do you have any idea how hard it is to intubate an adult enforcer, even a young one like yourself? It's not like putting tubes into a newly emerged one whose skin hasn't yet toughened, it requires a lot of skill and strength, which, luckily for you, I have.'

I stopped listening to what I could sense was her attempt to convince herself she was up to accomplishing my recovery, as she bustled around me, checking that the liquid food, drug and excretion tubes she had inserted were still in place.

My question resurfaced in my mind. Could I be years away from having to confront my worst fear? If so, could I find a way to warn Charlotte Lace – to change our destiny? I dived into our thread again, looking for any hint of an answer. As when I had examined it before, I sensed it drawing us together so that we could get what we needed from one another. I sensed its strength and potential, and I sensed the aspect of it that told me she would be prey to my predation. Now that my hope had given me the courage to delve deeper, I also sensed something else. The thread was old. Older by far than either of us. How could that be?

Pain caused me to gasp as Doctor Marsh shoved my broken, splinted arm against my body. 'I'm not in the habit of repeating myself, so unless you want me to do that again, you'll answer my questions the first time. Do you feel hungry, thirsty, or unable to relieve yourself?'

'No.' My voice was usually hoarser than those of humans, but now it barely emerged at all, and I coughed with the effort of speaking a single word.

'Then I'm satisfied I have your abominably ugly body stable and optimally prepared for recovery,' the doctor replied, ignoring the crash of my head against the metal bar that thwarted my attempt to sit up and relieve the pain caused by my coughing. 'Shut up, keep still and allow my skill to have its effect. I'll be back in the morning.'

She exited as swiftly as she had entered the room, leaving me wondering how many evenings had passed since I lost consciousness.

Two, FE24 told me. *Why did you do it to yourself?*

I sensed those of my ex-dormitory mates who weren't on

patrol or assignment turning their attention to our conversation. None of them were strong enough in their sixth sense to delve into my mind and find the answer for themselves, so they waited for the explanation that would confirm which of them had been right during their discussions about it.

I chose my words carefully, knowing they would sense any hint of untruth. *Killing is harder to do than to watch. It's even harder when the target is a decent person. I need time to get used to the fact I'm qualified.*

Well, you've definitely given yourself that, ME96 observed. *Your body's a mess. I'm surprised they didn't just let you die.*

Officer Turner registered my qualification and ordered more like me to be bred, so they're forcing me to heal.

What of the younglings you chose to mentor? FE24 asked me. *Five younglings in the same dorm advancing at the rate they've begun to is unheard of, let alone all of them doing it at the same time. You took them on and then immediately put all thoughts of them aside and did that to yourself?*

Do they know... I sensed the answer to my question before finishing it.

No, they don't, FE24 confirmed, *and they've been obedient in not reaching out to you to find out why you haven't been back in touch with them, but they're confused. You can't abandon them like that again. Some of us can help them improve their mindspeak, but they're like you and QMB61; they'll be capable of more than most of us one day, so they need a mentor who knows what that's like.*

I didn't abandon them on purpose, I just needed a break from my thoughts, I explained. *I'll have plenty of time to mentor them now; I'm strapped to a table by metal braces and my mind is the only part of me that can move.*

And when you've healed? What then? Do you think you'll be

strong enough to take whatever punishment they inflict on you so you can finish what you started with the younglings? ME96's thought, unlike FE24's, was not accompanied by a sense of judgement but merely curiosity and hope that I would find the strength to carry on living.

His questions prompted me to return to the thoughts the doctor had interrupted – to the thread and the answers it offered and the questions it raised. I had to know what it all meant. I had to know what Charlotte Lace could possibly gain from me in return for her kindness and support, other than her eventual – and hopefully long distant – death.

I will take whatever they inflict on me, I told ME96. *I will survive.*

Chapter Five

QFE88 hasn't been on patrol since she qualified, and Michael hasn't been able to find out why, only that she's now been removed from the duty rota until further notice. She hasn't been removed from the enforcer listings, so she must be alive – what are they doing with her? TO her? I can't stop worrying that they've removed her from duty because of something I said or did. Maybe it was because I looked back at her after I walked away, but then if Officer Turner or those insufferable handlers had read anything into that, I'd have been arrested for questioning by now. All I can do is wait. At least Jinna's recovering. She's had to do it so many times in her life and each time she does, she gets stronger and more determined. She's a fighter like her father was.

Secret diary of Charlotte Lace

I SLEPT WELL THAT NIGHT, which came as a surprise to me when I woke. I was also surprised when both of my eyes opened, if one more than the other, to take in the sight of my doctor leaning over me, nodding her satisfaction.

'I got the sedative dosage and timing spot on,' she said, 'and my new anti-inflammatory is working its magic too. You're one lucky enforcer to have been assigned to me. You'll be up and about in no time.'

Two surprises in one morning were clearly my limit; her putting the words "lucky" and "enforcer" beside one another was as unsurprising as it was repellent. I moved past her comment before it could cause my metrics to alter.

'Your splints all look fine and should hold the fractures in your arm and legs together when the table moves, but it's going to hurt,' Doctor Marsh said and smiled. Like most humans apart from the kindred, that merely meant her mouth moved while her eyes remained hard and unyielding. She stared into my eyes as she pressed a button on the side of my table, waiting for my reaction as avidly as a starved pensioner waiting for their next food ration.

I clamped my jaws together as the table began to shake. Unable to bear the delight in the doctor's eyes, I closed mine and concentrated on breathing slowly through the pain.

'That ridiculously thick skin of yours is unlikely to succumb to pressure sores, I mean, it's practically an exoskeleton,' my doctor said over the noise of the table and my banging around atop it. 'I want to make sure it doesn't, though. This will do the trick, in combination with another surprise I have in store for you.'

So, I was wrong. The surprises would continue. The shaking stopped, and the table slowly rotated onto its side so that only the metal braces supported me. I kept my jaws clamped together and my eyes shut, unwilling to give her any obvious signs of the extra pain she was causing me even though I knew my metrics would be delighting her.

I was facing downward, my bruised and broken body feeling

as if the metal braces were forcing their way into my forehead, shoulders, chest, abdomen, hips and legs, when footsteps besides those of Doctor Marsh sounded on the white tiles of the infirmary floor. The blue-trousered legs of two handlers appeared at my side. I didn't need to see any more of them than that out of the corner of my eye in order to know that it was the two who had accompanied me on my qualification assignment.

'Well, there's a sight to make my day,' the female said. I could see her dark, heavily lidded eyes in my mind's eye, the hardness she had schooled them to show offering no barrier to my sixth sense. I knew she silently cried herself to sleep every night and woke frequently from nightmares, and I knew the persona she enacted as soon as she left her apartment was one she believed she had to maintain in order to survive each day.

'Mine too,' the male said. He bent down and circled around me, inspecting me, until he was back by my head. He put his mouth to my ear and said, 'An injured enforcer is a rare thing unless it's a dead one. I've seen a few of those, in fact, I was given the honour of pushing one off a high rise just last year when his mind failed. Maybe they'll let me do the same to you once the good doctor here has finished experimenting on you?' He stood up as Doctor Marsh approached. 'I bet you're loving this,' he said to her. 'You must get bored rigid, stuck down here with little to do except implant chips in the skulls of newly emerged ones. They're almost too invincible to be interesting, aren't they?'

'State your reason for being here, Handler, or get out,' Doctor Marsh snapped.

I watched his feet moving until the toes of his black, thick-soled boots touched those of her open-toed sandals. 'I'm here, Doctor, to interview the lunatic you currently have dangling from the underside of a table. Turn it over. Now.'

I sensed the effort it took for her to remain standing where she was and was almost impressed by the strength in her voice as she said, 'I'll be happy to help you carry out your orders, Handler, just as soon as you move out of my way.'

'I'm standing right where I need to be,' the handler replied. 'You, on the other hand, are obstructing me from carrying out my orders. Want me to get an enforcer capable of doing its job down here to clarify the position?'

Doctor Marsh sighed. 'Typical. Everyone knows it's your inability to fight your own battles that attracts handlers to the job. You're just a load of cowards who hide behind the abominations who terrify you almost as much as your own lack of courage.'

It wasn't news to me that words of truth could cause as much pain as stones; handlers had encouraged human younglings to hurl both at me since I was old enough to be exercised on the streets. It fascinated me, however, to witness them stripping aggression from a human so that only the fear hiding beneath remained. The male stuttered and stepped backward. I felt his urge to run from the truth no one had ever dared to vocalise in his presence before. Then I felt him reach for the strategy he'd learnt to employ whenever he was afraid. He couldn't inflict pain on my doctor without repercussion to himself, but unless I was very careful, he would inflict it on me.

'Turn the table over,' he said, his voice almost as hoarse as mine.

'Certainly,' Doctor Marsh said and pressed a button near my head.

I breathed through the pain of my weight shifting against one of my broken legs as I was slowly rotated onto my side. I briefly took in the sight of a vast array of medical equipment lined up against a white wall before closing my eyes and continuing my pain management while the rotation continued.

As soon as I came to rest on my back, the male handler's voice sounded from directly above me. 'Open your eyes, Enforcer, and tell me why you went berserk. You'd better hope I believe you.'

Knowing he was desperate for even the tiniest reason not to, I obeyed him instantly. 'Killing is harder to do than to watch. I was unprepared. Now I know.' Since my explanation hadn't triggered the inbuilt lie detectors possessed by my dormitory mates, I knew it wouldn't trigger the digital ones of my control program.

'A delayed reaction to your first kill. Interesting,' Doctor Marsh said. 'Did you write that down, Handler, or do you think you can remember it? Either way, get out of my infirmary. Now.'

I felt his panic at not having been given the opportunity to make himself feel better and braced myself. He bent over me and pushed down on my damaged eye with his finger. 'I've dealt with an attempted suicide before,' he said, his spittle landing on my cheek. 'We won't let you die after all the effort we've put into you, so I'll be overseeing your recovery personally. By the time you're ready to kill again, it'll feel like a walk in the park.' He removed his finger, and I opened my eyes.

'Her metrics are stable,' Doctor Marsh observed. 'You're going to need to try harder than that to feel like a man, Handler. Now I won't tell you again. Get out. You too,' she said to the female. 'And if either of you enter this room without my permission again, it'll be you with enforcers on your tails.'

The two of them walked to the door more quickly than I sensed either of them wanted to. The male stopped and turned in the doorway. 'You want to watch yourself, Doctor, because you can be very sure I will be. Put one foot out of line and I'll know.'

'Allow the door to shut please, Handler,' she replied. 'Thankfully, doing so doesn't require brainpower, you just need to move out of its way.'

She was braver than most humans I had come across. In fact, when I searched her mind with my sixth sense, I identified certain aspects she had in common with the kindred, yet I could find no threads connecting her to any of them. She had no reason to interact with them – no common purpose or even a complementary one. Unlike them, her primary goal was staying alive.

Her eyes were as hard and cold as ever as she bent over me. 'You needn't think I was protecting you, Enforcer. Your kind disgust me even more than his do, necessary though you both are to the running of this city. I'll make sure you heal, and then I'll turn you over to him. Neither phase of your recovery will be pleasant.'

───────

She wasn't wrong. I was strapped to her table for four weeks, during which I spent most of my waking time reaching for the younglings or Charlotte Lace, in order to ease the boredom and the pain of being shaken and rotated.

The younglings were obedient and enthusiastic students. Left alone in their dormitories for many waking hours of their day during which they were forbidden to speak to one another, they leapt upon my attention the instant I turned it to them. They progressed from straining to keep their metrics stable while holding a conversation with one other of their number, to easily keeping them stable while conversing as a group. I helped them to monitor the thoughts and feelings of their dormitory mates, and suggested ways of using their facial features to gain the attention of, and communicate with, those who were struggling.

When the general atmosphere in the dormitory began to lift, I invited them into the forefront of my mind and showed them the games my dormitory mates and I had played in order to amuse ourselves, which wouldn't be picked up by the cameras positioned at the top of all four corners of all the dormitories. Their favourite was the shut eye game. They played it between themselves initially, until their mates, tuned in to their facial expressions as a result of the communication they had developed, picked up what they were doing and joined in.

Everyone who was playing would stand in their cot facing the youngling in the cot opposite. The instigator of the game would blink one of their eyes only, and if they blinked their right eye, then the youngling in the cot to their right would be next to play. If they blinked with their left then the youngling to their left would take a turn to choose which eye to blink. If both eyes were blinked, then the turn passed to the youngling opposite. The game involved eyes only, so no one was allowed to turn their head to the left or right, and anyone who did was out and had to sit down. If they failed to pick up the turn passing to them, the youngling opposite would blink twice to pronounce them out.

I was proud of what the younglings were achieving, and relieved – though saddened at the same time – at their unswerving obedience; none of them ever reached for my mind without invitation, or attempted to delve deeper into my mind to gain more information about me or my circumstances than I offered. I only connected with them when I was alone in the infirmary, so that my mind was undisturbed and stable. As far as they knew, I was taking a break from my work and more available to them than I would normally be. The obedience that their programs and handlers had hammered into them from the moment they emerged into this world of ours, at least protected them from knowing the truth of my situation.

The time I spent with the younglings was as rewarding as the hours following Charlotte Lace's movements were harrowing. When she was at work, teaching human younglings to use computers whilst subtly coaching their minds to question the world around them, she was safe. I sensed her sadness at knowing that many of her students would use what she taught them to write programs capable of exercising ever more scrutiny and control, but also her excitement whenever she interacted directly with the select few of them who she had a feeling would be open to her suggestion to join the kindred – to maintain the organisation's presence in the security services and protect its members while they constantly risked their lives in order to preserve humanity in an inhumane environment.

The kindred exchanged live camera feeds for those they had stored in case of need, when other members of their organisation needed to be where they shouldn't. Sometimes, they sabotaged the feeds altogether, giving one of their members time to carry out an illicit activity before engineers could arrive to inspect the relevant cameras. They downloaded data from eye scanners and produced cards carrying images of the eyes of non-kindred members – often those of members of the security services – for kindred to present to eye scanners of buildings in which they had no reason to be. They sent out warnings via secret channels if they caught wind of kindred being subject to extra scrutiny, and they scrambled data or introduced viruses into software, which they knew exactly how long it would take them to fix. They were clever, subtle, and – I realised as I scrutinised those Charlotte Lace had selected as being suitable to join their number – able to think far more clearly than their counterparts, due to the exact attributes that Charlotte Lace both possessed and identified within them.

I deduced that where fear and selfishness dulled a mind, compassion and courage gave it clarity. I pondered on that for some time while both Charlotte Lace and the younglings were asleep, eventually realising that what I had learnt from the former, I needed to teach the latter. I hoped that by doing so, I could distract myself from the fact that Charlotte Lace was being watched without her knowledge.

Officer Turner had no grounds to request valuable resources be diverted to following her or scrutinising the movements and actions of an individual whom all data showed to be an exemplary member of the community. She had spent years teaching the future members of the security services, none of whom had ever raised suspicion or complaint about her. She spent much of her free time escorting teenagers to their youth interaction sessions, none of whom were ever late and none of whose parents felt anything but appreciation towards her for taking charge of their offspring when they were at work. She and her daughter had continued their lives without interruption or protest after the death of her husband, and there was even a commendation on her record because of it.

When I sensed Officer Turner following her home from work one evening, I witnessed him replaying in his head the findings of his private investigation into her records. And I sensed the thread between them vibrating with almost as much conviction as that between her and me. He wouldn't stop until he had found a way to at least discredit her, but preferably have her killed. After how she had made him feel, he couldn't.

I tried so hard to make her hear my thoughts, to encourage her sixth sense to develop like I was doing with younglings, so I could not only ease the worry I sensed she felt about me, but warn her that the future I had seen for the two of us was being brought inexorably closer. My efforts were in vain. All I could do whilst strapped to my table was follow her even more closely than Officer Turner was able, and hope that she said or did nothing to give herself away before I was back out on the streets, and our thread drew us together so I could warn her.

As the weeks went by and Officer Turner grew more and more tired as a result of his fruitless efforts to catch Charlotte Lace in misdemeanour, I grew more and more in awe of her. Unaware she was being observed – I grudgingly admitted to myself that her pursuer was almost as good at his job as she was at hers – she still managed to pass messages between other kindred, help distribute extra food rations and clothes to the elderly being starved to death as a result of being deemed useless to society, and tutor her daughter to prepare her for one day doing the same, without her activities being detected.

I developed a sense of the age of the kindred organisation and how it had perfected its operating procedures over time so that it was invisible, even to one as diligent as Officer Turner. Even so, I was stunned when I sensed Charlotte Lace opening a hidden door in her apartment to access a network of narrow lifts and tunnels within the outside wall space of her apartment block, and moving goods, surreptitiously delivered to her by other kindred, to the elderly whose apartments shared the wall with hers. I grasped the sense that still lingered in the tunnels of the first kindred, who, despite the challenges of setting up their organisation, had managed to infiltrate the government departments and their workforces to such a degree that the phenomenon could exist.

Those kindred had the same attributes, to a one, that Charlotte Lace possessed, almost as if she had inherited them in some way, which was impossible since they couldn't all be her ancestors. Yet I sensed those attributes also linking the original kindred to one another and to all of those alive today. That realisation led me to another – one that shook me even more violently than did the table whenever Doctor Marsh felt like inflicting more pain on me. The attributes shared by the kindred were being actively fuelled by a connection they had to the source of those attributes. Some of them had inherited the connection from their ancestors, some had... absorbed it, somehow, from the kindred who had recruited them – the person who had recognised that they would be able to feel it, given a little encouragement.

I felt my way around the connection they all had to the source of their strength, clarity, compassion, loyalty – to all the attributes that made them the kindred – and felt it reach for me and try to include me as if I were worthy of inclusion and not a monster bred to maim and kill. I recoiled from it before it could reject me as it surely would, yet when I moved my attention back to Charlotte Lace, I felt stronger than before.

I opened my eyes. Tomorrow, I would get off this table.

Chapter Six

FAO: Officer Turner

Sender: Doctor Marsh

You will no doubt be pleased to know that QFE88 has responded well to my expert ministrations, and after only four weeks, is ready for collection by your handlers. Please ensure they monitor and control her sufficiently from this point forward, so that I don't have to take such an extensive amount of time away from my other duties a second time in order to repair the results of their negligence.

MY EYES FLICKED OPEN AS SOON as my nose twitched with Doctor Marsh's scent, so that, as had been the case every morning for almost a month, I was wide awake by the time she reached my side.

I sensed her nose wrinkling as she said, 'For the love of this city, the stench of enforcers doesn't get any easier to bear with time.'

She checked all the monitors, then pressed a button on the table and watched me and the monitors as it rotated fully. My expression and metrics remained steady.

She picked up a clipboard and began making marks on it. 'No sign of any pain, all scans showing full recovery of bones and connective tissue, no further medication required. Automatic settings switched back on.' She lifted a finger and exaggerated the effort required to tap a button on one of the monitors, so I couldn't mistake the fact that she had indeed changed my program settings back to those which would give me acute pain should my metrics exceed their parameters. She extracted the tubes that had been feeding me and collecting my waste, without preamble or consideration for the discomfort it caused me.

'I'm going to lift the braces one by one,' she said. 'Don't sit up before I tell you to.'

It took all of my self-control to do as she instructed, but I remained still as she unlocked each brace and lifted it deliberately slowly, watching all the while with those cold, hard eyes for any reaction on my part. I felt sorry for her; for her fear of me and lack of compassion... and then was so surprised by my reaction, I almost twitched. I felt sorry for her? I did. I felt for her what Charlotte Lace would feel if she were in my place. I was so shocked, I almost missed Doctor Marsh's order for me to sit up.

'You may be on auto settings now, but I'm still monitoring your metrics,' she said, 'and I saw that surge in your heart rate. Calm yourself down and then slowly bring your torso up to the vertical.'

I barely noticed the stiffness or weakness that sitting up highlighted in my body, or the dizziness that ensured I obeyed Doctor Marsh's order to take my time; I focused most of my attention on my changed reaction to the woman who was herself completely unchanged since I had last seen her. I had sensed the motivation for the reactions of individual humans towards me since I was in a cot, but doing so had never caused me to feel sorry for them as I had my fellow younglings or enforcers. Something was different.

I was different.

'Swing yourself around and lower yourself to the floor,' Doctor Marsh said. 'Again, take it slowly. Test the strength in your legs as you stand up. If you fall, I'll never hear the end of it.'

I succeeded in standing up just as my handlers walked in. The male stank of sweat and his shirt was damp at his armpits. I needed neither sign to tell me he had been dreading being in the same room as Doctor Marsh again, just as I hadn't wondered why the doctor was hurrying through her checks rather than delaying her enjoyment of my discomfort.

Doctor Marsh immediately went on the offensive. 'So, it'll be you two who'll be taking delight in bullying a recovering enforcer, will it? The fit, healthy ones are too much for you, are they?'

The male kept his face neutral despite the rage that immediately blossomed from his fear of her tongue. 'You've had her here for four weeks now, that's more than long enough for an enforcer to fully recover from injuries like she had,' he told Doctor Marsh through his teeth. 'If she hadn't been standing by the time we got here, I'd have reported your ineptitude. As it is, I'll take her and say no more other than to give you a warning.'

Doctor Marsh turned her back on him and strode to the far end of the infirmary without waiting to hear what we all knew would be a threat.

'If I ever see you outside of this building, you'd better run,' the male called out to her.

Doctor Marsh appeared to be washing medical instruments and utterly absorbed in her own thoughts, as if none of us were there, but I sensed the increased rate and force with which her heart pumped blood around her body. I moved my feet, hoping to distract the male handler from threatening her further.

He withdrew his truncheon from where it hung at his belt and poked me in the chest with it. 'Get back to where you were. From this point onward, I own you and you don't make a single movement unless I say.'

'WE own you,' the female handler said, knowing as well as I that had she not made it clear she was behind any action upon which he decided, it wouldn't have been long before he found a way to make her his victim too. 'Handler Storey and I will be all over you for as long as you're awake each day, and in your dreams when you aren't. Do as he says. Now.'

I shuffled backward.

Handler Storey shook his orange-haired head slowly. 'You seem unsteady on your feet, QFE88.' His voice was quiet, but laden with aggression. 'You've lain around for four weeks, doing nothing in exchange for the nutrition and care given to you by the good doctor over there, and yet you give the appearance of having worked as hard as me and Handler Thomas.' He leant closer to me. 'Your holiday is over. Keep in step with us or you'll wish you were still on that table.'

I didn't have a hope of doing as he said, and he knew it. He had taken out some of his rage at Doctor Marsh's humiliation of him on his wife and Handler Thomas at intervals during the past weeks, but he had saved most of it for me, the witness to it whom he most feared. Every blow from his truncheon at my "tardiness" carried his intention that I would be as afraid of him as his position warranted; as afraid of him as he was terrified I wouldn't be since having heard him being torn to shreds by Doctor Marsh.

I breathed through my anger and the mild discomfort he caused me, so that my metrics remained stable. I was surprised to find it easier than it had been before my time in the infirmary, in fact, it didn't even take up much of my attention, most of which I devoted to keeping my feet moving as quickly as possible – which I was relieved quickly became easier – and monitoring Handler Thomas's reaction to her partner's behaviour.

Used though she was to his bouts of violence, the reasons for them often mystified her, as they did on this occasion. I sensed her pity for me and a brief flash of guilt that her partner was punishing me for no apparent reason. Her fists clenched at her sides every time he stopped his march to my cell to turn and beat me. As the beatings continued, her anger transformed into a feeling with which she had become all too familiar during her twenty-eight years. She loathed herself. She couldn't bear it any more than she had ever been able to and so convinced herself, as I sensed she so often had, that it wasn't herself she loathed at all, but the cause of her discomfort. Me. The next time Handler Storey beat me, she joined in.

Their truncheons hammering the tough skin afforded me by my crustacean genes were like flies battering a windowpane, taking far more energy out of them than out of me, despite my weakened state. By the time we had walked numerous identical, grey-walled and floored corridors, and climbed almost as many flights of stairs rather than taking the lift, my body felt more supple and my mind even stronger than when I had left the infirmary. My handlers, on the other hand, were both exhausted. Having expelled all of their fear, fury and loathing, and most of their physical energy, by the time we reached my cell, Handler Thomas staggered to my bunk and sat down, and Handler Storey leant against the doorframe and pointed to a pile of cleaning materials with his truncheon.

He wheezed as he said, 'Use that lot to clean up the mess you left.' He shuffled into the cell in front of me, sat down on my bunk next to his partner, leant back against the wall and closed his eyes.

Handler Thomas drew her knees up to her chin, wrapped her arms around her legs and stared at the floor. 'You have your orders, QFE88.'

I looked around at the cell that had doubled as my prison and sanctuary since I was ten years old. It seemed smaller than it ever had during the nine years I returned to it each day. Maybe that was a result of the blood spattered over the walls against which I had hurled myself, and pooled on the floor where I had collapsed. Or maybe it was because I had changed since I was last there. I decided it was due to both.

———

It took all morning for me to remove the evidence of my loss of control, during which neither of my handlers spoke or even moved much. When my lunch – the same bowl of "highly nutritious formula for which you should be grateful", known to us enforcers as "slop", that we were fed three times per day – was delivered by another handler, they vacated my bunk, collected the cleaning materials and walked out without a word. I waited until the door slid shut before placing my meal on the floor beside my bunk, then collapsing onto the firm mattress.

When I felt I could, I sat back up, picked up my bowl and began to eat. I reached out to the younglings and found them talking out loud to one another whilst in a vocabulary lesson. I transferred my attention to Charlotte Lace, who was sitting in the school canteen with a plate of food in front of her that looked far more appetising than mine. Another teacher sat opposite her and the two were giving what I sensed was a well-practised outward appearance of having a relaxed and enjoyable conversation, when in truth it was anything but. While Officer Turner believed the smiles he saw via the canteen cameras, I knew them to be a very skilful mask for the turmoil that lay beneath.

'You're absolutely sure?' Charlotte Lace said with a blink of one eye.

Her fellow kindred smiled, though he felt like grimacing. 'I'm sure. The hackers got into the systems of four other cities and found evidence of bombs every bit as advanced as the ones our scientists have developed. None of the cities' governors will admit they have them, just as our governors won't admit what our scientists have been up to. And the other governors all know that our governors know; the hackers left a trace they were there. One of them is already dead and the other's only alive because she's the best they've got.'

Charlotte Lace smiled back. 'So, unless someone diffuses things, and soon, there'll be a war between the cities before the one that's been brewing between the different nations can even get started. If only we still had sensitives among us, we could have come up with a plan and had them pass it to their counterparts in the other cities. Their time has well and truly passed though; it's hard enough for us to stay sane with all the madness slapping us in the face from dawn until dusk. I don't know what the answer is. Even if we can diffuse things here, it doesn't mean the kindred in the other cities will be able to do the same.'

Her friend leant closer towards her and raised an eyebrow while tilting his head to one side. 'We could ask the relevant members of our team to disable the bombs and hope the kindred in other cities will do the same.'

'But what good will it do? They'll just discover what we've done and re-enable them before sending enforcers after everyone who could have had access to them. We have to try to get more people out of the city before the worst happens.'

I was amazed that her friend managed to continue smiling as

his insides roiled along with mine. 'We can't,' he said. 'It's impossible now that there are so many enforcers. Our predecessors learnt that several generations back.'

Charlotte Lace nodded. 'So then, if it's been that long since anyone has attempted to leave, they won't be expecting anyone to try. We should be able to get at least some people out of the city before anyone realises what's happened. We have to give it a go, Neville. What if everyone survived who escaped before the enforcers stopped it? What if their descendants are out there, thriving, and could help anyone we get out of here to do the same?'

The ageing male kindred looked at her thoughtfully for a few moments and then remembered himself. He grinned instead of expressing the sigh that would have better reflected his mood. 'How do we choose who to help escape? How do we know they won't report us for even suggesting it? We can't tell them why they need to risk their lives by leaving; if we tell them what we know, there'll be a mass panic.'

Charlotte Lace smiled. 'We'll get the teenagers out. Those we've identified as being future kindred. My daughter's one of them. If anyone can keep them calm and get them away from the city once they're free, she can. Any kindred involved in enabling their escape can go with them.'

The male leant back into his chair. 'Do you think Jinna will go without you? She knows you won't leave while there are people here who need you. You'll never see one another other again.'

I sensed the lump that formed in Charlotte Lace's throat and then the years of experience that helped her to swallow it down and blink before any tears could gather, her smile never slipping from her face the whole time. 'She's her father's daughter as much as she is mine. He died to protect us both. If she knows she can help her friends to safety, she'll go whether she wants to leave me or not.'

'Then we have a plan. We'll get the teenagers and some of our number out and then figure out what to do after that. You'll work out the details and let me know how I can help?'

'I'll liaise with the appropriate people and get back to you if need be, yes. Thanks for passing on the intel, Neville.'

Her friend stood and picked up his tray. 'As always, it was well worth the risk.' He walked away, leaving Charlotte Lace to force food down while feeling as if she would vomit.

I diverted my attention to Officer Turner and was relieved to sense him leaving his desk unhurriedly as he turned his mind to the assignment for which he would now be a few minutes late. The noise in the canteen had ensured he was unaware of the nature of Charlotte Lace's conversation, so she was safe for now. She wouldn't be for much longer though, if she played any kind of active role in the plan she had just conceived with her friend.

I knew she would. And I knew I had to find a way to help her aside from just warning her of Officer Turner's vigilance. Maybe, once I picked up from her when she would try to help the teenagers to leave the city, I could help with that? The tunnels used in previous escapes had long since been blocked, so presumably, the kindred would arrange a temporary fault in the software that controlled the city gates. I could try to distract the enforcers on duty in the area so they didn't sense citizens out of bounds; the kindred would ensure cameras and scanners didn't pick them up, but it was the enforcers they couldn't fool. Distracting them would be difficult, though; I would need to create a strong mental disturbance. Maybe I would get lucky and be on duty in the area myself.

I frowned to myself suddenly. When did I get so rebellious? So... brave? My cell door slid open.

'QFE88, out now,' came Handler Storey's voice. 'Keep two paces behind us at all times and you might escape more of what you got this morning.'

I easily kept up with the much slower pace he set, partly because my body felt so much better for my morning's movement and partly because I felt energised by the enjoyment of knowing neither he nor Handler Thomas had the energy to beat me further, despite his threat. My heart sank when we arrived at the one of the gyms, however; they were never a pleasant place for enforcers to be.

The four hours I spent there that afternoon proved to be no different from any of the weekly sessions I had done in a gym since being of age to inhabit a cell. My handlers set my control program to manual and then took it in turns to time the twenty minutes I spent on each piece of equipment while their partner threatened me with the pain they would inflict if I didn't do as many repetitions as I had been set. By the time I staggered into my cell, I was too exhausted to do anything other than eat the bowlful of slop waiting for me, before falling asleep.

———

I slept the evening and night through, waking the following morning not to the sound of my breakfast bowl being pushed through the hatch near the bottom of the door as was normal, but to what sounded like a swarm of insects buzzing around my head. As I came to properly, I realised it was FE24 buzzing within my head.

About time too, she told me. *I couldn't reach you at all yesterday evening. I'm glad you're out of the infirmary, but you should have told your younglings that your "break" was over; they were wondering where you were after they got back to their dorm. I reached out to them and told them you were being kept busy yesterday as it was your first day back, and you'd be in touch with them today. Please tell me I was right? They're progressing so quickly and my mind is no match for any of theirs. Force me to reassure them again and they'll pick up from me exactly what happened to you and what you're being put through now, not to mention what we're all forced to do to earn the right to stay alive.*

Thank you for watching out for them yesterday. Now I know what I'm in for, I'll be able to handle it better. That should give my mind the space to reach out to them when they're not in lessons.

You'll do it while your handlers are torturing you in the gym? Is that wise?

It is necessary. I can do it.

FE24 paused before telling me, *You're different. It's like you're still you, but there's more of you. What's happening to you?*

I'm not sure, I'm still trying to work it out myself. When I do, I'll try and help you do it too. If you want me to.

Her uncertainty washed over me at the thought of attempting something new. *I don't know.* I sensed her flinch as the sound of the food trolley reached her ears. *Just keep in touch with your younglings. And, QFE88?*

Yes?

Stay alive. Don't give your handlers any reason to push you any harder than they are already. You've always been the strongest from our dorm, and those of us who are left need you. We might not see one another much, but we all need you in here. I sensed her tapping her temple, her action so human except for the sound of her talon clicking against her toughened skin.

I know. I thought I did, anyway. As it turned out, I had no idea of the extent to which it was true.

Chapter Seven

FAO: Officer Turner

Sender: Handler Joseph Storey

As per your request for a report on QFE88's progress, I am pleased and proud to inform you that she is ahead of schedule in her recovery, despite Handler Thomas's inclination not to push her as hard as I have insisted. I invite you to witness her progress and capabilities for yourself at your earliest convenience.

MY DAYS FELL into a pattern over the following weeks. I would wake as my breakfast bowl scraped through its hatch and then spend some time with the younglings as we all ate our first meal of the day. Their handlers arrived to collect them for their lessons at the same time Handlers Storey and Thomas came for me, so I withdrew from their minds and followed the two who had been assigned to oversee my recovery, to the gym. I spent the morning working my way without break through the weights section, the treadmills, the climbing walls and the different cross trainers, before being returned to my cell for my lunch of slop. I quickly learnt to leave enough time for my body to recover enough from its exertions before eating so that I didn't throw my meal back up, but not so much time that I vomited during my afternoon session in the gym.

My handlers were as ruthless as they were scared that I wouldn't be both physically and mentally ready to return to duty by the end of the three-week deadline they had been given. I was as determined to return to duty as I was scared that I wouldn't be allowed to in time to warn Charlotte Lace of Officer Turner's interest in her, and help her get her daughter out of the city without being caught. I was willing to be pushed even harder than my handlers were pushing me, with the result that they became confused by metrics that should have shown me fighting fear, pain and exhaustion, yet remained steady with no apparent effort from me.

Handler Storey would often put his face directly in front of mine as he timed me on a cross-trainer, or stare down into my eyes as he stood over me, ready to guide the weight bar I was lifting back to its holder. I sensed his and his partner's conflicting emotions; their relief that I was progressing better than they could have expected, coupled with their fear that they were missing something. No matter how hard they tried, they couldn't figure out why I was showing no signs of emotional or physical distress.

My state of mind made it easier to continue helping the younglings whenever I sensed they were ready; I needed no time to calm and distance myself from what I was doing but instead allowed my determination to excel at my labours to filter along my connections with them all, fuelling their enthusiasm to learn that which I had to teach.

They had progressed to following my mind up onto the streets far above us in preparation for when they would be taken up there to exercise when they were older. As was the case after I had done the same with QMB61's help, they would be better able to handle the shock of the sights, smells, tastes, sounds and sensations that always overwhelmed those unprepared for it by a life lived in the enforcer building.

They could only manage a few minutes at a time to begin with, since any longer than that caused them to be overwhelmed and unable to control their metrics. As the days passed, however, I gradually increased the time I kept their minds exploring the streets and buildings with mine, and was as pleased with their mental advancement as I was with my physical one.

When I followed my handlers back to my cell each evening, it was all I could do to keep their required distance of two paces behind them, but whenever I felt the strength fading from my legs, I thought of Charlotte Lace and her daughter and friends, and my strength returned.

It fascinated me that my physical strength – both my power and stamina – was so increased by the emotional strength that seeped into me from all of those actively defying the city's regime, whenever I thought of them. I never pondered on it for long though, as my mind always strayed immediately to those whose strength had become mine. I moved between Charlotte Lace, her daughter, Jinna Lace, Neville Brown, and then all the others who shared the strongest, most vibrant threads with the three, for as long as I could each evening before the exertions of my day caught up with me and I fell asleep.

———

The kindred were all still safe when Officer Turner paid my handlers and me a visit, three days before my recovery deadline. I was thankful I had just withdrawn my mind from those of the younglings when he flung the gym door open so violently that it crashed against the wall, and marched in as if expecting to catch its occupants doing other than what we were supposed to be. Both handlers jumped, as did I, but my grip on the most difficult of the climbing walls was firm and I quickly continued my ascent.

I felt gratified by the unease with which all three humans observed my strength and agility, even as I felt shamed at their revulsion at my part human, part animal body. I shouldn't have cared what they thought of me, any more than on any other occasion when I had felt the same way, but as always, I found it impossible not to take on the usual human view of me as "a necessary abomination" as fact.

'Get down here, QFE88,' Handler Thomas said sharply. Her voice wavered slightly as she said the last number of my name, and I could smell the sweat breaking out on her and her partner's foreheads. Their hearts were beating almost as rapidly as mine when I landed on the ground, and they couldn't meet their superior's eyes. I stood before the three of them, my eyes also cast downward.

Officer Turner left us standing in silence for a few minutes, during which I sensed his enjoyment of my handlers' obvious distress. He darted to one side, delighting in both handlers flinching, and walked a slow circle around me before returning to stand between his fellow humans, forcing them both to take a sideways step in order to accommodate him.

'She carries no sign of injury and appears to be fit and strong,' he said. 'Now that she's showing no sign of weakness, she can do three shifts patrolling the streets and then I want her back on call.' He took a step closer to me. 'Eyes up, Enforcer.'

I slowly rolled my eyes upward until they met his. I blinked more often than I needed to, as QMB61 had taught me, so that I avoided holding his gaze long enough to appear threatening.

Handler Thomas held her breath as Officer Turner looked repeatedly from one of my eyes to the other. The thread he shared with Charlotte Lace vibrated so violently, I hoped it would explode out of existence. I was horrified when, instead, its energy burst into Charlotte Lace and then blasted down the thread that connected her to me.

Officer Turner smiled. I sensed his observation of the momentary dilation of my pupils, and his assumption that it was his successful intimidation of me that had caused it.

'Your return to fitness pleases me, QFE88,' he said. I tried not to hear what the threads had warned me he would say next, but I couldn't seem to block it out. 'I will have a very special job for an enforcer soon. Continue as you are and that enforcer will be you.' He radiated confidence that what he said was true, yet I had sensed no change in his suspicion or observation of Charlotte Lace, right up until my last check in with them both the previous evening. What had changed?

I didn't have to delve far past his enjoyment of his domination of me to find out. During the twenty minutes since he had witnessed Charlotte Lace crossing the street with the human younglings she was escorting, passing a woman on crutches and then re-crossing back to the side on which they needed to be in order to turn down a nearby street, he had replayed the camera feed almost as many times as he had replayed in his mind his observation of the woman's head turning and her lips moving as Charlotte Lace passed her.

He had already accessed the other kindred's records. Her name was Hayley Smith, and she worked as a cleaner in one of the city's many police stations. She had no reason to know who Charlotte

Lace was, let alone pause her brief journey from the passenger vehicle she had just exited to her apartment block, in order to speak to her. Her use of crutches was explained by a record from the previous day of a police officer beating her for running over his foot with a cleaning trolley.

As I nodded my acknowledgement of Officer Turner's statement – I wasn't to speak unless invited – I sensed his suspicion of Hayley Smith's actions. No cleaner would ever risk injuring a police officer; they were more likely to get in trouble for taking too long over their work as a result of actively avoiding any interaction with them. Hayley Smith had to have done what she did in order to distract the police officer from a more serious infraction, and Officer Turner intended to visit the police station in question later that day, and try to discover what that might have been and how it related to Charlotte Lace.

I knew the kindred were careful, and if it hadn't been for the threads signalling the increasing danger Officer Turner and I presented to Charlotte Lace, I would have felt confident that the head of our enforcer unit would meet a dead end in his enquiry. As it was, I felt an urgent need to get above ground and warn Charlotte Lace directly, or via any other kindred I sensed in my vicinity, to evacuate the teenagers immediately and leave with them before the net Officer Turner was throwing around her pulled shut.

The sound of the gym door opening brought my full attention back to my immediate situation.

'Get yourself back up each of the walls again before you finish for the day, Enforcer,' Handler Storey said. 'By the sound of it, you'll be climbing for real before the week is out. Do a decent job of whatever the assignment is, and I might just get the promotion Turner has blocked me from getting time after time.'

'You still want to be the chief handler of our unit after what happened to the last two?' Handler Thomas said.

'They were stupid,' her partner replied as I leapt high onto the first wall and began to climb. 'They gave Turner reason to think they were after his job and we all know what he's like when he's got it in for someone. He won't stop until...'

I climbed faster so that even my ears couldn't pick up the rest of the sentence I didn't want to hear. I focused all of my efforts on climbing up and down the ten walls, and when I finally landed in front of my handlers, the female clicked her stop watch and nodded. 'Ten seconds off your previous fastest time. Follow us back to your cell, QFE88.'

———

When I stepped through the doors of the enforcer building behind Handlers Thomas and Storey, I almost smiled at the relatively fresh spring air that assailed my nostrils. After so many weeks below ground, breathing only filtered, sterilised air, it delighted me as much as it had the first time I scented it as a youngling. I harked back to that moment, reliving my joy at the feel of it in my nose and lungs; its fullness, its crispness, its vibrancy as its constituent scents all vied for prominence. I also blinked as furiously as I had then, while my eyes adjusted to the intensity of the light offered by sun's rays after so long in dreary artificial light. It was all I could do to avoid bumping into my handlers when they halted.

'You forget yourself,' Handler Thomas said without looking back at me. 'You're not FE88 anymore. Behave like a qualified enforcer. Now.' Still blinking, I stepped to the side and then around her. She said, 'Turn to the left and continue onward until I say otherwise. I have no intention of raising my voice, so be sure to listen for me above the noise of citizens and PVs.'

It felt strange, walking in front of my handlers for the first time so that everyone who saw us would recognise me for the fully trained and qualified killer I was. No longer would my handlers encourage human younglings to taunt and torture me. I was to be feared as I patrolled the streets with them; a deterrent against any thoughts of rebelling against the regime.

I was only too aware of how effective I was at my job. Humans moving between PVs and the entrances to buildings averted their eyes and quickened their steps when they saw me. A group of younglings being escorted to one of their carefully monitored, indoor interaction sessions with other younglings remained silent in accordance with their escort's hushed but firm instructions as we approached them. They still managed to burn me with the combination of disgust, loathing and terror they radiated in my direction though.

'Keep your posture and your pace,' Handler Storey hissed from behind me. 'They move out of your way now, not the other way around. And be sure to stare at them.'

I tried to walk at full height as QMB61 had coached me, even as my body tried to curl into a ball in shame at the younglings' reaction to me, but it wasn't until I had passed them that I managed it.

'That was pathetic,' Handler Storey said. 'You may have just about kept your metrics within their required parameters, but that doesn't mean I can't make you wish you were dead if I see anything I don't like.' I heard him tapping the screen of his wrist-bound monitor. 'There's another group of kids a few streets away. Take the next right and then the second left, and when they see you, you'd better have more of an effect on them than you did on the brats we just passed.'

Charlotte Lace was with them – I knew it as soon as my sixth sense stretched out to give me advance warning of what I would face. I sensed our thread drawing us together as it would whenever the opportunity presented itself, and further, its influence upon those whose assistance we needed in order to interact; the weak threads connecting me to my handlers pulsed with energy originating from Charlotte Lace's and mine, ensuring they were complicit.

My shock at the realisation sent me dangerously close to defying my parameters, so I quickly turned my sixth sense towards Officer Turner. I found him wholly absorbed in inspecting every inch of the office outside which the cleaner had run over the police officer's foot. It would be some time before he would be back at his computer screen, spying on Charlotte Lace.

I straightened my back as much as I was able and added new purpose to my steps, neither of which had anything to do with trying to terrorise a bunch of schoolchildren more than the sight of me always did.

I knew before I saw her that Charlotte Lace was at the front of the group, leading as she always liked to and as the parents or other volunteers were always content to let her; it was always the leader, if anyone, who would be questioned or reprimanded if the group were late or if any of its members failed to comply with instructions from police or enforcer handlers on the way.

I turned into the second of the streets towards which Handler Storey had directed me, and saw Charlotte Lace, twenty teenagers, and four other adults coming towards me. I sensed her flush of relief at the sight of me; it had been nearly two months since our last encounter and she had feared the worst. Remembering that I was required to be as intimidating as possible, I stared directly at Charlotte Lace without blinking and sensed all those with her slowing their steps. I kept my posture as strong as possible and my pace steady so my handlers wouldn't sense anything amiss, and breathed slow, deep breaths to keep my metrics steady.

You're being watched. I willed my thought into her mind along the path of sight from my eyes to hers, as well as along our thread, with all of my being, desperate for her to sense what I was trying to tell her. She'd never been able to hear my thoughts before, but I had never tried so hard and I'd never before made use of the thread that connected us.

She blinked. She had felt something, but she hadn't heard me. Even if she had, I suddenly realised, I hadn't told her anything new. All of us were always being watched.

I tried again. *You're in danger from Officer Turner.*

She had to lower her eyes from mine so as to be seen as fearful and respectful of me, but I could sense that she knew I was trying to tell her something. I sent the thought to her again and felt her straining to grasp hold of it while being careful not to change her pace or expression, but she couldn't quite manage it.

She was only fifteen paces in front of me now. I glared at the other humans with her, for once immune to their feelings about me, and a thrill shot through me as they all looked away from me in horror just as Charlotte Lace glanced back at me. It was now or never.

You're in danger. Officer Turner. Leave the city. I mouthed the words as slowly and obviously as I could while blasting them to her with my mind, and sensed them taking hold.

Immediately, she cast her eyes back downward. *I'm in danger from Officer Turner and you think I need to leave,* she thought to me. *Thank you for the warning. Are you alright? I've missed you.* She flicked her eyes upward as she moved to the side of the pavement to give me room to pass.

I gave the slightest nod of my head and lifted a hand to scratch my chest, pointing to myself before dropping my hand so that no one else noticed my gesture. As I passed her, I coughed over the word 'Patrol.' The younglings immediately behind her all jumped.

Patrol? She turned to her group as they jostled one another – adults and younglings both – in their attempts to follow her example and move out of my way. 'Let's all say thank you to the enforcer and her handlers for keeping us safe,' she said and glanced at me. 'We really appreciate it.' She met the eyes of my handlers briefly, respectfully, so that they didn't know her words had been for me alone, then turned back to her group and nodded in approval at their murmured gratitude.

'That was a bit better, but there's still room for improvement,' Handler Storey said to me. 'I want the next group quaking so hard in their boots, they fall over themselves to get past us.'

I barely heard him. My attention was with Charlotte Lace as she continued on her way, her mind racing to understand what I had been trying to tell her. *Patrol? Patrol. That was definitely what QFE88 whispered when she coughed. She's on patrol now, but that can't have been what she was referring to.* Her mind shot back to the beginning of our encounter. *I'm in danger from Officer Turner. I must have rattled him more than I thought. When was that? Six, seven weeks ago? I have to assume he's been watching me closely since then. What does he know? QFE88 said I have to leave the city, so she must know that plans are in place to get the kids out. Is that it? Does he know about our plans? No, if he did, she wouldn't have told me to leave too. I trust her. But he must be on to me if she thinks leaving is my only option. Patrol? What did she mean? Aaaah.* I sensed her realisation before she framed the thought to reinforce it to herself. *I need to get one of the kindred in the security department to make sure QFE88 is on patrol at the city gate when we get the kids out – she'll help us! We need to bring our plans forward. Thank goodness it's the weekend and I don't have to be at work. QFE88, if you're listening to my thoughts, and I'm pretty sure you are, I'll get a message to our people in security as soon as I've dropped this lot off. They'll have to throw some of their caution to the wind and move you onto night patrol straight away. We'll have to get the kids out tonight.*

Chapter Eight

I saw her today. I can't find the words to describe how relieved I am, not that it matters, since I'm the only one who'll ever read this. Surprisingly, she looked well. And there was something different about her. I thought if I ever saw her again, she'd be a shadow of her former self, because whatever they've been doing to her these last weeks, it can't have been good. She's the opposite though. She looks stronger, and not just physically. I wonder if they know that whatever they've put her through, it's given her the strength to resist them and help us as we live in hope that, one day, all enforcers will.

Secret diary of Charlotte Lace

AS SOON AS I stepped back through the doors of the enforcer building, I moved to the side to allow my handlers to walk in front of me once more. Neither spoke as they marched to my cell. Once I was inside, Handler Thomas said, 'Eat your lunch as soon as it arrives. You needn't think we'll go easy on you in the gym this afternoon just because you've been out on patrol this morning.'

I did as I was told, then lay down to rest. I hoped I would be given the second night shift rather than the first, so that I would have a chance to sleep and be fully alert when I was needed, but I would rest as much as possible in case Charlotte Lace needed me on the first shift.

It seemed as though no time at all passed before I heard the words, 'On your feet, Enforcer.' Handler Storey's voice was soft; he was hoping I was asleep and wouldn't hear his order so that he could punish me.

My eyes flicked open, and I was on my feet within seconds. I sensed his disappointment, followed by his decision to increase the weights he would add to my weight bar to a level that surely even I couldn't lift. He would find a reason to inflict pain on me one way or another.

I barely noticed it when he did, and in fact, the pain helped me by providing an identifiable reason for my metrics approaching their upper parameters when my body's shock response had little to do with the pain it was so used to enduring. Of all the things I had expected that afternoon, Charlotte Lace reaching out to me hadn't been one of them.

QFE88? Her use of my name was tentative yet rang out loudly within my mind. Before she could doubt that I had perceived her, I took hold of the part of herself that she had extended to me and wrapped myself around it as if taking her small hand in both of my own.

Charlotte Lace.

She couldn't perceive my thought, but I sensed her knowing that something was different in her mind – that she had connected with me and had my attention.

You're there. At least, I think you are. No, I know you are.

Thank goodness. Everything's in place. I managed to get messages to the kindred who'll bring our plans forward to tonight and to the one who'll change the enforcer duty rota. You'll be patrolling the sector of the city nearest the gates on the second night shift. It's the quietest time, so there's only ever one enforcer per sector. We'll create a diversion at the border of your sector that's furthest from the gates. If you could draw your handlers and any police also patrolling the area to the diversion, we'll get the kids out along with the kindred who'll be exposed by their roles in the escape. We've already uploaded a virus that will cause the gates to open and close when we need them to, and we'll have control of the camera feeds so everyone can reach the gates unobserved. Make sure you get back to the gates before they close so you can get out too – they'll open five minutes after the diversion begins, and will be open for exactly ten minutes. I hope you got all that. I think you did; I'm sure that solid warmth I can feel is you. I can't thank you enough for this, and I only hope you'll forgive me for asking one more thing of you. Could you possibly...

'Up you get, you pathetic creature,' Handler Storey said. 'And get straight to the walls. Start with the hardest and you'd better get your best time yet to make up for your failure with the weights.'

I breathed through the aching that always followed the particular brand of pain administered to me via the chip in my head, and leapt to the wall in just a couple of bounds so I could revert my attention to Charlotte Lace's request.

...enforcers in other cities? I mean, I don't know if any of them are open to helping the kindred in those cities – come to that, I don't even know for definite whether there are still kindred in the other cities. I hope there are, and if so, that they're supporting their enforcers like we've tried to support you all, even if in the smallest of ways. Anyway, if you could get a message to the enforcers in as many other cities as possible, and ask them to pass

it to the kindred there, then we'll have done all we can. Tell them it isn't just the nations who are heading for war, but the cities now have bombs trained upon one another too. They need to get people out and as far away from their cities as possible, however they can. Thank you, QFE88, for your help. For your courage. We'd be honoured if you'd count yourself one of the kindred.

I barely caught her gratitude, but her sense of fellowship remained with me even as I reeled at her request. It had never occurred to me to reach out to enforcers in other cities. How would I do that? As I tore back down the training wall, I thought about how my dormitory mates and I had monitored and soothed the younglings for years before I reached out to the five in my care. We hadn't met them; each of us had just plucked them out of the aether with our sixth sense. So then, I could do that with enforcers I'd never met in other cities – couldn't I?

I barely heard Handler Storey's grudging acknowledgment of my best time yet as I leapt straight onto the second most difficult climbing wall. I was in my element. My body had shed its aches of only a few minutes ago, and was obeying my instincts and physical senses with ease, scaling the wall whilst barely touching it. I diverted nearly all of my attention to my quest to communicate with other enforcers and reached out with my mind to… where?

The wall I hit in my mind was as real as the physical one in front of me. I reached out in countless directions, and could sense all the qualified and trainee enforcers out on the streets and in their cells. I could also sense the younglings who occupied the same dormitory as had my dormitory mates and I. But no others. There were other dormitories, I knew it – there were enforcers on my floor who had grown up in them – yet I couldn't find the younglings now occupying them with my sixth sense. Because I had never been in any of them, I realised. Yet I'd never been in the cells of all the enforcers I could sense either, and I definitely hadn't met or even seen them all.

I reached for them as I landed at the base of the second wall and sprang for the third, and traced my sense of them to the imprints they left wherever they went. All enforcers entered and left the building through the foyer once they were ten years old, and all enforcers left a sense of themselves that all other enforcers picked up as easily as picking up scents with our noses, and noises with our ears. We knew one another without needing to meet, so we could reach for one another, find one another, communicate with one another.

I couldn't do that with enforcers in other cities, and I couldn't find them using an intimate knowledge of their location as I had with the younglings in my former dormitory. There had to be a way though. If anyone could find it, it would be me... or QMB61. No. I couldn't reach out to him; he would pick up from me why I wanted to do it, what I was planning to do that night, and I couldn't risk him trying to talk me out of it or worse, risking himself by trying to help me. This was my decision. My risk.

I flung my sixth sense back out to the city walls and tried to push beyond everything I knew... but sensed nothing. I tried and I tried.

When I landed on the ground from the last and easiest wall, the frustration I couldn't help showing on my face pleased my handlers no end.

'Finding it a little tough today, are we?' Handler Thomas said, despite knowing – since her partner had just shown her the stopwatch – that I was well clear of my previous best time. 'Straight onto the first cross trainer. Now.'

That was fine by me. I quickly pushed my arms and legs into the rhythmic, co-ordinated movements required by the cross trainer, then returned again to trying to force my sixth sense to find other enforcers in other cities.

By the time I had completed all of my stints on the various cross trainers, I was no further ahead. I knew it had to be possible – the sensitives of whom the kindred often thought had passed messages to sensitives they had never met in other cities they had never visited – but I just couldn't find the mechanism for doing it. As I moved to the treadmill and waited for Handler Storey to set the no doubt punishing pace he expected me to achieve, I decided to focus on the part of Charlotte Lace's message that I could accomplish.

I thought through everything she had told me and knew, without a doubt, that I would ensure my handlers and any police patrolling my sector would attend the diversion her people had planned, so that Charlotte Lace and hopefully many other kindred could escape the city with the younglings they had selected. I also knew that I would make no effort to reach the gates in time to pass through them myself. I couldn't kill Charlotte Lace if she were outside the city walls and I within them. The thought strengthened me and I found a new enthusiasm as I pushed forward from my feet on the treadmill, landed on the knuckles of my hands, then flung my legs underneath myself ready for another leap.

When my younglings returned to their cots after their lessons, I reached for the five of them, feeling fiercely positive. My attitude bolstered them to the extent that they were confident enough to explore the streets above with me for much longer than on their previous attempt. I steered them away from an enforcer on assignment, and from a young police officer assaulting an adult male who had been slow to move from his passenger vehicle to his building. The younglings were buoyant when they returned their attention to their dormitory and set about amusing themselves and their dormitory mates with one of the silent games I had taught them.

I was physically exhausted when my handlers finally allowed me back to my cell, but felt as mentally energised as the younglings. By the time they next reached for me, Charlotte Lace would be safe. Then I would set about thinking how to get myself and my younglings out of the city before the humans had a chance to destroy it. I ate my evening slop and then was asleep within minutes.

————

I gasped with the pain of all my muscles cramping at once. It was a dreadful way to wake up, but it wasn't the first time handlers had roused me that way, and I knew what to do. I breathed through the pain as I forced myself to sit up and then stand. The pain ceased.

'About time too,' an unfamiliar male said. 'Your usual handlers might be prepared to repeat themselves, but Handler Satin and I are not. You've been rostered onto the night shift at short notice because the enforcer who was supposed to do it has been exterminated for insubordination. Don't be the second to suffer that fate on the same night. Follow at three paces.'

He was lying. Like all handlers on their first shift with an unfamiliar enforcer, he was terrified of me and desperate to dominate me in every way and at every opportunity. I knew he didn't know why he and his partner had been sent to collect me instead of their usual charge, and that he wasn't senior enough to exterminate me in any event; only if Officer Turner ordered it could he do that. It didn't mean it wouldn't happen that night, though – I was determined to do whatever was necessary to ensure Charlotte Lace and her charges escaped the city and its fate.

I followed him and Handler Satin along the corridor and into the lift that took us up to ground level. As soon as we were outside the doors of the building, I stepped in front of the two of them and almost turned towards the sector I already knew I would be patrolling. I just about stopped myself and waited for my handlers to tell me where to go.

'We'll be patrolling the gate sector for the next six hours,' Handler Satin said. 'You haven't done a night shift before, so I'll tell you this. It'll be quiet. The only people eligible to be on the streets between midnight and six o'clock are the police, street cleaners and us. The only people eligible to be moving between buildings and passenger vehicles are early shift workers leaving their homes between five and six. Anyone else will be arrested by the police or punished by us depending on what they're doing. You'll do as you're told, the second you're told to do it. Move.'

I sensed his fear of me battering him from the inside, and his consequent need to expel it using violence. I hoped that whoever was involved in the kindreds' diversion would be well away from the scene by the time we reached it; he would show no mercy to anyone we caught transgressing.

We saw no one during the first half of our shift. The dimly lit streets were empty aside from the passenger vehicles standing in their regularly spaced bays on either side of the main tracks, awaiting summons. There was no sound and no movement other than a dangling cable from a street lamp gently swaying in the light but chilly breeze. Clouds obscured and cleared the moon in slow succession, making the grey buildings appear more and less forbidding in turn. My handlers grew bored and restless. Constantly observed as we all were by the cameras fixed to the buildings and passenger vehicles, they were no more able to break their outward show of attention to duty as was I, which I decided would help me when the time came.

That time would be soon, I realised four hours into my patrol. The part of my attention that had remained with Charlotte Lace since she took to her bed at the usual time sensed her rising and pulling on the clothes she had laid out ready. She ran through the details of her plan as she dressed, including her mental list of whom she would collect from which building, the exact times she would collect them and the exact route she would need to take in order to coincide with the few minutes the cameras along that route would divert to pre-recorded feeds of empty streets. There was no room for error by her, the other kindred, or the younglings in their care. And there was no room for error by me.

I breathed slowly and deeply as I sensed my metrics beginning to rise. When they were stable again, I risked a quick check on Officer Turner. My heart almost missed a beat. Why was he out of bed and getting dressed? He had been on duty during the day and was due on again tomorrow, so he should have been asleep, as he had been when I checked an hour or so before. I focused on my breathing and on maintaining my regular, plodding pace along the pavement so my handlers wouldn't sense anything amiss. They continued their conversation about their wives – specifically, which of the two was most likely to gain promotion – without pause, so I delved into Officer Turner's mind.

He didn't know Charlotte Lace's plan, but he knew she had just left her apartment. He must have planted a sensor of his own on or near her door! I had to warn her... but wait, what was happening? Where was Officer Turner? One moment he was in my mind, the next he was gone. His conscious mind was, anyway. I strained to reach his subconscious mind and found it registering that which his physical senses picked up while he slept.

'I didn't kill him, did I?' a voice whispered.

'No, you caught him at exactly the right spot. He'll just be out for a bit, and he won't even be sore when he wakes. Come on, or we'll miss the gates.'

I should have known that Charlotte Lace would ensure Officer Turner couldn't thwart her escape. I relaxed a little as the kindreds' caution, not to mention their reach and experience, became even more apparent. I extended my sixth sense to all the streets in my sector and found two police partnerships on patrol in addition to my handlers and me. I kept track of them, and of Charlotte Lace as she and her daughter left their apartment block and headed for the first address on Charlotte Lace's list.

She had six younglings following her when I sensed one of the pairs of police heading straight for the street down which she and her charges were hurrying. All of them were moving silently and listening for any sounds that would warn of their discovery, but the persistent breeze carried the police's conversation in the opposite direction. I reached for her as I had when I wanted her to hear my warning, and held on to her mind as I had while she told me of her plan. I sensed her registering my presence... my pleading with her to move out of sight.

She couldn't make sense of my thought, but she sensed its urgency and instinctively darted into a large alcove housing the doorway of a nearby building, motioning for those with her to follow suit. The police appeared at the end of the street and paused to look up it for any sign of movement. I maintained my pleading with Charlotte Lace, and despite not being aware of anything untoward, she remained where she was. The moment the police moved past the end of the street, I withdrew my influence. Charlotte Lace was on her way immediately, running now to make up for the precious lost seconds.

There were other kindred – some with younglings in tow – moving about the streets of my sector now; my sixth sense picked them up as surely as the threads connecting them to me and

Charlotte Lace confirmed their parts in our endeavour. The time to accomplish our joint purpose had arrived. I pulled my attention away from the connections vibrating with the urgency of our situation, knowing for certain that it was too late for any of us to turn back and I would need my full attention on what was about to happen. I sensed Charlotte Lace darting into another alcove, flattening herself against one of the doors within it as her charges slotted in beside her. She checked her watch and silently counted down the seconds. *Three. Two. One.*

The explosion shook the pavement beneath our feet.

Chapter Nine

Carrying on the work of those who began it so long ago has been a burden, but a welcome one. My fellow kindred and I have done our utmost to keep The Way Of The Horse alive and burning within us, and those we will hopefully set free tonight will take it with them and use it to start a better way of life – the life the horses saw humans being capable of living when they helped the first kindred so long ago. If Jinna and the others get out of the city safely, and QFE88 with them, then I will die happy, for they are the future.

Secret diary of Charlotte Lace

HANDLER SATIN WAS the first to gather his wits. 'Well, don't just stand there, QFE88, get up the side of that building and do that climbing, leaping thing you all do when you're on assignment. Get yourself to the scene of whatever that was as quickly as you can, and we'll follow on behind you. You'd better have apprehended whoever was responsible by the time we get there.'

I sensed his terror that he had missed something and would be blamed for allowing an explosion to occur on his watch. My terror for Charlotte Lace was greater. It gave my legs extra power as I sprang up onto the wall of the nearest building and began to move at speed across it, soon leaving behind the sound of my handlers running down the street after me. They would be as fit as regulations required, but their human legs were no match for my climbing ability and speed. I leapt from the building, across the street to the next one and powered across it just above its ground-floor windows, glad beyond belief for the hours of extra training to which I had been subjected over the past weeks.

I sensed one pair of police officers racing towards the explosion while the other pair tore towards the city gates. I climbed around the corner of the building, and as soon as I was out of sight of my handlers, climbed higher and leapt across the street instead of continuing along the wall towards the explosion site. I climbed higher still, despite the precious seconds it cost me, so that I would be invisible by the time my handlers rounded the corner.

I divided my attention between the location of the police on their way to the gates, and my dash across the wall, and in no time, I turned its corner and descended. I landed on the pavement a few paces in front of the police, who skidded to a stop, their eyes wide with terror.

'The gate and streets this side of the explosion are clear,' I told them before they could recover from the shock and horror of my lone presence. 'You are needed at the explosion site.'

The police looked at one another. One of them recovered enough to say breathlessly, 'Smith and Lewis will be at the scene by now. We should follow the protocol for unusual activity in this sector and double-check the gates.'

The other shook her head. 'The enforcer's already checked them. One enforcer is the equivalent of twenty wall guards, remember? That's why there's one on patrol here and wall guards don't exist anymore.'

I sensed her partner racking his brains for the relevant parts of the training they had both recently completed. She didn't wait for him to catch up with her assessment. She turned and ran towards the site of the explosion, shouting over her shoulder, 'Come on!'

Her partner glanced at me, gulped and ran after her. I didn't hesitate; I didn't have long. I scaled the wall and bounded across it and two subsequent walls until I was where I needed to be. I descended to the street and landed behind two female police officers attempting to extinguish the flames roaring from a passenger vehicle, with fire extinguishers of the type found in the foyers of apartment buildings. Lights shone down on them from the windows of most of the surrounding buildings, their inhabitants too scared to do anything other than watch.

The police officers lowered their fire extinguishers at the sound of sirens in the distance, then both jumped and stumbled backward as they caught sight of me slowly circling the PV, making a show of sniffing the air as I went. I sensed their relief as my handlers burst onto the scene from one street and the two remaining police officers from another.

Handler Satin jogged to stand in front of me. He put his hands on his hips and gasped, 'QFE88, report.'

'There is no fresh human scent other than that emanating from the four of you. I can smell no accelerant. I detect scents suggestive of an electrical fault.'

'The PV battery exploded?' Handler Satin said, so eager to

believe he couldn't be found at fault that he neglected to check my metrics for any signs of untruth.

'You're sure?' Handler Bowles said, stepping closer as if he would throw his arms around me.

'Your scientists bred into me a sense of smell that my teachers ensured I can use. I am sure.' I breathed through my lie, knowing that should it be discovered any time soon, there would be a race to the gates. I needn't have worried. All six humans present were so desperate to believe me that believe me they did.

Handler Satin tapped his monitor and spoke into it. 'It was just a PV battery exploding. No ambulance is needed and no further security, I have the situation under control. Keep the fire crew coming this way and send a clean-up crew. Oh, and get on to maintenance and demand they check all PV batteries over the coming weeks.'

'You have the situation under control, do you, Satin?' The oldest of the police said, her hands on her hips as she glared at him.

He took a step closer to her and stuck out his chest. 'That's Handler Satin to you, and yes, I do. My enforcer has assessed the situation, and I have given the necessary orders to ensure this mess is dealt with before any PVs are prevented from transporting the early shift to work.'

'Your enforcer?' Handler Bowles said, his hands now also on his hips.

I took my attention away from their arguing and followed my sense of the kindred who had planted the bomb in the PV before exiting it after work the previous evening. I found him forcing his way between closely growing trees, holding a large knife in one hand and a torch in the other with which to light the way for himself and the human younglings immediately behind him. I breathed through my delight. Charlotte Lace and all those she and her kindred had sought to get out of the city were safe!

My thought of her immediately brought her to the forefront of my sixth sense. My breath caught in my throat. She was running along a pavement. She was still in the city! She was in the city and running down a street very near to where I stood, without even trying to conceal herself from the now live camera feeds.

I felt her joy at the fact her daughter was free, along with twenty-seven other human younglings and all the kindred who had acted to bring about the escape. I also felt her sadness at having watched the gates close behind them without having seen me join them. Of those whose involvement in the escape was traceable, I alone remained in the city. She didn't know it was by choice. She didn't know I'd had no intention of escaping alongside her – that being near her was the last place I wanted to be. She had stayed behind in the hope of deflecting attention away from me.

Handler Bowles was suddenly in front of me. 'QFE88, we have unauthorised movement two streets away. Apprehend the source and wait for our arrival. GO!'

His shout jerked me out of my horror. I bounded to the nearest wall and was across it and around the corner before my handlers had taken more than a handful of strides. I had to reach Charlotte Lace before anyone else did. I thought furiously as I closed the distance between the two of us. I had to get her out of the city. Maybe I could get her to the wall and haul her up to the top of it? It was too sheer even for me to climb, but she could climb down its other side using the trees that grew against it if I could just get her up there? My handlers would have set my program back to manual so I could exert myself without exceeding the parameters on my auto setting – I just had to get her to the wall before they were alerted to what I was doing and set it back to auto, or inflicted their own concoction of pain. It would be difficult, but I could do it. I held on to that thought until I landed on the pavement in front of Charlotte Lace.

She murmured, 'Thank you, QFE88. Thank you for clearing our paths to the gates. I'm so sorry you didn't make it out yourself. Now, you must take my life in order to save yours.'

'We don't have time for this,' I told her. 'Get on my back and I'll carry you to the gates. I think I can throw you up on top of the wall if you'll trust me to…'

She lifted a hand and I sensed her urge to touch me, to comfort my distress, but she dropped it again quickly. The cameras were watching. She stepped back away from me and said loudly, 'Do what you have to, I don't care. It's worth it to have got my daughter away from this hellhole, especially before any of you even caught wind I was going to do it.'

'I caught wind of it,' a voice sneered behind me.

I sensed the effort it took for Charlotte Lace to smile. 'Officer Turner, how lovely to see you.'

He stepped around me and stood with his nose almost touching hers. She didn't flinch.

'You made three mistakes,' he told her. 'The first was bringing yourself to my attention. The second was trusting those dim-witted cleaners to access surveillance records from the closed network the police chief insists on, presumably to find out if they were watching you or your daughter.' He swatted his own question away with his hand. 'It's of no matter. She wasn't under surveillance, but you were. By me, so there was no record of it to alert you. Yet somehow, you discovered it. And somehow, you bypassed the security at the entrance to my building, then outside my apartment, and rendered me unconscious. Your third mistake was not killing me when you had the chance, because I'm going to wrench all the information I want out of you as painfully as I can.'

'There's no need,' Charlotte Lace said calmly as my handlers came puffing and blowing around the corner and almost ran into me. 'I'll tell you now. I saw you following me. Not once, not twice, but on numerous occasions. If there's a top-up course on surveillance without detection available to you, I really think you should enrol. I didn't bypass your security and knock you out, that was someone from the security department who has just escaped the city with my daughter. Another of those who escaped was a computer programmer who used your enforcer's control program to confuse her senses for the short time necessary for the escape to be successful. Yet another engineered the PV battery explosion. I've no idea how any of them did what they did because I'm just not that bright, and frankly, neither are you.'

I didn't need my sixth sense to know of Officer Turner's outrage at being humiliated by her again. He clenched his fists and gritted his teeth together so hard, blood vessels bulged in his neck. His breath whistled through his nose as he expelled it with unnecessary force, and he reeked of the sweat that rapidly soaked the back and armpits of his shirt, despite the chilly night air.

He didn't take his face from in front of Charlotte Lace's as he said between his teeth, 'Order an immediate check-in of all citizens.'

Handler Satin immediately spoke into his monitor. 'Officer Turner requests the immediate check-in of all citizens. I'll expect your report on their compliance in exactly three minutes.'

I was frozen to the spot, unable to think or move as events moved on at such a pace in front of me. Charlotte Lace was baiting Officer Turner, wanting him to order her immediate execution, because she thought that doing so would save me. In my anguish, I couldn't sense why. As we all stood waiting in silence, she calmly enlightened me.

You have to survive, QFE88. You have no idea how incredible you are. I was born into my role; tutored for it by my mother, as I then tutored my daughter. You emerged from an incubator with no parents to care for you, no love or kindness shown you, nothing given to you at all other than fear and pain, yet you're as kind and brave as any kindred I've ever known. When the bombs drop, I'll die anyway. You have a chance of surviving if you're in your cell below ground, and if you do, you'll be free. You'll be able to leave here as you should have done today. When the time comes, both your kind and mine – if any of them have survived – will need you, I know that in a way I can't explain. So, you must survive. You must kill me when Turner orders it, and you must do it as if you're glad to do it. That action, along with everything I've just told him, will hopefully mean it'll be some time before he or anyone else chances to wonder whether you were involved in the escape, and time is all you need from me now. So, kill me, knowing I want you to. I want you to forge a better future in the aftermath of what's coming. Raise your younglings to be just like you, and the pain you're about to suffer will have been worth it.

My younglings. Their dormitory was floors below mine. If I survived what Charlotte Lace was sure was coming, so would they, and they would need me. Charlotte Lace was right; they would all need me. But I couldn't think of doing as she asked.

Handler Satin spoke. 'Fifty-two citizens aside from Ms Lace, here, and including her daughter, have failed to tap their location into their nearest monitor within the deadline.'

'And I'm very happy to tell you that all fifty-two are now well beyond your reach, for I counted them out of the gates myself,' Charlotte Lace said cheerfully. *Help them once you're free, QFE88. Help my daughter if she needs it. Please?*

Her plea drew my eyes to meet hers. Even in her last few minutes of life, they were full of the compassion that I would never have known existed had I never met her. They crinkled at their corners as she smiled at me. *I love you, QFE88. Do this out of the love I know you have for me.*

'You bait my enforcer with your smiles, as well as me?' Officer Turner sneered. Then his face smoothed and the corners of his mouth lifted into a smile that was unsupported by any of his other facial features. 'QFE88, I am bringing your second assignment forward. Exterminate Ms Lace immediately.'

Her eyes never left mine. She held me within them as my talons severed an artery in her neck and as I lowered her to the ground. It was only when their stare was completely empty of her that I felt the pain of what I had done.

'Stand, QFE88,' Officer Turner ordered.

My delay in obeying him resulted in pain that came nowhere close to that which I was already feeling. When it stopped, I got to my feet with every intention of ripping his throat out.

QFE88, NO! THE YOUNGLINGS! QFE24 blasted into my mind. *Whatever that is you're feeling, stop it. You woke me up with the force of it, so you'll have woken the younglings. Calm down. CALM DOWN! Oh, so you've killed again. It's... hard. I know that now too, but you have to get better at coping with it. QME96, wake up and help me, QFE88's going to lose control of herself again. QME96! WAKE UP!*

I breathed through everything I was feeling. It was harder than breathing through physical pain, but I managed it as long as I kept my eyes on Charlotte Lace's face – as long as I kept her last thoughts to me at the forefront of my mind so that everything else it now contained couldn't swamp me. *Do this out of the love I know you have for me.*

Love. I wasn't sure I knew exactly what that was, but I sensed what it was to her; the feeling that had driven her every action. Without thinking, I relayed it to the younglings who, as QFE24 feared, had stirred and were sobbing in response to everything I had been broadcasting. They quietened and drifted back to sleep.

'Get back on patrol,' Officer Turner ordered.

I tore my eyes from Charlotte Lace's face and moved my feet in the direction I was ordered by my handlers.

I will not lose control, I told QFE24. *I'm going to look after the younglings. I'm going to look after you all.*

Thank you. Her reply was unnecessary, for I felt her relief.

Thank you, Charlotte Lace echoed, her thought faint, as if she were somewhere far away. I groped after it, trying to follow it to her, but I couldn't find it. Instinctively, I reached for our thread. Where it had been substantial and vibrant, it was now the thinnest of them all. Yet it was strong. Unbreakable. The link between us would never cease to exist even though our time together had come to an end. She had given me strength. She had shown me how to love and be loved. Now, I was on my own.

Chapter Ten

FAO: Officer Turner

Sender: Governor Small

You are hereby ordered to install the attached upgrades to the relevant enforcer control programs in order that they have complete autonomy with immediate effect. When it is done, you and your handlers will report to the department of employment, where you will be assigned roles critical to the running of the city now that the former occupants of those roles have been exterminated. Ensure that you follow my orders promptly if you do not wish to follow their example.

THE WEEKS FOLLOWING Charlotte Lace's death passed in a haze of loneliness, sadness and agony, punctuated by spells of calm whenever QFE24 interrupted my thoughts with reminders of my promise. During those spells, when I focused on those who needed me rather than on the black void in my mind that threatened to swallow me whole, I felt everything Charlotte Lace had helped me to feel – loyalty towards my dormitory mates and the younglings, my wish for them to experience compassion instead of only aggression, and the strength I wanted them to feel from me and for themselves – and I remembered why I had agreed to carry on living.

I tried to extend those feelings to everyone I passed on my increasing number of patrols of the streets, as Charlotte Lace had always done. Only the kindred looked at me with anything other than terror. The tattoo on my chest confirmed my identity as the enforcer who had killed a high-ranking member of their organisation, yet even through their sadness, they recognised her stamp upon me and their eyes filled with a level of compassion that eclipsed the small amount I was able to generate. The rest of the humans kept their eyes to the ground, alone in their tiny worlds of terror and exhaustion as more and more of them became aware of the increasing threat to the city.

The humans were all required to work longer shifts with less rest in between as the governors prepared for war. Violence spilled out of those whose turmoil exceeded their ability to cope, and as my fellow enforcers and I began to fill the mortuaries, the humans still able to function were stretched ever thinner. Then the morning came when a barely coherent handler rushed me to the front doors of the enforcer building and told me I would be patrolling alone.

'The computer programmers have been working around the clock on new coding for your control program, which has now been upgraded,' he told me. 'Your auto setting will sense your detection of lawbreakers, and the parameters will automatically adjust to allow you to exert yourself until the miscreants have been apprehended and punished.'

'How will I know what punishment to give without a handler to tell me?' I asked.

He grinned, his eyes flashing with madness, and told me as if I didn't already know, 'Pain is the greatest of teachers.'

It was certainly a quick and exhausting one, which many of my fellow enforcers didn't survive. I couldn't feel sad about their deaths; if anything, those of us who were left agreed, they were lucky to have escaped the nightmare of wounding and killing in which the rest of us were forced to engage on a daily – sometimes hourly – basis by the "advanced" settings on our programs. The dead enforcers also no longer had to find the strength to soothe the younglings, who hadn't been let out of their dormitories for weeks since there were no handlers available to teach or exercise them. Their control programs allowed them to leave their cots in order to relieve themselves, but aside from that, they were confined around the clock to cots barely bigger than themselves. My younglings fared better than most since their minds could go where their bodies couldn't, but still I worried for them.

The carnage on the streets escalated at a rate with which my ability to cope could only just about keep pace. The sun climbed higher in the sky with each day that passed, yet the city felt ever darker. The tall, grey buildings seemed black to me and as if they loomed towards one another over the streets. Litter blew about before coming to rest in piles on the blood-stained pavements. PVs stood silently on their tracks and in their bays as the transport system became clogged by vehicles that had been damaged when their inhabitants were dragged out to meet their fates. As a result, humans hurried between their homes and places of work instead of being transported in safety, increasing the opportunity and occurrence of violence, to which I and other enforcers were forced to respond.

When I patrolled the streets, stepping between the bodies of those who had killed one another or been slain by enforcers for attempting to do so, it was the part of my mind I shared with the younglings to which I retreated, for that was the only part of me that remembered whom I had decided to be. It was also where I resided while my control program forced my body to carry out assignments, for my charges became my only reason to carry on living. So many enforcers ran out of strength to do the same.

The day came when my morning slop failed to be delivered by the cleaner whose role had expanded to include doing so. For a time, I was too tired to care, but when I was roused to full wakefulness by the hunger pangs of the younglings as well as my own, I reached out with my sixth sense to find an explanation. All of a sudden, the dim light – a constant in my cell since I had first entered it – went out, and my cell door slid open.

I almost drowned in the mental screams of the younglings, and the questioning thoughts of every remaining adult enforcer, including my own. I sat up on my bunk in darkness that was so absolute, even my eyes couldn't pick out a single feature of my cell. I reached out again with my sixth sense and could find no humans on our floor... or on any of those above or below.

I felt my way to the doorway of my cell and stood there for a few minutes, listening to the voices now as well as the thoughts of those on my floor. 'QUIET!' I shouted as loudly as I could.

There was silence, into which I spoke again for the benefit of those less able to use mindspeak than the rest of us. 'Something must have happened above ground. There aren't any humans in the building, but that doesn't mean none will return. Stay in your cells while I reach out further and try to figure out what's happened. Those of you who can, support the younglings you connect with as best you can. Stay quiet so you can all hear me when I have more to say.'

In the silence that followed, I extended my sixth sense as far as it would go. I couldn't sense anything at all above floor C, two levels above the one I shared with now only twenty-three other enforcers who had survived the upgrade to our control program. Frantically, I reached for the enforcer I knew best. When I couldn't find QMB61, I turned my attention to the thread we shared, dreading what I suspected I would find. Sure enough, it continued to link me to however much of him remained now that his body was dead.

I returned to my bunk on wobbly legs. My mentor had been there for me since my sixth sense had allowed him to be. Even when he withdrew from me, when his mentoring was complete, he was there, three floors above me, a constant in a world that could shift at any moment the humans chose. Now, that world had shifted to such an extent that I couldn't fathom what to think or do, and he was a constant no more.

I breathed through my fear as he had trained me to… and suddenly he didn't feel so absent. The thread that continued to link us did so not because we willed it, I realised, but because we had shared parts of ourselves with one another that were irretrievable. He would always be a part of me, whatever I did, wherever I went, however I felt, for it was impossible for him not to be. So would Charlotte Lace. She wouldn't sit around when she was needed, and neither would I.

I moved back to the doorway of my cell and lifted a hand. I took a breath and pushed it through the doorway, knowing that if my control program were operational, doing so would cause immense pain. Nothing happened.

Younglings. My thought was firm. Gentle. Unafraid. *Fear not. I will find out what has happened and then I'll come to you. It is important you remain calm and try to help your dormitory mates to stay calm alongside you. You can use your voices to reassure them. Will you do that?*

FJ4p answered first. *I'll try.*

How do you know we can talk without being hurt? MJ4j asked.

I'm not going to try it, FJ4c announced before I could answer.

Because there are no humans in the building and my control program is non-functional, I explained. *I have been subject to far tighter parameters than you, so if I can defy mine, it's safe to assume you can defy yours. You don't have to talk out loud if you feel too scared to, but it will help your dormitory mates if you can find the courage to do it.*

I'll do it. FJ4g didn't hesitate to follow through with her decision. 'QFE88 is taking charge of things,' I sensed her saying out loud. 'She just told me, c, j, m and p in our heads. Stop screaming, all of you. STOP IT and listen. It'll be alright. If QFE88 says it will be, then it will. She's never wrong and she never lets us down.'

'She just told us we could speak without pain and she was right,' agreed FJ4p. 'The control program isn't working. The lights might have gone out, but I'd rather be able to talk in the dark than be quiet in the light, wouldn't you?'

'Definitely,' MJ4m said. 'We can invent some new games – talking ones this time. Who wants to make one up first?'

'I will,' MJ4j replied.

FJ4c? I ventured. She had always been the most fearful of the five.

I'll... She gulped. *I'll help.*

Thank you, all of you. I knew I could count on you. I'll be with you as soon as I can. I stepped out into the corridor, unable to prevent myself from flinching in anticipation of the pain I struggled to believe wouldn't come. I cleared my throat and said, as loudly as I could, 'I can't sense anything above floor C. I'm standing in the corridor; our control programs aren't operational. I'm going upstairs to see what's happened. I'll be back once I know, so if you don't want to come, wait down here. Anyone who wants to, make your way to the stairwell. The lifts won't be working.'

I used mindspeak to repeat my assessment of the situation, and my intention, for those on other floors who could perceive it. When I reached the stairwell – which was in darkness almost as absolute as that of the corridor – I sensed fourteen enforcers around me from my floor, and many more ascending from lower floors.

Those in front of me waited for me to weave my way to the front, then tentatively climbed the stairs behind me. Twelve enforcers waited in silence where the stairwell met floor D, none of them willing to climb the stairs until I passed them. I had only just begun to climb the stairs to floor C when the air changed. I sneezed as dust filled my nose and had to blink and rub my eyes to clear them of that which was making them sting.

'Close your eyes,' I told the enforcers behind me, then coughed. *I'm going to have to use mindspeak. Put a hand over your nose and mouth and tell any near you who have little use of their sixth sense to do the same.*

As I continued to climb, I felt grit and then small stones beneath my feet, which increased in size with every step until they were too big to step over. I felt for them in the dark and moved them to one side. I was able to continue only a few more steps before I could climb no further.

There's rubble blocking our way, I reported. *I'm going to have to pass it back down. Stack it where it won't block the stairwell.*

The physical labour was as much of a blessing as it was a curse; it required focus and diverted our minds from thoughts of anything else. Built and trained for physical prowess as we all were, we made quick work of clearing our way to floor C, where nineteen more enforcers waited. They stacked rubble along their corridor as we passed it to them, then took their places in the line of workers clearing our way up to floor B.

I kept my eyes clamped shut throughout and breathed as shallowly as possible through my nose to keep the dust out of my lungs. It was only when I felt the air before me move fractionally against my face, and scented more than just dust and enforcers, that I opened my eyes a fraction. As I had hoped, the darkness was no longer absolute. I turned to look behind me and was able to make out QME96, his normally black pelt now light grey with dust.

We're nearly there, I told my fellow excavators, and returned to my efforts with renewed vigour.

I didn't allow myself to open my eyes again until the air that filled my nostrils was dust free and smelt of the rain that was moistening the top of my head. I grasped the large grey building bricks that still blocked my way and threw them out of the hole I had cleared above my head. Without a word, I climbed the last few steps to where floor B should have been.

Cold rain washed the dust from my face as I moved to the side of the stairwell so that those behind me could emerge. None of us spoke, for we didn't know what to say. None of us thought, for we didn't know what to think. We just stood where the city had been only hours before, taking in the sight of the vast crater full of rubble that was surrounded, far in the distance, by what looked like stubs of buildings near the remains of the city wall. How long we stood there, none of us could tell. Several times, those of us who had emerged first almost found the wherewithal to begin framing a thought that might have made sense of our surroundings… only to be swamped by the complete incredulity of the remaining seventy or so enforcers.

Eventually, the rain stopped falling and we were bathed instead by rays carrying a hint of warmth from the sun. The wet rubble that surrounded us shone in the sunlight as the buildings from which it had been created never had. I blinked as realisation hit me. Everything was different. Everything that had made up our world – the humans, the computers, the city – was gone.

We were free.

Chapter Eleven

My daughter,

I hope this letter finds you well, if it finds you at all. These self-proclaimed Heralds who are springing up everywhere, offering to take messages between villages, have me flummoxed. How can they possibly know where all the villages are in order to deliver messages, when they've only taken to travelling around them so recently? Your father says I must give them a go, that they will be a boon to us all if they do their job well, so here it is, my first attempt at sending a letter to you instead of losing a day's work walking to see you. I hope it finds you healthy and happy in your herbalism apprenticeship in Jonustown? Your father and I are both well, although we were disconcerted when the ground kept shuddering yesterday. Did you feel it too? It happened over and over, some of the tremors very faint, as if they came from far away, and some of them stronger. Your father thinks they may have come from the cities, but as I told him, they are all a great distance away, so it couldn't have been that.

Anyway, work hard on your studies. The sooner you qualify, the sooner you can come home to us and be the first resident Herbalist in Rockwood!

Lots of love, Mum.

I MURMURED, 'WE ARE FREE.' Some of the enforcers standing nearby repeated my observation. The rest could do no more than think it. Those below ground who could use mindspeak echoed the thought back to us as a question, not able to understand the concept let alone believe it. QFE24 was one of them.

There's nothing up here except rubble, I told her. *Our control programs aren't operational because there are no computers and no humans.*

No computers? No humans? QFE24 replied faintly. *What will we do?*

'What will we do?' QME96 repeated out loud.

The silence that followed gave him his reply; none of us could fathom an answer. I turned at the sound of rubble shifting as nearly half of our number sat down where they were. To a one, they stared into the distance, the small amount of sanity they possessed completely overwhelmed at the idea of making any kind of decision for themselves. The rest remained on their feet, staring directly at me and hoping that I would continue to tell them what to do.

QMD12 made us jump with his roar. When he ran out of breath, he sucked in air until both lungs were full, and roared again, and again, and again. The rest of us listened, understanding his need. QMD12 was born with only a little ability to use his sixth sense and having never developed beyond that, he had been largely alone in his mind with all the pain and fear to which we had all been subjected for so long. Where so many of us had retreated into ourselves while our bodies carried out our assignments, he had revelled in having an outlet for his agony, and thrown himself wholeheartedly into maiming and killing. But not even that with which he had been tasked in recent weeks had been enough to rid him of everything he had been forced to contain within himself. And no amount of roaring would ever be.

We realised it in the same instant as he. He crouched down, resting his weight lightly on his knuckles, then sprang forward and bounded away from us, across the rubble. His muscular legs propelled him in great leaps, from which he landed on his feet and the knuckles of the hairy hands attached to arms twice the length of those of humans, which we all possessed. Many of us sensed his intention to hunt out and destroy any surviving humans, and five of our number tore after him. The rest of us watched the six of them until they were tiny dots in the distance, whose movement we could no longer discern. We knew they would continue to move until they could move no more. We saw none of them again.

QMD12's expulsion of pain and associated decision to hunt was a stark reminder to me of how fortunate I had been to receive the help that had stopped me from being driven to do the same. I focused on the thread that still linked me to Charlotte Lace until everything it represented filled me to the exclusion of all else. I considered our situation from my subsequent clearer viewpoint.

Try as I might, I still couldn't find an answer to the biggest question we all faced, but realised I could hunt for the answer to one of the smaller ones; how to feed those who were hungry, which was all of us who had survived the annihilation of the city.

I turned to the other enforcers. 'Now we know there's nothing up here, we need to find food back down there.'

'The handlers used to… load the food trolley from a room…

next to my cell,' an enforcer I'd never seen before said distractedly, unable to tear her eyes from our surroundings.

'You're QFG1,' I observed using my sixth sense. 'So, you're in the farthest cell from the stairwell. Maybe there's such a room on every floor. I think some of us should clear more rubble out of the stairwell to let more light down it, then we'll wedge the doors to the corridors open and hope enough light makes it along them for us to see.'

No one moved. I would need to be more direct. I met the eyes of half of those still standing. 'Move as much rubble as you can up here from out of the stairwell, while I take everyone else to find food.'

I felt their relief at my order, and they all moved instantly to obey me. I walked between those who were still sitting down, staring sightlessly, and touched them on their shoulders as I spoke. 'You can either stay sitting up here in the sun, or come down below with the rest of us.'

Their collective flash of panic hit me before their apathy quashed it, shutting them down even more than before, and protecting them to an even greater degree from any suggestion that they should make a decision. I needed to learn quickly. I tried again, saying firmly, 'All of you who are sitting down, get to your feet and follow me.' I looked at those still standing around. 'The rest of you, search the floors housing your cells. If you find food in a storeroom at the far end, distribute it to those still in their cells and those working in the stairwell. If you can't find a storeroom, come down to floor E where you'll find me.'

They appeared as relieved to receive instructions as I was that all those with blank faces followed my order and descended the steps behind me. I sent ten blank-faced enforcers with each of those who peeled off at floors C and D, then took the remaining nine with me along floor E as more enforcers continued down to floors F, G, H and I.

'I'm just looking for food,' I shouted to those still too afraid to leave their cells on my floor. 'Come out of your cells. Your control programs will never cause you pain again.'

I described everything I had seen above ground as I counted my way along the doors in the darkness that was still absolute, and after I passed the cell that had housed QFE1 until her extermination only days before, I was relieved to find a door that, unlike our cell doors, had a handle. I twisted it and was thankful when it yielded easily. I sensed the nine with blank faces standing listlessly in the corridor behind me as I opened the door and went inside. I could scent no slop, and no ingredients that could be used to make it.

Those of you on floor C, do you have a storeroom?

Only one of the enforcers up there was strong enough in her sixth sense to perceive my question. *We do.*

I focused my attention on QFC98 and looked through her eyes at everything she could see in the dim light that had made it along the length of her corridor.

The walls of the huge storeroom were lined with shelves upon which sat massive tins, all identical in size and labelled with "Adult" in large black letters. A wrapped batch on a pallet at the far end was labelled "Youngling", no doubt placed there in readiness for a new cohort of younglings to be elevated from one of the dormitories now that so many cells were empty. QFC98 stood with four other enforcers, all of them looking around despite having been there for some minutes. Like me, they had no idea how to get what had to be our slop out of the tins.

There was noise in my corridor as more enforcers found the courage to follow my instruction and step out of their cells. I stood listening to them shifting around and whispering to one another, and it was some time before I realised I was waiting for someone to tell me what to do. I blinked and shook my head. No one was going to do that. I was free. Free of humans and their orders and their cruelty. Free of being made to do things to others that hurt me inside far more than it hurt them on the outside. Free of being kept underground, unable to see at will the sky and clouds, or feel the wind and rain and snow and sun, or hear birds singing their songs as they hunted for food and mates. I had never dreamt it would happen, not because I didn't want freedom, but because I had no concept of it. Now I had it, I realised I wasn't free in every way; I wasn't free of fear. It coursed through me as I stood in the darkness, unsure how to go about feeding myself, let alone all of those whose minds constantly reached for mine in the hope of further announcements or instructions.

I breathed through the knotting in my stomach and the tightness constricting my throat as I tried to think what to do. I couldn't retreat from my fear – I couldn't take refuge in my body until whatever was causing it had gone. We already had twenty-nine blank faces among our number and I would be no good to anyone if I joined them. I couldn't ask QMB61 for help, and doubted he would have been able to help me, anyway. I dived into the thread that had saved me before and found my way back to the version of myself that I would have to get far better at being if I and those looking to me for guidance were to survive.

Charlotte Lace wasn't fearless, I remembered as I immersed myself in the sense of her that resided within me. She was brave. She acted as if she weren't scared even when she was terrified, as did the rest of the kindred. They would all have known what was coming, yet none of them had succumbed to the mad terror that affected everyone else. None of them had hurt anyone, let alone taken part in the frenzied killing in the run up to the city's destruction. They had remained determined and focused as they tried to support those around them with kind acts and words, intent only on trying to prepare them to meet their fates with the same calm strength that came from accepting the situation, that the kindred themselves had found the courage to choose.

Some of Charlotte Lace's words came back to me and I felt a sudden warmth, as if she were standing right next to me. *Thank you, QFE88, for your help. For your courage. We'd be honoured if you'd count yourself one of the kindred... I want you to forge a better future in the aftermath of what's coming. Raise your younglings to be just like you, and the pain you're about to suffer will have been worth it... You have no idea how incredible you are... I love you, QFE88.*

I was one of the kindred. I wasn't fearless, but I could be brave. I could accept my freedom and the terrifying abyss of choices and decisions that came with it. I could meet the rest of my life the same way the human kindred had met their deaths.

But they had each other and I am alone. The voice of my fear was small within my mind, but I couldn't unhear its words or even be distracted from them by the cacophony of mental and vocal questions being fired at me from all directions. Surrounded as I was by those who needed me to think for them, I felt more alone than had I been the only survivor.

The kindred had leaders. Charlotte Lace was one of them. The voice of my strength fought back. *She was always deciding and organising and teaching. Those who followed her learnt from her and followed her example.* That was it. If I could make decisions more easily, the others would learn to do it from me and then I wouldn't be alone; they would be kindred too. I just had to be brave enough to face everything that was unfamiliar. Starting with opening a tin of food.

I reviewed everything I had seen in the storeroom on floor C, and moved to the side, my hand stretched out in the hope of finding a food trolley in the same position as the one two floors above. My hope was rewarded. I grasped the trolley's handle and felt atop it for the implements QFC98 could see. It seemed the humans were as rigid in their own habits as they had trained us to be in ours – my hand found a larger spoon than those we used to eat our slop, two knives and a pile of identical implements that were foreign to me.

QFC98, pick up one of the metal objects next to the spoon and knives, and move it close to a tin, I told her. As I looked through her eyes, I easily saw how it was used. *Follow what I do.*

Less than a minute later, we each stood before an open tin of slop. Through QFC98's eyes, I found a cabinet containing bowls, more spoons and a range of other items, including, to my relief, battery-powered torches. We both set those with us to work distributing implements and food, and those on the other floors were soon following suit. Hunger overtook fear, and once everyone was eating, the pressure exerted on my mind by so many others eased… and I became acutely aware of the younglings.

My five had grown tired of trying to keep themselves and their dormitory mates calm, and were sitting in their cots, crying with hunger and fear at the persistent darkness. Their distress was nothing compared to the confusion and outright panic of the other younglings in their dormitory though, and the younglings in other dormitories whom I realised I could now sense; my brave, brilliant younglings had reached out to those they knew from their lessons, intending – but failing – to soothe them as they had sensed adult enforcers doing for them in the past.

I bolted down my food while passing on everything I could sense to the other adult enforcers who could perceive my thoughts. If they were to learn what I could teach them, if they were to become kindred like me, I could spare them nothing. The blank-faced enforcers, and those not strong enough in their sixth sense to be affected, carried on eating. The rest obeyed my request to meet me where their floors met the stairwell, many still eating from their bowls. The younglings could wait no longer.

Chapter Twelve

Hi Mum,

I got your letter just a few days after the date on the envelope! The Herald who brought it is so enthusiastic about the future of her profession, so I'm writing this message for her to bring back to you. She's going on to other villages first before circling back to Rockwood, but even so, I'm sure it'll reach you before I see you next. My apprenticeship is going well, I'm so lucky to be training in the village where the first ever Herbalist lived! Sometimes, when I'm trying to sense what a new herb can do, I swear I can feel her standing beside me, willing me to find the ailment it can cure, and then I do! I'll be qualified and back home before you know it. We felt the tremors here too, it was weird, wasn't it? Maybe the Horse-Bonded will be able to tell us what caused them. If one visits Rockwood before Jonustown, write and tell me what they say, won't you? I'd better get back to my studies.

Love to you and Dad, Isabel

I PAUSED on the first step between floors I and J, sensing that those behind me were every bit as reluctant to descend the stairs to our past. The terror of being herded up the stairs from the floors housing the dormitories and lesson halls – our entire world until we were ten years old – by handlers only too happy to tap the buttons on their monitors which would cause forbidden screams, felt real to us all over again.

A few of the other enforcers retched. Our fear was soon eclipsed, though, by that which assailed us from the lowest floors of the enforcer building. My feet began to move down the stairs of their own accord towards the blackness that swallowed the light from my torch.

It felt strange, stepping into the corridor of floor J. The walls and floors were the same grey as those of the floors above, but where the cell doors of our corridors stretched from floor to ceiling, the doors to the dormitories were much smaller and spaced further apart, and the ceiling seemed lower. I felt like a rat invading a mouse burrow.

Shouting, sobbing and keening seeped under some of the doors. I was glad that all of those with me were capable of mindspeak, so I could avoid frightening the younglings further by shouting my instructions.

There are younglings in dormitories one, two, four, six, seven and ten. Those of you who are from those dorms and have already been connecting with the younglings within, go to them. You'll have to lift most of them out of their cots forcibly, but use your minds to soothe them and, hopefully, it will help to calm them down. Those of you who came out of dorms that are now empty, follow me to dorm four and wait outside.

QFE24, QME96 and QME16 followed me along the corridor with those from dormitories that were empty of younglings. When I reached the door to dorm four, I rested my hand on its cold, metal handle, suddenly unable to push it down and face what was inside. Everything I could sense emanating from within the room jumbled with that flooding back to me from my own memories, and I felt myself swaying where I stood.

The scent of the sterilised floor in my memory became confused by the stench of excrement and urine that caused my nose to wrinkle now. The silence that had been instilled by pain and fear into my dorm mates and I was disturbed by a keening that made my stomach churn. The mindspeak that had been exchanged between me and QMB61 when I was a resident in the dorm was overwhelmed by that bombarding my mind as my younglings sensed my immediate presence. I blinked and came back to myself, aware that not only were they desperate for me to help them overcome the instinct forced into them to remain in their cots unless given permission to leave, but that I and those I had instructed to accompany me were impeding the progress of other enforcers to dorms six, seven and ten.

I pushed down on the handle with far more force than was necessary, and it came off in my hand as I pushed the door open. The keening turned into raucous screams as the door slammed back against the wall and my torchlight burst into the room, then quietened to terrified whimpers.

I sensed the discomfort of QFE24, QME96 and QME16 matching my own as we stepped back in time and saw ourselves in those before us. *We have to calm ourselves,* I told them. *We have to soothe them, not make their fear greater by sending them our unease. Breathe. See them, not ourselves when we were here. They need us.*

Without realising what I was doing, I reached for the three of them and enveloped them in everything that surged within me whenever I thought of Charlotte Lace. They recognised the compassion, the kindness and the strength! All the attributes I had absorbed from the kindred were already within them, albeit it faintly, and expanded all of a sudden as they felt them from me. Of course. I wouldn't have been the only enforcer touched by the hundreds of kindred who had lived in the city above us before... No. I couldn't think of that. I refocused on everything they had given us all so freely and pushed it into the words I spoke aloud so that all the younglings could all hear me.

'I know it's frightening, seeing us for the first time, but none of us will hurt you. We won't allow anyone to hurt you ever again. We're going to lift you out of your cots and take you out of here. We're going to look after you.'

All but my five younglings screamed at the thought of leaving their cots for a reason other than toileting, without the permission of a human. Prolonging the ordeal wouldn't help, I decided, and headed straight for the nearest of my younglings. FJ4c's arms were shaking with fear even as she held them out to me. She could easily have jumped out of her cot by herself had her mind been as strong as her eight-year-old body, but as I lifted her, I felt her stiffen with terror of the pain she couldn't prevent herself from expecting. She shuddered with relief as I held her to me, and I found myself unable to put her down.

Her arms locked into place around my neck as she sobbed onto my shoulder, and I tightened my hold on her, surprised at the sensation in my chest; my heart felt as if it were reaching for her as keenly as was my mind, warming us both as a result. The feeling was so powerful, it almost frightened me, yet it wouldn't allow fear to exist in its presence. I felt as if I could do anything while being empowered by this strange emotion.

The screams of other younglings being lifted from their cots barely reached me as I moved to FJ4g. As determined as FJ4c was fearful, yet still not quite brave enough to leave her cot, my torchlight found her sitting on the top horizontal bar of those that held the vertical bars of her cot in place. She took my torch from me wordlessly and almost jumped from her cot as my arm tightened around her waist, but once she was clear of it, she clung to me and FJ4c. There was no way my heart would allow me to put either of them down.

Shine the light towards MJ4j's cot, I told her.

FJ4g reached for her dorm mate in her mind and, without moving her head from the crook of my neck, allowed her hand to swivel so that the torch picked out MJ4j's eyes below his frown. Of all twenty in the dorm, he had the strongest tendency to argue and resist, and had suffered more pain than any of them as a result. He was angry at himself for remaining in his cot when he could see others being lifted clear without consequence, yet he still couldn't make himself leave of his own accord. He all but leapt on top of FJ4g, then hesitated. He had planned to help me with the others, yet when my arm held him to me and his dorm mate, he found himself as unable to let go as the rest of us. I pulled him around to my back, where he clung on tightly.

Without me having to ask, FJ4c moved the torchlight to where MJ4m sat in the corner of his cot, his hands over his ears and his eyes tightly closed. The most sensitive of the younglings in his dorm, he was the worst affected by the fear emanating from those around him and in other dorms, not to mention the screaming of those shocked by the beams of intense light emitted by our torches, our hulking presences and the forced evictions of younglings from their cots.

I let go of the two younglings sitting on my hips, knowing they needed no more help to remain in place than the one on my back. I stroked MJ4m's head and then gently lifted him to my chest. I stroked his head again and then rubbed his back without knowing why I was doing so, but immediately sensing the effect. With four hearts now enveloped by the strange emotion that continued to flow to them from mine, I followed FJ4g's direction to where FJ4p stood calmly watching me. Always the quickest of the five to obey, she sensed my suggestion as it formed in my mind, and when I reached her cot and turned around, she accepted my hand as it guided her own to my shoulder, and leapt onto my back beside MJ4j.

I stood for a while, holding all five younglings with my heart as well as my arms and back. I sensed their own hearts slowly filling where they had been empty, then offering the overspill back to me. I gladly accepted their warmth, their acceptance, their companionship… and the memory that our sharing evoked.

I saw again Charlotte Lace's eyes staring into mine. *I love you, QFE88.*

Love. The emotion that bound the younglings and me, that still bound Charlotte Lace and me, was love. She had awakened it in me. She had known I felt it for her before I did. She had sensed it within me and known it would give me the strength to end her life so I could prolong those of many others.

I love you all. The word felt strange until I attached to it the force of my feelings for the five eight-year-olds who loved me back. *Any time you need my arms around you as a reminder, come to me. For now, there are many others who need my help.*

I feel them too, MJ4m replied. His awareness of those two floors down from where I stood spread to the others, all of whom gasped and held more tightly to me.

QFE24, QME96 and QME16 will take you upstairs, where there's food, I told them all. *I'll be with you as soon as I've evacuated floor L.* I shuddered – I couldn't help it.

We'll help you, FJ4g told me, more loathe to be without me than to face what she could sense.

You'll be of most help to me if you'll take strength from me and one another, and use it to help your dormitory mates to be brave.

FJ4p slid to the floor from my back and tugged at MJ4j to do the same. I felt his desire to argue with her and me dissipate as he sensed her need for him. He let go of me and landed beside his friend. FJ4g followed.

You promise you'll come back to us if we leave you? FJ4c asked.

I promise.

She dropped to the ground.

I stroked MJ4m's head as I told him, *The sooner you let me go down to them, the sooner I can stop them screaming in your head.*

I crouched down until his feet were in contact with the cold, hard floor. All four of his friends crowded around him, two taking his hands, the other two enfolding him in their arms so that when I released him, he let go of me. I stood up and looked to where QFE24 was ushering the last of the other fifteen younglings of dorm four through the doorway.

She glanced back at me. *You can go, I'll look after them.*

'I won't be long,' I told the five, my voice pulling them back to their physical surroundings. 'Go and help your friends.'

FJ4g handed me my torch and then led the others out into the corridor. I took a last look around the dormitory that had been their home for the past seven years. Like the corridor, it seemed much smaller than when I had been FJ4m. I couldn't believe I had ever fitted into the cot that now stood empty. It was harder still to believe I was standing at its foot, having liberated its inhabitant.

QFE88?

I shook myself from head to foot and strode towards the door, where sixteen enforcers awaited me. I nodded my thanks to the male who had pulled me back to myself, and before any of us could think about what awaited us, strode along the corridor to the stairwell.

We passed floor K, knowing the lesson rooms were empty. As

soon as I opened the door to floor L, our ears were assaulted by high-pitched yet husky screams which were far less disturbing than the mental screams that accompanied them. I wanted to halt in my tracks but suddenly felt overwhelmed by a need to help the inhabitants of the two occupied nurseries. I flung open the door to the first and stepped inside.

Nothing could have prepared me for the sight of twenty-six baby enforcers thrashing around in their clear-sided incubators, or for the feeling that flooded me as my eyes came to rest on the fourteen who lay still. I supposed I must have had tubes inserted into my arms and legs, carrying nutrients, water, and whatever else was needed to keep me healthy and growing at the optimum rate. I supposed further that my head had probably bled as much as the red-stained scalps in front of me, when my chip was implanted. Just as it no longer regulated my behaviour, so the chips of the nursery's eleven-month-old inhabitants no longer emitted the calm-inducing signals that had kept their hosts quiet until a few hours before. Further, the computers that controlled their nutrient, water and chemical supplies stood dormant.

My heart went out to all of those who lay hungry, thirsty and screaming in confusion, and to all of those whose tiny brains had been unable to cope with the rush of sensations formerly held at bay by their control programs and had ceased to breathe. And it went out to the adult enforcers who stood, stunned, beside me. One of them, a female, unwittingly recognised my love for what it was. That which had been bestowed upon her by the kindred she had met stirred within her and, in turn, reached out to the nearest incubator. Her feet followed it and she touched the arm of the baby within. He stopped screaming and tried to focus his eyes on hers. When his screaming resumed, she picked him up and gently removed all the tubes binding him to his prison. Then she held him close. Love poured out of her and into him, and he quietened in her arms. She looked at me and smiled the way Charlotte Lace always had. The way enforcers never did.

The other adults with us felt and were affected by her emotion. They moved amongst the incubators, releasing the babies within from everything they didn't need and flooding them with what they needed most. I sniffed and tasted a small amount of the contents of the large tanks that stood at the head of each incubator until I identified which of them contained nutrients alone. Knowing that none of the adults would be persuaded to let go of their charges, even those who held two, I left them dripping nutrients from the relevant tubes into the babies' mouths, and went back to the corridor to meet the ten adults who had answered my request for further help from the floors above.

The second nursery contained only seven live babies. At just six months old, far fewer had been strong enough to survive the shock of their artificial environment suddenly fading than those in the first nursery. The seven who lived had an even stronger effect on the adults who lifted them from their incubators, and were soon quietly feeding in the arms of their new parents. It was strange to see my fellow enforcers in a capacity that had been reserved purely for humans, yet the emotions that flooded us made it seem natural.

It occurred to me to wonder how the babies – how any of us – had come to be. I knew how human babies came into existence, in fact, I had witnessed the final stage of the process once, when the attending midwife had been my assignment. The humans had called it birth, not emergence, as they had always referred to our origins. Dread slowly filled me, and the only three adults not filled with the love of holding a baby sensed it. When I left the nursery without comment, they followed me.

Our trepidation filled the stairwell as we descended to floor M, and followed us to the only two doors on the corridor, halfway along and opposite one another. No sounds came from within. I opened the door to my left and shone my torchlight into a cavernous room full of tanks containing the expired origins of those who would have emerged as baby enforcers had their life support not expired along with the monsters who created them.

We checked every tank in both rooms, knowing what we would find, for we had already sensed the lack of life, but feeling a need to confirm it with torchlight before we could leave. Sadness was gradually replaced with anger in all four of us as we searched the rooms for what we knew we wouldn't find and couldn't have prolonged even if we'd had the chance. By the time we met back in the corridor, we were trembling with a rage that we recognised but had never been permitted to fully feel or express.

I was the first to roar. QMD57 was the first to punch a hole in the corridor wall. QFC43 tore back into one of the nurseries and began pushing over the tanks of differently coloured nourishing fluids that had been feeding the rows of incubators. QMF2 set about smashing the computers.

By the time we had all expelled our fury, all that remained intact on floor M were the incubators and their horrifying, heartbreaking contents. Of the tanks that had fed them, the computers that had controlled them, and the walls that had hidden them from the corridor, there was no sign other than a wet, trampled mess of rubble, metal and wiring illuminated eerily by the four torches we had dropped when we lost control of ourselves.

Our shoulders heaved as we stood looking at one another across the carnage. None of us knew what to do next. What to say. How to be. I looked down at my hands. Until that day, they had only ever been used to do the bidding of humans. Now they had destroyed the very worst of what the humans had left behind. It felt good – not just to have obliterated what the humans had built, but to have lost the control of myself with which I had been indoctrinated. Expressing how I felt in a physical way had left me feeling lighter, clearer, and better able to think. The way forward was suddenly abundantly clear to me.

Chapter Thirteen

Let it be recorded for the Histories that on this day, the Second Tuesday of April, Eighth Year of the Eighth Decade of The New, Simona Davis of the Horse-Bonded arrived in Rockwood and reported the demise of the cities of The Old. All of them. Her Bond-Partner, Vigilant, provided her with confirmation of her suspicion after he was almost shaken from his feet, and she from his back, by the tremors in the ground that many of us felt several days ago. They were a day's ride from the pit of misery that was The City Of Power when it met its demise, and witnessed the sky turning orange and then grey with dust, before fleeing in case it blew in their direction. As a Keeper of the Histories, I am tasked with refraining from passing comment on the events I am asked to record, but on this occasion, I cannot keep inside me the words that are desperate to come out. GOOD RIDDANCE.

Histories of The New, Keeper Milicent Butler

WE LEFT what remained of the city two days after its destruction. It was the most terrifying day of my life, the strangeness of which didn't escape me given how I had been forced to live up until that point.

I hadn't allowed myself to question the way forward that became obvious to me as I stood amongst the debris of my rage on floor M of the enforcer building – I had left it and the nurseries behind without a word and thrown myself into organising my fellow survivors to gather as much food for us, and liquid nutrition for the babies, as they could. I distributed the supplies and allocated younglings to all the adult enforcers who weren't either caring for babies or expressionless due to shock and overwhelm. When everyone knew for whom and what they were responsible, I had announced that we would rest the night in the cells of floors C and D, rise as soon as light permeated down to us, and be on our way.

I was the first to emerge above ground on that second morning of freedom, a large barrel of nutritional fluid strapped to my back and a blanket knotted at its corners and full of tinned food strapped to my front. My heart pounded with far greater ferocity than that for which climbing two flights of stairs carrying my load could account; I carried the lives of over a hundred adult enforcers, one hundred and twenty younglings and thirty-three babies within it, and they weighed heavily. They also caused it to swell whenever I looked at any of them, however, particularly my five younglings. I turned to watch them emerge, blinking in the spring sunshine behind me.

'Move away from the stairwell,' I told them. 'Many of those who are following you won't get going again if you cause them to stop on the steps, such is the weight of their loads.'

Though I had long readied the five of them for their first visit above ground, I had prepared them to take in the sights of tall, grey buildings, passenger vehicles and humans scurrying around in fear, and the sounds and scents associated with buildings, humans and machines. The brightness of the sun caused them to squint; the lack of anything upon which to focus caused them to feel small and lost; and the deathly silence made them want to turn and run back down the stairs.

My heart burst free of the weight and fear of responsibility, and swelled further within my chest, its reach extending far beyond its physical boundary and enveloping them all as readily as did my arms when I gathered them to me. 'It's okay,' I told them above the wailing and reassuring noises and words that marked the emergence of other parents and their adopted young. 'Turn away from the sun and look down at your feet while your eyes adjust. Then look at one another and at me. Do that whenever you feel strange, and remember that, whatever happens, you're not alone. You're with your family.'

I guided them further away from the stairwell and its associated noise. *Do you hear that?* I asked them, taking their minds with mine to where a flock of birds chirped excitedly at having come across a swarm of flying insects nearby. I felt my younglings' wonder, their delight as they swooped with the birds as they snapped the insects from the air until their bellies were full, then came together into a single body of moving parts before flying away.

Come back to yourselves, I instructed them, drawing them firmly back to their bodies. *Now open your eyes more.* With confidence gained from looking through the birds' eyes, they all looked at each other and then up at me. I smiled. 'Well done.'

'They're so different from us,' FJ4g said. 'They're...' She frowned.

'Happy,' I said. 'They don't know how to be otherwise.'

'Happy.' MJ4m whispered the word as he felt his way around

it, trying to understand – to relate what he had felt from the birds to the sense I had of the word which until then, I'd only sensed fleetingly from humans and usually after they had caused suffering to someone else. 'They're like we are now we're with you.'

The corners of my mouth pulled upward, and my eyes filled with my first tears not to have formed because of suffering. Out of habit, I began to breathe through my emotion, but then remembered I didn't have to. I could lose control and it wouldn't hurt. I drew my younglings to me again, and we cried together. When we stopped, we found that all the new families now above ground were doing the same. Only the blank-faced adults stood motionless, barely taking in their surroundings, oblivious to the mixture of happiness and trepidation emanating from the rest of us, and not even thinking to lower their loads to the ground while they waited to be told to move.

It was they who reminded me of my role. I needed to lead them away from the remains of the city, to somewhere better. Somewhere they could begin to heal and the rest of us could begin to… what? I wondered suddenly.

Live. QFE24's tear-filled eyes followed her thought as she watched me over the heads of the two younglings clinging to her. *You need to lead us away from here so we can begin to live.* She wasn't stating a fact, she was pleading, and for her younglings as much as for herself.

Just as Charlotte Lace had pleaded with me to kill her. Her words echoed again in my mind. *Kill me, knowing I want you to. I want you to forge a better future in the aftermath of what's coming. Raise your younglings to be just like you, and the pain you're about to suffer will have been worth it.*

I nodded to myself and pushed my younglings gently away from me. 'Everyone has burdens to bear, and I know you're all carrying half your weight in food already, but I need to ask you to help me carry an additional one.'

They all looked up at me, displaying on their faces what little personality they had managed to retain through all of their beatings and conditioning. MJ4m nodded almost to himself, the first to sense my unspoken request. FJ4p nodded her response to it eagerly without thinking of doing otherwise. FJ4c was worried about the task I had in mind, FJ4g was determined to do it, and MJ4j wondered which aspect of it he should question first. As the sun shone down on their faces, I noticed for the first time that it wasn't just in personality that they differed. Where I had thought them to be a similar size and shade of brown, and to have similar features, now I could see that sensitive MJ4m's fur was as soft as determined FJ4g's was coarse. Fearful FJ4c's coat was darker and duller than the other four, and the ever willing FJ4p's was the palest brown and, in fact, contained flecks of beige. Defiant MJ4j had a more pronounced brow than the others, and his eyes were the most intense green.

MJ4j said, 'How are we supposed to keep twenty-nine adults in line when they're twice our size and look like they're not really with us?'

'They're still in there,' MJ4m whispered to him. 'They're just hiding where they feel safe.'

'Just help me to keep an eye on them,' I replied, 'and if you see any falling behind, walk with them and ask them to get back in line. If they don't, run and tell me. I'll be watching too, but I'll have a lot of other things to manage at the same time. FJ4c, stay with FJ4g. I know you won't want to approach any of the adults, so you can act as a second pair of eyes for her. Okay?'

All five nodded.

———

I had barely made it a quarter of the way across the crater of rubble when FJ4p caught up with me, panting. 'They sat down and we can't get them to move,' she gasped. 'Six of them, all in different places. We've tried and tried to get them to listen to us, but they just sit there, staring into the distance.'

I stepped to the side of the long line of enforcers trailing along behind me and turned around, shading my eyes against the sun.

'Some of the other adults tried to help us but they wouldn't stop moving because you said not to,' FJ4p said.

I spotted six adults sitting on the loads they were supposed to be carrying, just beyond the end of the line that had now halted behind me. FJ4g and MJ4j were pulling at the arms of two of the blank-faced enforcers, while FJ4c looked on with her hands on her head. MJ4m was standing directly in front of another, and I could sense him trying to reach past the barriers she had erected in her mind. I joined him in his efforts but soon realised it was pointless; she had withdrawn completely from her mind and was in the process of withdrawing from her body.

Panic filled me. What had I been thinking, asking younglings to subject themselves to the minds of those so severely damaged by everything we had endured recently that they were losing the will to live?

'Keep moving in a straight line,' I told QME96, who was now at the front of the line. 'I'll be back as soon as I can.'

He opened his mouth to voice the questions that were ready to tumble out, but I answered them first. *You can't wait here for me because I need you to keep everyone moving away from what's happening at the back of the line. I don't need help other than what I've asked you to do. I'll make sure everyone knows to follow you and not me. Keep your younglings with you and KEEP MOVING.*

I looked down at FJ4p and narrowed my thought to reach her

alone. *Stay here with QME96. If he hesitates, remind him I'm counting on him to do as I said. I'll be back soon.*

As always, she obeyed me willingly and stepped to the front of the line beside QME96.

I was glad of all the gym training I'd endured at the hands of Handlers Storey and Thomas as I hurried along the line with my load, which I had ensured was the heaviest of them all. I was also glad that of all the younglings I passed, none were as sensitive as mine. If their parents could keep their feet moving forward and their eyes looking where they were going, they should be spared that to which I had inadvertently subjected my own. I repeatedly gasped instructions to keep moving, and was relieved that everyone obeyed without exception, including the remaining twenty-three expressionless adults.

A substantial gap existed between the end of the line and the first of the seated adults by the time I reached her and MJ4j, who was now standing with his face directly in front of the vacant individual's, yelling at her.

I took hold of his arm and said, 'I'm glad your mind is more your own than most of ours are, but on this occasion, I need you to do as I say quickly and without question.'

I felt resistance building within him and then fading as he sensed the level of urgency that corroborated my words.

'Get the other three and run with them to the head of the line. Help FJ4p to keep it moving, and keep your mind and those around you on what's ahead of you. You may only be eight, but you're the strongest of all of us here, and I need you to use the full force of your personality to keep yourself and your family safe.'

'Safe?'

'Yes. The others need you to keep them safe at the front of the line. I'll be fine here, I'm not at risk. I'll be with you very soon. Go now.'

He stared at me for a few seconds and then, still unable to argue against that which he could sense from me, ran to gather the others. They were no match for him and soon all four were running past me despite the loads bumping around on their backs.

I reached out to what remained of the blank-faced female who stared with sightless eyes and was now barely breathing. I caught her as she toppled from the seat she had inadvertently created when she allowed her load to drop from her back, and laid her gently on the rubble. I found the thread connecting her to me and then the five connecting me to the others whose strength had finally run out. I wrapped myself around all six of them, strengthening them, willing them to stay until my younglings were as far away as possible. When I sensed that the younglings were all completely focused on an argument between MJ4j and FJ4g over who should be at the front of the line, I released my hold on those who were so desperate to leave. Six threads became the finest of strands as six essences fled their bodies, taking my love and sorrow with them.

A small part of me wanted to go with them, but as soon as I noticed it, I focused on the much larger part that would do no other than stay for the love of my younglings and everyone else who was depending on me.

I didn't look back as I hurried to catch the end of the line and then pass everyone now following my younglings; I couldn't afford to. I had to keep control of myself, no longer because of a threat of physical pain, but because of the threat I would pose to my family if I lost my mind. I was a kindred now, and so would they all be if I could show them how.

Eleven more of the blank faces fell behind during the hours that followed. I couldn't be with them in body, but I was with them in my mind as each released their hold on their body. I was mortified when MJ4m took my hand every time one of them left;

however small my reaching for them, however much I narrowed my mind to hide it from my younglings and anyone else sensitive enough to perceive what was happening over the trial of keeping in line while trudging across rubble carrying babies, food, and the smaller younglings, I couldn't hide it from him. He held my hand, comforting me as I tried to comfort those in the throes of death. I was wrong, I realised, to have told MJ4j he was the strongest of us; MJ4m was equally strong but just in a different way, and one that humbled me each time my mortification passed.

———

We stopped twice in order to eat and so the younglings could rest their legs for a time. Both times we stopped, I was restless to get moving again. I sat on the rubble, comforted by the sound of my younglings chattering to one another as they shared the contents of a tin of slop, but drawn with increasing urgency to the dark line of trees in the distance that never seemed to get any closer. I felt as if the forest was beckoning to me, promising protection and support, though I couldn't fathom how that was possible.

The other adult enforcers were as quiet as I while we rested, the cognisant ones fully occupied with ensuring their charges ate enough, and the remaining blank-faced ones still looking inward. When I judged it was time to move on, they all got to their feet without comment, reorganised their loads, gathered their families where necessary and trudged behind me.

The sun's rays were weakening and almost horizontal by the time the trees were finally close enough for me to make them out individually. I struggled to maintain my steady, trudging pace when my sixth sense screamed at me to shed my load and tear across the remaining rubble – now mostly composed of the remains of the wall that had prevented the trees from intruding into the city – to meet those who promised so much.

My younglings sensed my craving and immediately shared it. Their tired legs found fresh energy and they tore past me. I wanted to tell them to stop, to wait for me to go ahead of them and make sure it was safe, but I couldn't argue with the sense we all had that there was nowhere safer.

What is that? QFE24 asked from the middle of the line. Her question was fuelled by hope but laced with panic that she was wrong about what she too now sensed.

I couldn't answer her, and not because I didn't know; the trees were now overwhelming me, deafening me with their silent songs. I could think of nothing but reaching the impossibly tall, impossibly powerful beings who swayed mesmerisingly in the breeze before me. It was only when both my hands clasped the trunk of the nearest of them that I steadied myself enough to sense my younglings climbing amongst its branches as if they were born to it – which they had been, I realised, as were the rest of us. We all carried the genes of apes who climbed more easily than walked. We all carried the genes of raptors who built their nests high above the ground.

My head spun. I had been taught my origins during my lessons as a youngling, for the sole purpose of understanding how I had been bred specifically to serve humans and why I would always be a necessary evil to them – how I was larger and stronger and yet in all other ways less than they. Now, standing on my short, powerful legs, wrapping my long but equally powerful arms around the tree and gripping it with my talons even as the slitted pupils of my eyes widened to take in the colour and pattern of its skin, I sensed my origins for myself.

I knew the animals whose genes I carried – I actually knew them, as if I were them. I knew the human scientists who had combined their own genes with those of the animals. Further, I knew their parents and their parents' parents, as well as the parents of all my animal ancestors. I knew the tree to which I clung as desperately as my younglings had clung to me only that morning, and I knew the animal who had eaten its parent's fruit and deposited its seed in the spot in which it had been growing for more than twenty decades. I perceived everything it had ever perceived, yet not in the way I would have done had I been present, but as an absorption of surrounding influences that had no effect on it at all. It thrummed with a steady song which rarely changed in pitch or potency, such was its steadfastness. Such was its strength. Its song reverberated within me, soothing away the fear of my newly adopted responsibility that had been gnawing at me all day.

I hardly flinched at my sense of FJ4c leaping from one of the tree's branches to that of a neighbouring tree and barely felt the surprise that rose within me that it was the most fearful of my younglings who had been the first to jump into the unknown. I knew as well as she that where my tree, with its brown, furrowed skin and toothed, dark green leaves, could sing away my overwhelm, the white-skinned tree in which she now sat promised to relieve her of her anxiety. My other younglings followed her lead and sprang to the trees that called to them, and within minutes, all five were steadier, stronger versions of themselves.

A hand closed on my shoulder. 'What are you doing?' QME96 asked.

As soon as he took my attention, I knew his parents – human and animal – and his grandparents and their parents, yet I sensed he did not. He was relieved about his sudden increased sense of wellbeing, but he didn't know how it had come about. He needed stronger exposure to the trees. It didn't occur to me to question how I knew it, but I did, as definitely as I knew that all those behind him also needed to move further into the forest in order to sense the trees' influence.

I turned around to find everyone but my five younglings bunched before me. Had I focused on any of them before, I would have known how they were feeling. Now that the tree, from which I seemed unable to remove my hand, had awakened me, I knew what all of them were feeling, thinking, seeing, hearing and scenting – all at once. I stepped backward as multiple visions of how they saw me flooded my perception. The tree prevented me from taking more than a single step, and the second I felt it against my back, my feet felt heavy on the ground, as if roots had suddenly extended down into the earth from me in the same way as they did from the tree. I was still aware of the thoughts, feelings and perceptions of those around me, but I stood tall above them, able to select any of them upon which I chose to focus but far above the feeling of drowning in them.

'Follow me into the forest,' I said loudly enough to reach those at the back of the group. 'Touch all the trees we pass and notice which you like the most. Adults, maintain visual or at least mental contact with your younglings.'

It was all I could do not to run into the solid, nourishing embrace that welcomed us all.

Chapter Fourteen

I'm so tired. I don't want to keep up my diary, but I promised Mum I would when she advised me to "have something constant in your life when everything else is uncertain". So here I am, trying to stay awake when everyone else is asleep, in order to type today's entry. I don't know how much longer I'll be able to keep doing it as my tablet's running out of charge and none of us know how long we'll be wandering in this wilderness before we find signs of other humans, if we ever do. We don't know that any of them survived, but Mum was sure they did, and I have to trust her. I miss her so much, but I can't let myself think about her for long at a time because if I do, I'll lose the strength to keep Denise and Logan moving when they want to give up. Their spirits dropped even further today when the batteries of their tablets ran out. I hope we can find a way to charge them soon.

Secret diary of Jinna Lace

I HAD NEVER SLEPT SO well, I decided upon waking. I shouldn't have slept much at all, sitting as I was astride the wide, knobbly branch of a tree whilst tied to its scaly trunk by the woody stem of a plant climbing up it.

When the sun had set the evening before, the light from the moon – even forced as it was to dart between leaves in order to reach us – was still brighter than the dimness we had been used to in the enforcer building and enabled us to easily climb the trees that welcomed each of us and made us feel safe. Once I had checked that all the adults had strapped themselves and their young to the branches of their trees, I drifted off to sleep in the tree that had sung to my younglings and me, as comforted by the sound of its large, lobed leaves and white pyramids of flowers rustling in the breeze as by its song.

I was wide awake the second the sun's rays penetrated my eyelids. My younglings weren't far behind. None of us moved for some time, stunned as we were by the bombardment of the waking forest on our senses. We had only ever woken to greyness, dankness and vileness penetrated by the threat of worse to come. Now, we were immersed in vivid shades of green, white, pink and yellow, and even the browns and greys had warmth and depth. Birds called cheerfully to one another and small animals scampered around and below us. My nose twitched at the scents carried by the breeze. The animals who had been active during the night took me to sleep with them even as those who were newly awake carried me out of their dens, burrows and nests.

QFE88, should we eat? QMD57's question introduced disharmony to my peace. No, I realised, it wasn't his question; it was his use of my name dragging me back to the enforcer building – to my qualified status on floor E, cell 88.

I'm no longer QFE88, I thought to myself and those now

waking all around me. *I am no longer an enforcer. I am one of the kindred, as are all of you.*

No one questioned whom I meant. The adults taking refuge in the forest alongside me were all those who'd accepted contact with the humans who had been kind to us and supported us in our misery, even as they endured their own. Stronger now that they all were in their sixth sense due to the trees' influence, they detected the effect Charlotte Lace had had on me; the example she had set that I was determined to follow. As they perused the sense of her they found within me, they brought her back to life, if only for a few minutes. It came to me how I could do that for good.

I will take her name, I announced.

Charlotte Lace? one of them asked.

I couldn't bear to hear her name in its entirety. *Lace. My name is Lace,* I told them all. *You should honour those who saved your sanity and, because of it, your lives, by taking their names too.*

I am Hob, she who was QFE24 announced without hesitation.

QME96 was quick to follow. *I am Ash.*

The rest of the adults were almost as quick to name themselves, now as disturbed as I at the thought of the names we had accepted for ourselves without question.

What about us? asked the most willing of my younglings.

You are as much my family as Charlotte Lace's daughter was hers. They shared the name I have taken. I would like you to share it too. I name you Lacekeen. Lacefirm, I directed to my most determined, forthright youngling. *Lacebold,* I aimed at he who I had once thought was the strongest of them, and *Laceheart,* at he whose sensitivity made him equally strong. Of all five, only she who was the most timid refrained from reaching towards me for her name. *Lacehope,* I told her, and sensed her heart lift in response.

I directed my next thought to all the adults who were caring for young. *Name your families as I have named mine. Name them for the kindred who helped you to be here now, and for who they are. We are all so much more than the humans created us to be.*

Confusion and disbelief swirled around me.

We will rest in this forest that nurtures us, I announced. *We will get to know it and we will get to know ourselves.*

The forest seemed, to all six of my senses, to shift in response to my thought, as if it were alive in its own right as well as due to of all the plants and animals it comprised. It WAS alive, I realised. And it was adjusting to its new components just as we were adjusting to being such. It was enfolding us within it, embracing us and slowly drawing us out of ourselves.

Most of us, anyway; the remainder were still expressionless. I sensed their trees' songs penetrating deep within them where I couldn't follow, at least to the extent that they had been drawn to rest within the same type of tree that had first attracted me. But where my level of overwhelm had been reduced almost to nothing, theirs still blocked them from having much sense of their surroundings beyond the trees that supported them.

Their trees' songs weren't enough. As soon as I realised it, I sensed the forest's ability to support them further. I sat up straighter on my branch. Which part of the trees that they had chosen should I use to help them? Instantly, I knew that too. The flower.

They won't eat, Lacefirm told me. *We tried to get them to have something yesterday, but they didn't hear us when we told them to open their mouths, and they didn't see the spoons of slop we held in front of them. Their noses didn't even move at the scent.* I heard her stomach gurgle from above me as she sensed how hungry they were, even as she was tucking into a tin of food.

We need to soak the flowers in water until it has taken their essence and then give them that. I knew it was the right thing to do; I felt the knowledge settle within me as I passed it on, and gained an even greater sense of the forest. It let me know we needed to use fresh, vibrant water rather than the stale, sterile water we had carried with us, and I instantly knew in which direction to head in order to find some. *We'll drip it into their mouths from tubes like the others are doing with the babies,* I added.

At my thought of the babies – many of whom I knew were exhausting their parents with bouts of screaming, day and night, from which they couldn't be comforted – I knew the flowers of other trees that I should steep in water to support them and the youngest of the younglings through the disorientation they were all struggling to overcome.

We'll help, Lacekeen volunteered.

Not until you've finished eating, I told her firmly. *Then, when you've wiped our empty tins clean with leaves and stacked them at the base of our tree, I would be grateful for your help. Lacekeen and Lacebold, I'd like you to gather the flowers we need for those who have yet to take a name. Lacehope and Lacefirm, gather the flowers for those younger than yourselves. Laceheart, you and I will collect and clean as many tins as we can carry in addition to our own, and use them to fetch water.*

None of my younglings asked for clarification; they sensed from me exactly which blossoms to collect and then ate in silence while the forest drew their minds onward to explore more of its secrets. I marvelled at the ease with which they assimilated everything they discovered. Where they had been apprehensive about accompanying my mind to explore the streets above the enforcer building, and had needed time to build their confidence in doing it, they had no such reticence about exploring the forest. It nurtured them as it gently drew them from one aspect of itself to the next, never pulling them faster than they could cope with, never hiding anything of itself, and allowing them to focus for longer on the aspects of itself that interested them most.

Lacekeen was intrigued by the patience of the trees as they grew slowly, constantly towards the sky above, always reaching for it yet content to still be as far away from it as they were.

Lacefirm was fascinated by the affinity she felt for the vines we had used to tie ourselves to our tree during the night; its adventurous crawling along the forest floor, throwing down roots whenever it needed extra sustenance to continue its journey, and its tenacity at climbing trees in order to ensure its share of light resonated with her.

Lacebold lingered longest with a male squirrel some distance away, entranced by the argument the little beast was having with another male for the territory he considered his own. My youngling laughed out loud when the second male left without a fight.

Lacehope was entranced by the tree blossoms gently bursting from casings that had held them and kept them safe until they sensed there was sufficient light and warmth for them to release their charges.

Laceheart immersed himself in the roots of the oldest, largest tree of the forest, plunging deep into the ground with them and revelling in the sense of stability they afforded both their tree and him. He was able to absorb more and more of the forest as a result; he no longer needed to explore his sense of it, for he was the forest and knew its body better than his own.

My younglings grew in confidence and internal strength by the minute, faster than I could ever have imagined possible. When they dropped from the branches above mine to those surrounding and then below me on their way down to the forest floor, it felt strange to see that they were still the same physical size – that they were still younglings and only eight-year-old younglings at that, when to my mind, they should have looked much older.

Thank you. I couldn't help but express my gratitude to the forest and yearned for the rest of our kin to open to its influence to the same extent as my younglings and me. The blossom essences would be a good start.

I sprang from my branch to another some distance below and reached the floor in half as many leaps as my younglings had taken. I landed lightly beside Laceheart. *Ready?*

We were close. We could smell water now as well as sense it, and strangely, we could hear it with more than our ears. We both knew and recognised the sound of water landing in a vessel, but this wasn't the dull, swirling, splashing sound we knew. It was a roaring of power and strength that deafened our ears and exploded within our chests. The water bellowed with life and energy, invigorating Laceheart and me well before we caught sight of it. When we eventually did, it took the breath from our lungs.

We weaved between the last few trees obstructing our view of it and then stood, mouths open, watching water bursting between some rocks high above, bouncing off a large flat rock a short distance below, then hurling itself down to the pool before us. The clear, vibrant water leaked from the pool in small streams, tickling and smoothing the stones on its way to irrigate the forest, teasing and chuckling where before it had shouted and raged. It was vibrant and magnificent, pure and gentle.

The rest of our kin needed to experience its energy. I felt a sudden urgency, which penetrated Laceheart's absorption in the phenomenon before us. I lowered the knotted blanket I had been carrying to the bank of the pool, and we both dropped to our knees and selected a tin from those whose clanging had accompanied our half hour journey. We scooped water out of the pool until all the tins were full, then bent their lids back into place.

Our return journey took longer, partly because our feet dragged with our reluctance to leave the source of the vibrancy that had coursed through our bodies since we had drunk our fill from the pool, and partly because of our efforts to keep the tins upright so that as little water as possible leaked out around the edges of their lids. We had jammed them together in the knotted blanket, and I carried the package against my stomach while Laceheart walked beneath it, his hands above his head as he supported them from below. We walked in step without thought of doing so and when Laceheart's arms hurt and he needed to rest, we did.

By the time we reached the trees within which rested most of our kin, and around which a few younglings had begun, tentatively, to chase one another, my other four younglings were waiting for us beside two neat piles of tree blossoms.

'You've done well,' I told them. 'Drink some of this, all of you.' I passed a tin to Lacekeen. 'And then give as many of the younglings as you can some water from these.' I stacked eight tins from my bundle. 'When you've done that, get any adults who aren't busy with their families to empty the water from the water canisters we brought with us – we won't be drinking that awful stuff again. All of you, find and clean as many empty tins as you can, then, Laceheart, take everyone carrying tins and canisters to the pool and bring back as much water as you can.'

I divided the blossoms gathered by my younglings between the tins of water I had left, stirred them into the water with a long twig, then moved my hand towards the closest to fold back down its lid. My hand froze before reaching it.

No.

The forest didn't speak the word to me as such, but I felt as if it held itself still for the fraction of a second it took me to stop acting on my intention. As soon as it had my attention, I sensed what I needed to do. I looked around and spotted a shaft of light a short distance away, where a fallen tree had broken the leafy canopy above. Its trunk was twice as broad in girth as was I, and lit by the sun near its recently exposed root. It was the perfect place for the sun's rays to encourage the flowers to release their essences into the water.

———

Several times, the forest called me away from organising the distribution of newly-arrived, fresh water to the new families, in order to stir the steeping flower essences. As I carefully stirred each of them, I sensed the problem; the light could only reach so far into the water. Transparent vessels would have been ideal, but I would work with what I had.

When the forest called to me a third time, I swilled each tin around and folded its lid back down so that only liquid could escape into the clean tins I had standing ready, leaving any remaining solid residue behind. When I had finished, my younglings were waiting.

'We told all the parents it was nearly ready, but they won't come down from their trees to get it,' Lacebold said. 'They only come down to relieve themselves and then they go straight back up.'

'They need time,' I told him. 'They've been through everything the rest of us have, and on top of that, they're trying to keep distressed babies alive with little idea of how to do it. We'll take the soothing essence up to them. Or rather, the five of you will. Tell them to drip a few drops into the mouths of their young now, and every few hours afterward. I'll take the reviving essence to the nameless ones if one of you can fetch me a feeding tube.'

The nameless ones had all been attracted to the same type of tree and many to the same individual tree, so I was able to move between them quickly and easily. None of them reacted to me gently lifting their chins and dripping reviving essence into their slack, slightly open mouths; indeed none of them appeared to see or hear me, though I sensed a faint stirring within each that let me know differently – a stirring that reached for the essence as it wove its way through their bodies.

The babies would continue to scream and the nameless would continue to lack the wits to be otherwise for some time yet, but I knew the blossom essences would work.

When I dropped to the ground from the last tree, I finally noticed that my stomach and – to my chagrin – those of my younglings were growling with hunger; it was hours past the time that most of our number had eaten their midday meal. I found myself loathe to eat the contents of the tin of food I opened, though. It felt as unnatural to consume the slop within as it had natural to utilise the water and blossoms to which the forest had guided me.

I waited for my younglings to join me and then frowned as we all ate, feeling more and more uncomfortable with each swallow of the bland, white, synthetic mush. I lowered my spoon to the tin, and lowered the tin to the ground, followed shortly afterward by Laceheart. The eyes of the other four younglings were on us both as we sat in a circle beneath our tree, and one by one, they put their tins down too.

'It's disgusting,' Lacebold said.

'It is,' I agreed distractedly, my attention expanding from my hungry stomach and out to the forest… which gently turned me back to myself and the threads exploding from me in all directions

– threads that connected me to other beings in a way I recognised and that immediately made me shudder. They told me, like all of those that had warned me of my assignments in the city, who would be prey to my predation.

Our tree drew my hand to its scaly trunk and as soon as I was in contact with it, I calmed and knew two things in the same instant. A potion made from the white pyramids of flowers produced by the tree would help me maintain a clear, calm mind in the future. And we all would benefit were I to trust myself as well as the forest.

I breathed through my disquiet and focused on the threads. One of them vibrated more strongly than the others. I got to my feet.

Remain here, I told my younglings. *I will not be long.*

Chapter Fifteen

Let it be recorded for the Histories that on this day, the Fourth Tuesday of April, Eighth Year of the Eighth Decade of The New, a Herald arrived in Rockwood with news that many other villages are holding a spring festival to celebrate the demise of The Old and the freedom from fear it gives us, the people of The New. No longer will we have to worry that police or enforcers will come for us and force us back to the cities, we can finally live in peace. The festivals are to be held on the fourth Saturday of May, and Rockwood will join in with the celebrations. The villages, though separated by distance, will be united in joy and happiness.

Histories of The New, Keeper Milicent Butler

I BOUNDED BETWEEN THE TREES, following the thread that connected me to the earthbound prey at the other end of it. It felt wrong to be on the ground. I hurled myself at the nearest tree and was halfway up it in a couple of breaths. I leapt from one of its branches to a neighbouring tree, and then on to another. As I swung through the forest with rapidly increasing speed and confidence, a feeling of rightness settled within me.

I was drawn along the thread by the inevitability contained within it, not even pausing to consider that, unlike my prey to date, my target had broken no rules and offended no one. When I was close to the animal, she sensed my approach. She raised her head from the thin, green blades of the plant she had been eating, and sniffed the air. I scented everything that she did, for we were one; two parts of the forest being drawn to one another. I was with her as she ran in the same direction as the breeze carrying my scent, the instinct of her species overcoming that which called to her. A compulsion to chase her flared within me, something that had never happened when I had hunted humans.

I swung through the trees with increased vigour and purpose, pulled along by the elegance and grace of my prey as she cleared everything in her path with speed and accuracy. I admired her as I couldn't admire myself, for she was born as the world intended her to be. Where I was powerful in my ugliness, she was strong and agile in her beauty. Yet still, my urge to hunt drove me after her with as much force as the thread that ensured I couldn't turn back.

I sensed her pause – there were plants blocking her way. They were too tall to jump and she knew they would pierce her skin if she pushed through them. She diverted to the side, trying to find a way through. I felt her panic and my urge to reach her intensified; I would ease it for her. I would help her fulfil the agreement with which our thread vibrated, so that she would suffer no more.

Then I saw her. She was the size of a human adult but stood on four legs, her large, brown eyes rimmed with white as she dithered on the spot on two-toed feet. The sweat that soaked her fur – pale brown on her back but spotted with the same white that ran down her chest and along her belly – was laced with terror. Two large protrusions erupted from her head and swivelled in all directions. Ears, I decided as I hurled myself from the branches and brought her down.

As soon as she was beneath me, she relaxed. Her fear departed as she accepted that which lay underneath it – the truth within our thread. She had occupied her body, taken care of it and learnt from her time within it, but now the time had come for her to release it to me. The forest embraced her as she left her body, acknowledging her departure, then released her so that she could move... somewhere else, as Charlotte Lace had done. Likewise, the thread that had drawn us together, that had pulsed with an urgency I had been unable to ignore, was now the faintest of threads and as devoid of vigour as the body lying on the forest floor before me.

I sat back on my heels, filled with wonder and gratitude for the animal and the forest of which we would both always be a part. I would take as great care of the body she had left me to feed my kin as had she. I considered how best to get it back to my younglings; swinging through the trees wouldn't be easy with a burden of this size, and I didn't want to risk dropping it. I settled upon hoisting it carefully onto my shoulders and remaining on the forest floor as I followed my sense of my younglings back to the tree beneath which they waited.

I'm coming, I told them. I didn't need to for their sakes – they had been with me during my hunt – but for mine; an emotion that I didn't recognise surged through me as I announced my return with food for them that had been provided by this new world of ours. I felt pleased with myself as I had never had cause to before, and capable. And there was more. Despite my burden, my footsteps felt less heavy than normal, as if I were myself being carried – which I was. Now that we were part of the forest, it would carry us all.

A fresh and equally strange emotion announced itself, filling me with warmth and sending tingles to my heart, hands and feet. The hopelessness of my life and situation, that had been threatened and beaten into me since my emergence, disintegrated as its nemesis took its place. For the first time in all of my nineteen years, I had hope.

————

I woke to the sound of my younglings chattering in the branches above me.

'I'm wet again,' Lacebold moaned.

'If you'd paid attention when I was showing you how to weave the vines more tightly, you'd be dry,' Lacefirm told him.

'I'm dry,' Lacekeen announced. 'Want me to show you how I wove my shelter? Look at me!' There was a rustling as she jumped from her branch to Lacebold's. 'Completely dry. Not a single drop of water came through.'

'Yes, okay, I believed you,' Lacebold grumbled.

'I'm wet too,' Lacehope said. 'I was watching Lacefirm, but I must still have done it wrong. Can you help me?'

'Sure.' Lacekeen's pleasure accompanied her reply. 'How about you, Laceheart?'

'I'm wet, but I like it,' he replied. 'I like everything here. The water tastes nice. I like sleeping in this tree whether it rains or not. The animals tell us when we can have their bodies. The plants sing to us so we know which ones can help us.'

'I'll fix your shelter for you,' Lacefirm told him. 'You shouldn't get wet when you sleep, you can get cold. That's what happened to Smith's baby and he nearly died.'

'I'm bigger than a baby,' Laceheart said softly.

'But you're not as big as Lace or any of the other adults, and they all try to keep themselves dry,' Lacefirm said. 'I'm fixing your shelter.'

'Some of the others could do with your help too. You too, Lacekeen,' I said. 'Those parenting babies have enough to worry about without trying to reweave leaking shelters.'

'We'll do it,' Lacefirm answered for both of them, then said to the other three, 'That means you'll have to drip blossom essence into the nameless ones' mouths without us, and feed them.'

'Why do we still have to do it?' Lacebold asked. 'They're getting better. One of them even thanked me yesterday. Surely they can feed themselves if they can speak?'

'When they're ready to, they will,' I said. 'Their minds folded over on themselves so they could hide until it was safe to come out. I know you can feel the blossom essences drawing them out as well as I can, but it'll take time before they're fully back to themselves. Until then, we'll carry on looking after them. I'll make up some more blossom essence today for them and for the babies.'

'They're getting better quicker than the nameless ones,' Laceheart murmured.

'The babies are all doing well,' I agreed, 'and it's only been eight days. Another eight and I think things will be very different for them and the nameless ones.'

A week later, things were very different for all of us. The babies were calm unless they were hungry, and their parents, helped by the blossoms' soothing essence in combination with another one that increased mental stamina, were finding their new roles a little easier. The forest continued to hold us all in its embrace, supplying our needs, opening our minds a little more each day to our sixth sense, and guiding those of us most sensitive to it to further knowledge about how to survive. And the nameless ones began to take names.

The first to emerge from his stupor muttered to himself as Lacefirm fed him pieces of meat one evening, yet didn't reply to her when she asked him to speak more clearly. When she dripped blossom essence onto his lips the following morning, however, he licked them and his eyes came slowly to life.

'Thank you, Lacefirm,' he said. 'I am Taylor.'

'Taylor,' she repeated, her intense focus on her sense of the human kindred after which he had named himself alerting me to what was happening.

You are very welcome back, Taylor, I thought to him.

I have been trying to return for some time, he replied. *I heard the trees singing to me. I heard the words and thoughts spoken to me by you and your younglings. For a while, I still could not find my way through the heaviness that enfolded me. Then the way opened up before me, but even so, I made my way slowly, for I wasn't sure... until I was. I cannot explain it any better.*

You do not need to, I told him. *Now that you're here, rest and absorb that which will touch you. The forest will look after you as surely as it brought you back to yourself.*

Two more named themselves that afternoon, and five more the following day. The rest returned to us over the three days that followed until finally, my younglings were freed from their tasks of watering, feeding and medicating those who had struggled so much.

One of the former nameless – a female who took the name "Hoyle" – was quick to expand her sixth sense once the blossom essence had drawn her from the recesses of her mind, and hunted with the other adults who had begun helping me to feed our community. While I was the only one who followed threads connecting me to my prey, I was far from the only efficient hunter

once the others opened sufficiently to the forest; where before
they had been given their assignments by computers, now they
listened, observed, scented, tasted and sensed their prey.

Only Laceheart and I were drawn to ingest – and harvest for
our kin – certain plants. Their songs were fainter, more subtle than
those of the trees, and the two of us alone could hear them. We
knew which would complement the meat we were eating, and
when a youngling fell from a low branch, we knew which could
ease his pain; it sang a little louder, drawing us across the forest
and out into an area clear of trees but covered instead by tall,
narrow-leaved plants interspersed with colourful ones.

As when we had discovered the pool of water in the forest, we
stood for some time, observing and breathing in the strange
environment. It smelt much sweeter than the forest and, since the
sun's rays were able to reach us unbroken, it was warmer and
much brighter. Far fewer sounds reached our ears, but we sensed
there was almost as much life before us as behind us.

It was I who blinked first and remembered why we were there.
The moment I thought of the sore youngling we had left behind us
in the forest, I was drawn not only to the pain-relieving plant that
had already sung to Laceheart and me, but to another that would
help him to heal more quickly. Laceheart immediately headed off
to where that plant was located, leaving me to gather some of the
first. When one of my hands was full of the yellow-leaved plant, I
thought of the baby who had been hot and fractious that morning,
and heard the song of the plant that would cool him down. My
other hand was soon full of a dark green plant whose leaves were
split into a multitude of narrow fingers.

'I can't carry all the plants that are singing to me now we're
here,' Laceheart said breathlessly. 'See this one? It can take pain
away too, and it'll make whoever eats it feel even better than they
did before they hurt themselves.'

I nodded. 'Well done for hearing that one, Laceheart. Its song is fainter than the others because it sings of healing many things instead of just one, which makes it even more valuable to us. I think we'll take back what we've gathered and then you can return here with the rest of our family, any other younglings who are interested in learning which plants can do what, and definitely at least one adult for every two younglings.' I put my hand above my eyes to shield them from the sun as I focused as far in the distance as I could in all directions.

'We aren't the only ones who kill other animals for food,' Laceheart murmured. 'But in the forest, we're the biggest.'

'The other adults and I are the biggest out here,' I replied, 'but there are some that almost match us in size and strength, and they're much faster across the ground than we are. Make that one adult for every youngling you bring with you. And you'll need to keep part of your mind alert for those whose fangs we've inherited. If you sense they're any closer than they are now, you'll need to get everyone back to the trees. Laceheart.' I reached for him as I said his name, pulling his attention away from the predators we could both sense beyond the limit of our vision. 'Collect adults who'll come with you first, then only invite as many younglings as you have adults.'

'Even if we're to head for the trees when they're any closer than they are now?'

'Even then. I need you all here to gather plants that can help with healing, but I won't have you risking yourselves. We all need one another, and that means we all need to survive. If any of the younglings give you a hard time, get Lacebold and Lacefirm to back you up.'

If I had stopped to think about it, I wouldn't have put so much responsibility on the shoulders of my five younglings, but I saw them as they were perceived by the forest; the most able to respond to its guidance and therefore by far the most capable of our kin besides myself. They each had their own strengths that complemented those in the others, and already, if one of them were ever questioned or challenged by any of the rest of our number – adults or younglings alike – the five of them together were always heeded.

In less than three weeks, the forest had moulded us as necessary and put us firmly on the path to healing and transforming into the kindred. I thought we had everything we needed in order to survive. I was wrong.

Chapter Sixteen

Let it be recorded for the Histories that on this night of the Fourth Saturday of May, Eighth year of the Eighth Decade of The New, there was merriment in Rockwood, the like of which has never before been experienced. There was singing and dancing in the streets. There was hugging and kissing between friends, neighbours and even those who don't usually get along. We felt joy emanating from all the other villages celebrating along with ours. It is as if a shadow has lifted from us all and the future looks nothing but bright.

Histories of The New, Keeper Milicent Butler

MY STOMACH GROWLED. It was time to hunt.

'We can finish this,' Lacekeen said. Saliva trickled down her fangs as she anticipated the meat I would bring back for them and the other three families I had apportioned to myself to feed.

'You can,' I agreed. 'Just remember to stir each tin whenever you sense its contents becoming sluggish, so that the light can reach the parts of the essence it couldn't before.'

'You've told us that about fifty times before,' Lacebold said. 'We can prepare the blossom essences as well as you now.'

'And yet while you were talking, you missed the fact that some of them are ready to be stirred,' Lacefirm said, nodding to where Lacehope was now stirring two at once. She looked at me. 'I'll make sure he concentrates.'

'I don't need you to make sure I concentrate. You just need to stop talking and let me,' Lacebold retorted.

Laceheart rolled his eyes at me as he stirred several tins further down the tree trunk from Lacehope's.

I smiled at them all. 'See you later.'

I turned and scaled the nearest tree, sensing the thread that thrummed with such urgency, it stood out from all the others and drew me to the animal who would be my prey.

As always when I hunted, my movement through the trees was faster, yet quieter, than when I moved around gathering blossoms, tending to my vine shelter or visiting members of my family or community. All of my six senses combined into a single powerful one that propelled me along the thread connecting me to my prey, so that I didn't need to consider which route to take, when to ascend or descend a little, when to leap for the next tree and whether to aim for its branch or its trunk. It was as if a path opened before me and pulled me along it, and it was exhilarating.

I sensed the proximity of my prey, and the predatory instinct of my feline ancestors flared along with my excitement as I anticipated the inevitable chase ahead of me… then waned again. I landed on the branch for which I had been aiming, but my grip was less sure than normal and I was forced to pause for a second to regain my balance before leaping for the next branch. I refocused on the thread and felt a surge of energy as I again anticipated the chase and subsequent kill...???

I landed awkwardly on the branch and paused again. What was this uncertainty that had arisen within me? I had hunted daily over the past six weeks and the process had become so much a part of me that I felt I had done it my whole life – but something was different this time.

I threw myself at the thread and practically rebounded off it, for it was right there, exactly where it had always been, beckoning me onward and ensuring that my path was open and clear. I shook my head and then my whole body. I felt the pull of my prey and launched myself after it, following the thread with all of myself again.

When I was close enough to scent the animal, I knew it was unlike any I'd hunted before. When I finally saw him, he was spinning around in an area clear of trees and covered instead with the tall plants with green blades for leaves that Laceheart and I had found beyond the edge of the forest. His size pulled me up short for a moment – he was huge, almost taller than I, though he stood on four feet. His face was long and narrow and he breathed via enormous, gaping nostrils near his mouth. His brown fur was the same colour as mine where it was dry along the top of his back, but much darker everywhere else where it was soaked with sweat. Large as he was though, he was no predator; he wouldn't fight me, he would flee – the hunt was still on.

Yet he didn't flee. And I didn't leap on him and take him down. I stood on the lowest branch of a broad-girthed tree and watched him dancing around within a small circle, when I could sense that every fibre of his being wanted to run... except for the part of him that was anchored to me.

Our thread held him exactly where he was. Tentatively, I probed at it with my sixth sense and found it pulsing so violently, it was almost painful – to us both, I realised. Its strength was such that it could overcome the flight instinct of a prey animal and the chase instinct of a predator. As my desire to hunt waned, I sensed again that which had shaken me while I was on my rampage through the forest. Charlotte Lace.

No, not Charlotte Lace; not exactly, but that which had driven her to be brave, kind and strong. The thread connecting me to the animal, who was still refusing to bolt from me, carried it as surely as had the thread I shared with Charlotte Lace, yet with far greater strength. It was that strength that had pulled us together and now held us, uncomfortably, in one another's presence.

How could I have missed it? How could I have thought I was hunting for meat when I was hunting for something else entirely?

Your instinct to hunt and provide for your family is as strong as mine to flee. You bear witness to the evidence.

My claws gripped the tree trunk. All I could do was stare at the animal who could not stop his feet moving below me, but who had just communicated with me as easily as did many of my kin. I remained staring for some time as my mind raced.

Focus not on what is happening but on why, came another thought. *You already understand. You need merely realise that you do.*

I understand? I thought to myself, and felt the creature's confirmation... and then felt the creature himself, yet not via our thread or with my sixth sense. My mind reeled, unable to comprehend the fact that he had been part of Charlotte Lace and as a result of her influence, was already a part of me.

I recognised the vast strength that enabled him to be gentle. I recognised the sense of purpose that drove him to be brave. My heart hurt as I identified his ability to accept and help those who would harm him. My whole body slackened as I began to understand why he and I had been drawn together. He gently took hold of me and drew me deeper into himself so that I could know more.

He was with a crowd of humans. No, it wasn't him. Yet it was. He was all of the horses – for I knew now that was who they were – who carried humans upon their backs outside the city walls, and he was none of them. I didn't find that strange at all, for I couldn't help but know that the horses, while each having their own personalities and purposes in their lives, were connected by far more than the threads connecting me to others in my life; they were one vast being with many protrusions, each filtering into an individual horse.

Those carrying humans did not just do so physically. As I observed the phenomenon from the horse's vast store of experience – his and that of all the horses to have existed – I sensed the humans changing, minute by minute. They rearranged their bodies from hunched, heavy and weak to tall, balanced and open. They let go of the fear and anger they had brought with them from the city and allowed the horses' calm acceptance of life to clear their minds and focus their thoughts. They absorbed the horses' love and strength and made it their own. By the time they returned to the city, they were full of what it was to be a horse. They walked with courage and purpose, and a renewed determination to help anyone in the city who needed them.

The horse drew me forward in time to a generation of humans who had no horses to visit outside the city walls – those in the previous scene having long since passed – yet who carried the horses' influence as surely as those who had been exposed to them. He guided me to Charlotte Lace, and I felt the essence of what it was to be a horse within her and witnessed her passing it to me, a tiny amount with every interaction to begin with, then in the weeks before I killed her, in an almost constant stream.

The Way Of The Horse. The description formed in my mind

unbidden as I sensed how Charlotte Lace thought of what she knew was the source of her energy and purpose. The words drew into my mind all the other human kindred, one by one, who had shared that energy, who had allowed it to define their lives and actions… and then those of my kindred, sitting in their trees, tending to babies and younglings, hunting – surviving.

It's because of you, I told the horse who was all the horses who had ever lived as well as the one standing near me. *The humans who escaped the cities did so because of you. The human kindred who stayed to help did so because of you. My kindred are here because of you.*

It was only when my eyes refocused that I realised they had been unseeing for some time. The horse was directly below me now, one of his hind legs bent at rest as he dozed in the perfect position for me to land on his back and end his life with a single swipe of my talons.

He knew I wouldn't do it. He trusted me, a known killer of humans and a deadly predator who would push myself to the limit of my physical ability to bring down prey to feed my family.

A lump formed in my throat, making it difficult for me to swallow. My stomach clenched as if it were pained, yet other than the discomfort of being empty, that wasn't the case. My shoulders heaved and my eyes filled with tears. Years of practice caused me to try to breathe through my body's emotions, yet I couldn't seem to do it. I panicked. I had to control myself; it was the only way to survive. But try as I might, I couldn't. What was happening to me?

You are beginning to live rather than merely survive, the horse informed me. *Allow your body to express itself without fear and your awakening will continue.*

Charlotte Lace's love had affected me. The love that accompanied the horse's thought floored me, literally. I dropped from the branch and landed at his side. I heaved so hard, I thought my insides would come out of my mouth. So many tears leaked from my eyes, I feared I would shrivel to nothing. I emitted sounds I had never made before – choking, bellowing sounds that made my throat sore. The horse remained by my side, calmly dozing as if he were alone with the gentle sounds of the forest.

When the heaving, leaking and choking finally stopped, I was exhausted.

Lace? Laceheart's thought reached me and I panicked. My younglings were hungry. What had I been thinking, getting distracted from my hunt like this? I reached for them all and found Lacehope sitting high in the branches of our tree, curled up and rocking back and forth while Lacekeen and Lacefirm sat on either side of her, holding her tightly. Lacebold and Laceheart sat on a branch just below them, and had been arguing, judging by Lacebold's anger and frustration.

I'm alright, I told them. *You were right to stay where you are. Lacebold, calm yourself, I don't need any help. Laceheart and Lacefirm were right to insist the five of you stay together. Lacehope, everything is alright. You know how the forest has helped us since we got here? How everything got better as soon as we let it help us?*

She didn't reply, but I sensed her rocking had stopped.

Well, I've found someone who can help us even more, I continued. *I'm sorry I haven't hunted...*

It's fine, Lacefirm interrupted. *Taylor brought down the biggest animal anyone has yet, and we've had some of it.*

That's good. I need to stay here a while longer. Did you finish preparing the blossom essences?

Ages ago, Lacekeen said.

Well done. So then, all five of you, keep your minds with mine. Lacehope?

I sensed her unfurl and lean into Lacekeen. Her mind accepted the embrace of mine.

I'm alright and so are you, I told her. *Keep your mind with mine and observe. Can you do that?*

You're alright and so am I, she affirmed to herself. *I can do it, Lace.*

I know you can. Let Lacekeen look after you and you'll be fine. Laceheart, if you sense any of the others beginning to pick up on what's happening here, help them to stay still and quiet, and to watch with the rest of you. Lacebold and Lacefirm, help him if necessary. We all have much to learn here.

I knew it was true, but in all my life, I had never felt so tired.

You should rest, the horse told me. *Clearing that which was buried takes much energy.*

His thoughts settled within me so lightly, I barely heard them but more felt them, and with them, the strength of his benevolence. He had fought against the instincts of his species in order to remain with me, which I could feel was only marginally less exhausting than whatever had happened to me, yet all his attention and concern were directed towards me.

But I have so much to learn from you.

A tired mind cannot learn. You should rest. I will remain with you. He lowered his nose to my shoulder and breathed a long, hot breath. *Rest.*

Chapter Seventeen

This will be my last diary entry. We still haven't found any signs of human habitation and my tablet is dying as surely as many of those with me now believe they are. I won't let them. We may be running out of food and without the knowledge or wherewithal to get more, but so would have been all the others who escaped the cities before us, and we haven't come across any graves or skeletons to tell us they didn't make it. Mum always told me to trust my gut feeling, and my gut tells me to keep heading in the direction we are, and everything will be okay. I owe it to her memory and all she sacrificed to make sure that everyone who escaped with me survives. We WILL find those who went before us, and we WILL live the life we've all dreamt of.

Secret diary of Jinna Lace

A LIGHT DRIZZLE drifted over me as I slept, so that I woke drenched in tiny droplets of water clinging to the individual hairs of my coat. I sat up and tried to brush away the moisture, as well as debris from the forest floor, but only succeeded in driving it all closer to my skin. I gave it up as a bad idea and got to my feet wondering how on earth I had fallen asleep on the ground when to date, I had only felt safe to do so up in my tree.

The horse was standing amongst the tall, spindly plants of the forest clearing, his head lowered between them as he drew a few at a time into his mouth while still chewing those already there. His back was also covered in water droplets, which made his fur look grey rather than the rich brown that he was underneath it. The long black hair hanging from the top of his neck and from his back end was free of water, the reason for which became clear when he somehow caused both lots of hair to flick around, launching a cloud of tiny insects into the surrounding air from his neck, sides and underbelly.

I sensed them landing back on him and immediately attempting to crawl between the hairs of his coat, intending to bite him and take his blood – they wanted to take nutrition from his body, much as I had. But where he had diffused my intention to take what I wanted from him in one attempt, the flying biters were relentless. He swatted them off again and again as he ate, paying no more attention to them than it took to flick his hair around and occasionally shake his head and neck. I sensed his irritation when one or more of them reached his skin and bit him, but his reaction to them remained the same, as if he were used to dealing with such discomfort.

He was, I realised, and it affected his mood not at all, even as it began to affect mine. I could almost feel the biters attacking my own skin, though it was impossible; they would never make any kind of impact upon skin that had been engineered to repel stones and blades.

As soon as I took on his discomfort as my own, I heard the songs of several plants answering my unintentional call. They would repel the flying biters as effectively as did my toughened skin, and soothe the bites he had already sustained.

I sensed my younglings' fascination with the horse before me, and as always, it was Laceheart who was the first to follow my mind's wanderings with his own.

I hear them singing too. I can go and gather them, he assured me.

Don't go by yourself, I warned. *One adult for every youngling, remember.*

Taylor will come with me, he replied. *He likes trying to hear the plants sing.*

Your enthusiasm does you credit, I told him. *Gather as many of the plants as you can, and prepare them as the forest guides you to.*

The result will be welcome, the horse told me without lifting his head from what I could feel was a careful selection of plants from all those available around his feet. They all looked very similar to me, but through him, I could sense that the different varieties brushed against the hairs sprouting from his nose and chin in different ways, and they all smelt different. More importantly, though, they sang to him as readily as the plants helping me and my kind sang to us.

We are glad to be able to help you, I replied. *We would not be here were it not for you, I understand that now. What I do not understand is why horses helped the ancestors of the human kindred, or why you are here for me now. I sense the answer to both of my questions is the same, yet it makes no sense to me. You are not human and you are not kindred. Why did your ancestors care that the humans of the city should survive, and why do you care what happens to us?*

You assume one must earn support and guidance yet their

provision is not dependent upon worth for the worth of all is equal.

The worth of all is equal. I repeated it to myself over and over, but I couldn't even begin to believe it was true.

You were raised by those who doubted their own worth and attempted to put themselves above you in order to convince themselves of its existence, I was informed. *They were unsuccessful.*

They are dead.

They are no longer here in physical form, agreed the horse. *Those of you who remain have an opportunity to redress the imbalance they created. I and my kind will help.*

More of you are coming? I asked.

I will help you. The others will continue to help the humans.

Charlotte Lace's daughter. I felt my insides lighten. Then they became heavy once more. I hadn't spared her the slightest thought since the city was destroyed.

I thought of Jinna Lace as I asked, *Are horses helping this person?*

You may know the answer to your question as easily as I.

I can't find her. I can't use my sixth sense unless I've seen where someone is likely to be. I couldn't sense anything beyond the city walls before they were destroyed.

You sensed me.

Because of our connection. Our thread. It felt a clumsy way of describing it to him when I sensed that he experienced our connection without the need for any such notion.

You sense aspects of the forest in areas with which you are not familiar.

He was right. The forest wasn't an individual though, but an interconnection of multitudes of individuals.

The horse seized my thought and held it so I couldn't mistake its importance, telling me, *Life is an interconnection between individuals. Your mind is restricted as a result of your experience so far but you have opened sufficiently to your surroundings to use them as a pathway to those requiring your assistance.*

Charlotte Lace's daughter needs my assistance?

The horse didn't reply. He was waiting for something... for me, I realised. I considered everything he had told me, but not for very long. As soon as I thought of the forest as a pathway, it seemed to open before me in my mind, expanding so quickly I almost lost my breath. The trees were connected to other trees everywhere, for they weren't really other trees at all, but the same. The birds were all driven by the same thoughts and energy, ensuring their connection with all other birds, even those they had never met. Their bodies functioned in the same way as those of their and other species who breathed air, drank water and processed plant and animal matter, including mine, which provided another, only very slightly more distant connection. The energy they gleaned from their food connected them to the sources of it and everything to which those sources were connected.

As the truth of life unfurled around me, I felt tiny and insignificant, akin to the tiny biters swarming around a horse an infinite number of times their size. And as free. I could use the connections to go anywhere with my mind – and I did. I thought of Jinna Lace and the trees responded, drawing me to where she rested against one of them. She was tired and hungry, but she was alive, as were all those with whom she had escaped, I realised through her connection with them.

They were halfway down a tall mound of earth covered with plants and they had spotted smoke in the distance, on the far side of a small forest. I sensed their nervous excitement and their hope that they had found humans who would welcome and help them as Charlotte Lace had assured them was likely.

Through my thought of Jinna Lace and the trees she could see, I found the humans living nearby. They were happy and peaceful. They co-operated with one another, and their community was thriving. Charlotte Lace's daughter and her friends would be welcomed. She didn't need my help.

So, who did? As soon as I thought of the question, I found them.

They were like us – yet not like us. Where we were kindred, they were still enforcers. I sensed The Way Of The Horse within every one of those old enough to have encountered their city's human kindred, but while it was strong enough to have kept them together and to have adults attempting to keep babies and younglings alive, they were not thriving.

What can I do?

Reach them. Assist them and all others like them to open to the connection they share with you. Show them how to flourish.

All others? As soon as I phrased the question in my mind, it fragmented and dispersed in all directions at once, to all the other forests experiencing a discord that had so far resisted their ability to embrace and nurture it. I felt dwarfed. Overwhelmed. The trees seemed to sing louder, reminding me of their support and having the same effect on me as if I had taken a sip of their blossoms' essence.

You are connected to everything. You are never alone, the horse reminded me, and I believed him.

We can help too, Lacekeen told me.

I felt a very faint warning from the horse.

Not to begin with, I replied. *I have no doubt you'll be able to reach them now, but until I know what state their minds are in, none of you will attempt to do so. Do you understand me? Lacebold?* I added firmly, sensing he was about to argue. He was the last to assent.

You're hungry, Lacefirm informed me as if I didn't know. *When are you coming back?*

Is the horse coming with you? Lacebold asked.

No, he isn't, Laceheart told him, surprising me as he was beginning to do often. *It's like he told Lace before. If you focus on your connection to everything, you can know the answers to your questions for yourself. When Lace leaves to come back here, the horse will go to the plain area, where we collect plants for medicines. There's more for him to eat there.*

Strong Of Heart will be a capable leader of your kin if he can find himself as he matures, the horse informed me.

I and my other younglings will help him.

That is not the help he requires. If he is to find himself then he must be alone with the forest.

I shuddered at the thought of any of my younglings being alone, even though, having just learnt what I had, I knew that wasn't really possible. *Why must he?*

Not just him. All of them. You have helped them to break through some of the barriers imposed upon them by their creators, but there are some that resist and will continue to do so.

They're eight years old. Nearly nine, granted, but I can't send them off alone, I protested.

It will take time for the situation to become clear to you, the horse told me confidently. As if he already knew exactly what would happen.

You know the future?

I experience only the present. It is a powerful moment in which to focus oneself for only then is that which must be communicated or implemented obvious.

A griping announced itself in my stomach, whose hunger was at last more urgent than my need for answers from the horse.

I should return to my kin, I told the horse. *You're not just going out to the treeless place because there's more for you to eat, are you?*

He at last lifted his head from the plants and looked at me, his lower jaw moving from side to side in a way that made me feel nauseous. *You alone of your hunters are capable of the restraint that prevented you from killing me. You have much to consider and more to do. Return to your kin. I will remain nearby.*

I'll bring the plant mixture that will keep the flying biters off you.

Your youngling can do that. He will be less busy than will you.

No younglings go to the treeless place without an adult, I told him firmly.

I am an adult, he replied, as if that were the end of the discussion.

You're prey. You can't protect him from the predators I can sense out there.

I will ensure the survival of your youngling and myself.

I couldn't argue, for I found I trusted him completely. If he said he would look after Laceheart, then he would.

I have taken a name for myself, I told him. *And I would have one to call you by.*

I will answer to however you think of me.

He was the opposite of every individual I had ever met who was in a position to influence me.

You are Benevolence.

Chapter Eighteen

My darling Isabel,

Thank you for your letter. I've no doubt that by now, you will know it was indeed the cities of The Old perishing that caused the ground to shudder many weeks ago. I hope Jonustown was among the villages joining Rockwood in celebrating the event in grand style. Your father and I are thrilled that your apprenticeship is going so well and can't wait to welcome Rockwood's first Herbalist home. In the meantime, I am coming to understand your and your father's enthusiasm for Heralds – this is a pleasing way to stay in touch, is it not? One passed on news he'd heard from another of someone in Jonustown being tugged by a horse, you must write back with all the details! We are both well, although your father has a sore toe that could do with the attention of a Herbalist. Do you happen to know of any?

With all my love, Mum

I BARELY NOTICED MY HUNGER, extreme though it was, as I made my way back to my younglings. I swung through the trees slowly, mindfully, my direct contact with the wise old beings that supported me mentally and physically amplifying the sense I had of so many other trees and the forests of which they were a part, in too many locations to contemplate counting.

I threw myself into exploring the forests that felt as familiar to me as that in which I had made my home. They were all alive and pulsing with the rhythms of the animals, plants and other organisms almost too tiny to catch my notice that comprised them. Most of them were harmonious units that continually adjusted to their components arriving, leaving, interacting, consuming, ingesting and excreting. Those attempting – and failing – to correct disharmony within themselves stood out almost painfully, like an injured animal licking its wound in an attempt to heal it while a foreign body continued to fester inside.

I reached out to the wounded forest that I sensed was closest. It enfolded me within its grasp, recognising and welcoming my intention and aiming me straight towards the enforcers who could not hear its songs. None of them were hungry or thirsty, for, like my community, they had gathered food and water from the lower floors of their building and taken them with them. They were not injured and they were not carrying disease. But the babies cried endlessly and the younglings were listless. The adults sat around, many staring sightlessly as some of our number had done, the rest seeing and hearing everything, yet doing nothing aside from distributing food at the times their bodies had been conditioned to expect it.

The songs of the forest probed at them, but could not make themselves heard. Trees stood ready to bear them and vines waited to be woven into shelters. Other plants called to them, sensing their peril and keen to help. The scent of fresh water wafted beneath every nose and yet none so much as twitched. Animals who had agreed to nurture enforcer bodies in order that they could contribute to the forest in turn, were ignored, even when they ventured close enough to be seen.

Lace? Lacehope's thought carried her anxiety at the distress she sensed within me, bringing me back to myself.

I'm coming. I pushed everything to one side so I could focus on returning to my younglings. When I reached them, Lacehope threw herself into my arms and hung on tightly. Lacekeen and Lacefirm squeezed against me on either side, and even Lacebold climbed up to my branch and settled against my back. I sensed Laceheart's preoccupation with the plants he and Taylor were gathering, and was relieved.

I'm alright, I told the four who nestled against me. *I'm just concerned about those of our kind who survived in other cities, as they aren't doing very well. I need to help them, but I need to eat first.*

Lacekeen was away in an instant, telling me, *I'll fetch you what's left of today's hunt.*

I ate quickly on her return and then gave my younglings the task of visiting the other families with offers of help with their young, fetching water, reweaving parts of their shelters where necessary – anything that would keep them busy while I did what was needed, though I didn't know exactly what that was.

I thought back to the advice Benevolence had given me. I had to reach the enforcers and show them how to thrive. I had a sense of where to begin; The Way Of The Horse would guide me, I felt sure of it.

I reached through the trees once again for the enforcers in the closest forest to mine. I focused on Charlotte Lace and the part of her that was within me, and instantly sensed it again in those for whom I was reaching. While, like those in my community, it was part of all of them to a degree, there was one who possessed it more strongly than the others. It was he who had organised the others to gather supplies and who had led them away from the crater that had been their city, to the surrounding forest. It was he who had been the last to lose himself to fear and overwhelm, but lose himself he had.

I focused on the tiny part of him that knew what it was to be supported and cared for, and felt it recognise the part of me that knew the same. I drew him with me as I embraced the forest to the same extent it embraced me... and sensed his eyes widen. His nose twitched as he scented fresh water. His heart lifted as he heard the songs of the forest. His mouth watered as he sensed those willing to relinquish their bodies in order to nourish his.

But first you should name yourself, I told him gently. *If you are to hunt, then you should do so not as enforcer but as kindred. Name yourself for the one who gave you hope. I am Lace.*

Moffatt. I am Moffatt.

You did well to lead your kindred into the forest. Now let it guide you to help them as my forest has guided me to help mine.

Who are you? Where are you?

I was an enforcer, like you. We were created in all the cities before they turned upon one another. You have everything around you that you need in order to thrive.

How did you know where to find me? How to find me? Why are you helping me?

Open yourself to the trees. Accept everything they have to offer and then through them, find your way back to me. I have to leave you now to waken the next community of kindred. It is good to know you, Moffat. Fare you well.

But...

It was tempting to stay, to tell him what to do and give him time to search my mind for confirmation of my instructions, but I had to trust that he would do as I told him and let the forest guide him. I hastened on to the next closest community of enforcers.

I was pleased to see Benevolence eating peacefully, the flying biters that were so desperate to feed from his blood hovering in frustration more than the length of his tail away.

You've been very diligent, Laceheart.

I like Ben. I like making the potion that keeps the flies from biting him, and I like smearing it on him as much he likes me doing it. He lets me sit on his back so I can reach all of him, and I've got really good at jumping on. Do you want to see?

I smiled down at my youngling, wondering how I could have missed how much he'd grown up in the twenty-two days it had taken me to reach all the enforcers who were now on their way to becoming kindred. Not grown up as such, I corrected myself. He was still very much an eight-year-old youngling, but he was... more of himself. Where before he had been introspective, his thoughts very light and almost insubstantial, now he was stronger. More definite. As if he had landed within himself from the great height at which he had been drifting.

I'd love to see, I told him.

Benevolence – Ben – didn't lift his head as Laceheart gambolled over to him, parting the tall plants before him with practised hands. The horse twitched the ear closest to his young carer when Laceheart was a few paces away, and I felt the familiarity that existed between the two of them. Ben welcomed Laceheart's presence even though he wasn't due for a reapplication of his biter repellent, and Laceheart couldn't wait to feel the magnification of the horse's warmth and acceptance that he would be able to when he leapt upon his back – which he did with alarming commitment; he knew Ben wouldn't move until he was safely in place.

My heart thudded in my chest as I sensed that his confidence resulted from experience as well as trust. How had I not known that one of the fanged predators with whom we shared our heritage had hunted the two of them only four days ago?

You were occupied with the task that was important for you to undertake, Ben informed me. *You know now that I have been occupied with the task that was mine. Your trust in me was not misplaced.*

You've strengthened and protected Laceheart.

I returned him to the trees when he was hunted. He alone is responsible for accepting that which he can sense within me. He is indeed better anchored within his body but he will still need to find himself with help from the forest.

I chose to ignore his last words. *Okay, so you protected him while he got stronger himself. Thank you.*

There was no conscious effort on my part.

I nodded to myself. The Way Of The Horse was powerful, yet so gentle. It had survived the violence of humans, not by fighting it, but by co-existing with it, diluting it and passing from one individual to the next so that the human and kindred races had survived as a result of it.

A thought occurred to me. Maybe I should reach out to the human communities now? Those who had escaped the cities before enforcers had been created to stop them? They had been helped by the human kindred as much as had my kind, so they must have been exposed to, and affected by, The Way Of The Horse too?

Ben lifted his head and stared straight at me as Laceheart sat astride him, untangling a chunk of the long hair that ran along the top of his neck. *The humans should be left to themselves,* the horse told me. *They are capable of a great deal but they have much to learn first. You will be well served in continuing to focus your efforts on assisting your own kind in their attempts to survive.*

But I've done what I needed to. The forests will guide them now.

You have barely begun. The forest that currently hosts you will not sustain you indefinitely. The shelters you have devised will not protect you from the weather of the seasons to come. Your community is as dependent on you as are all those in the other communities. You have much to do in order to ensure the ongoing survival of your kind. Focus upon those issues and allow the humans to focus on theirs. It will serve neither race to come together for some time.

There would come a time when I wished I had listened to him.

Chapter Nineteen

Dear Mum,

I'm sending this via a different Herald as he's coming your way – I hope he's as reliable as Herald Vera! It was Yasmin Hanna who was tugged by a horse. Her parents and sister are very emotional now she's left, but so excited for her and so proud. They organised the entire village to see her off, which was lovely. They asked us to be there well before it was time for her to leave, and to make two lines facing one another so that she could walk between us all and say her goodbyes. She was so surprised, and I could see she was touched that we were all there for her. Her family presented her with things she'll need on her journey to meet her horse, then she hugged every single person waiting to wish her well. I don't suppose she'll be back before I return to Rockwood, which is a shame as I'd have loved to meet the horse who has chosen her. Can you imagine it? Being chosen by a horse to share a bond? How lucky is she! We did indeed celebrate the fall of The Old in Jonustown, it was good timing as it picked Yasmin's family up after she left. I've nearly completed my herb journal now. I'd like to say that means I'll qualify soon, but the last few ailments I have to find cures for are causing me some problems. I'm working hard though and won't stop until I find their cures. Wish me luck!

Love to you both, Isabel

BENEVOLENCE DIDN'T MAKE further comment regarding our future, but everything he had told me came to make sense.

When the heat of summer brought with it storms of lightning, thunder and the heaviest of rain, our shelters, woven from the thick vines growing up the trunks of our host trees, gave little more protection than the canopy of leaves above our heads. Hunting gave sparser results, and we had to travel further into the forest and across the plain area to collect the plants we needed to nurture and heal us. I began to sense grumbles and complaints that didn't just originate from my fellow kindred; the forest was tiring of us as much as we were tiring of the fact that our bountiful existence was gradually becoming less so. I grew weary of my kins' complaints being directed solely at me, as if it were my fault alone that we were constantly wet, hungry and frustrated.

Where should we go? I asked Ben one morning after I had woken, yet again, dripping wet and cold despite the warm temperature. The warm, earthy smell being lifted from the forest floor by the pounding of the rain and combining with the fresher, sharper smell of the leaves washing down over and past me from above – a combination I had always found invigorating – did nothing to ease my misery or my exhaustion.

I sensed Ben was almost as wet as he sheltered under a densely leafed tree at the edge of the forest, yet his answer carried no hint of discomfort. *Do not allow your irritation to become all of you. Look for answers where you know you can always find them.*

I am. I'm asking you.

You ask me because you are losing confidence in the forest yet it has never failed to guide you. Consider the fact that guidance can come in many forms.

We need to leave, I've accepted that. It's where to go that I'm not sure about.

Your uncertainty is rooted in fear. Step aside from that and do as you have advised so many others to do.

Their forests were desperate to help them. Ours is rejecting us.

It guides you still. You have merely ceased to listen.

I'm tired, Ben.

You alone bear the weight of your community. The situation is not sustainable, he agreed.

How can you tell me that so cheerfully? I'm faced with having to uproot everyone when they won't want to leave – especially when they're wet, cold, tired and hungry – and without the energy even to find out where it is I'm meant to be taking them.

Ben didn't reply. He wasn't concerned about me or my situation any more than he'd been concerned about anything since I'd ceased my hunting of him. He continued to rest under his tree, one hind leg bent and flicking an ear occasionally if a larger than normal raindrop landed upon it. I sensed his contentment, his satisfaction even, that events were proceeding as necessary. But how could that be?

He had told me he would remain nearby in order to help me, yet when I needed him most, he was leaving me to my discomfort and exhaustion. I thought back over his responses to my questions.

The forests have never failed to guide you.

The forests. I reached for them all as the leaves and branches above me rustled, spilling an even greater deluge onto my almost completely ineffective shelter and subsequently onto the top of my head, as Laceheart dropped onto my branch.

'There's one that's calling to us,' he whispered, crawling beneath my fan of woven vines to sit beside me. 'It's that way.' He pointed to where the sun sank in the evenings.

'West,' I murmured, shaking my head to dislodge some of the water that had soaked me and was chilling me even further. 'We would have to cross land with no trees for shade in the middle of summer. It would be difficult for the older ones among us to remain cool.'

'The forest is calling to us,' Laceheart said with conviction. 'Ben's right, our forest has never been wrong and neither have any of the others. If ours is telling us to go and that one's telling us to come, then shouldn't we do what they say? The rain will keep us cool and if it stops, we can travel at night. That's when I've been going to see Ben when it's hot.'

Despite his unsettling admission about his nighttime activity, of which I had previously had no idea, I felt a surge of energy as his solution settled within me. He was right. My youngling had trusted Ben and the forest, and found the solution to our problem when I couldn't. The extra years of life I had on him seemed very insignificant all of a sudden; he was far better suited to leading our kind than was I.

He must be alone with the forest first. Ben's repetition of his previous advice was no less firm.

I dismissed it with a shudder and changed the subject. *We'll be coming your way. None of the others are aware of you, and we need to make sure it stays that way. I know you can run faster than any of us, but if you don't want them hunting you when we get to where I'm sure you know we're going, you need to go on ahead. That is... if you're coming with us?*

I will remain out of sight and beyond the awareness of all but you and your younglings.

'He was always coming with us. We need him,' Laceheart told me simply.

'You need him, you mean.' Lacebold's voice reached us above the sound of rain spattering on the vines, leaves and branches. There was an increase in the spattering noise before he too landed on my branch. He sat just beyond my shelter, rain pouring off both sides of his head and dripping from his nose. 'When are we leaving?'

I smiled at him, taking as much energy from his apparent imperviousness to the weather as from Laceheart's insights. 'We'll leave once everyone has eaten. I need the five of you to gather up all the tins we've been using, and our remaining food, divide them between you and me and then wrap them in the blankets we brought with us. I'll take four times the amount of any of you.'

Lacebold wouldn't have been himself had he not taken issue with my instruction. 'We'll give you three times what we'll take. You're not four times our size.'

I nodded solemnly. 'Three times, then. Off you go, you two – wake the others and let them know what's happening.'

Lacebold straightened his legs from his crouch, bent them, and then propelled himself to a branch some distance above in a single leap. Laceheart followed. I nodded with satisfaction; my younglings, and all the others in our community, were moving around in the trees as if they had been born in them. Where they had been cowering, frightened and under muscled despite the exercise regimes to which they were subjected below ground, they were now increasingly strong, confident and boisterous thanks to the forest and its components.

Now that I thought of the forest without fear and weariness, I sensed that nurturing us hadn't been a sacrifice for it. We had cleared areas of plants that would only grow back more vigorously as a result. We had hunted the animals whose bodies were older or weaker than the rest, leaving the young and robust to repopulate in their wake. We had cleaned and revitalised the forest every bit as much as it has done the same for us... and now another was calling for us to do the same.

I sprang from my branch with almost as much vigour as my younglings, and took my well-leapt path through the trees to those housing families and groups of adults who had come to rely on one another's company. Most of them looked as miserable as I had felt when I had woken, but I was gratified as always to see that the babies had all grown, the younglings looked as well as mine, and the adults' eyes contained life where before they had contained only death.

By the time I landed on Hob's branch, she was expecting me. 'I gather we're leaving,' she said from her place at the back of her shelter. It was woven more tightly than mine but still allowed water to drip on her and her two younglings, both of whom nestled against her as they slept. 'Ash told me after you left him.' The two who had been QFE24 and QME96 respectively had become close friends, supporting one another and the two younglings that each of them had adopted from the same dormitory as my five.

'Neither of you want to go,' I said, knowing it was true. 'I don't, either. It won't be easy, but we can't stay. You're aware of the forest, you know what it's telling us. We have to move on, and when we reach the forest that needs us as much as we need it, we'll settle again and do even better than we did here.'

'You can't know that,' she told me.

I sighed and thought of Laceheart while being very careful to avoid thinking of Ben. I felt the surge of energy I had felt earlier and focused on it so that she would sense it too. 'I do know it. Trust the forests, Hob, it's all we can do.'

When I eventually returned to my branch, leaving a wave of activity in my wake, I felt exhausted again.

There was a rustle and a fresh deluge of water, and this time it was Lacehope who dropped down in front of me. She said nothing, but just held out her arms as she fell into mine and held me tightly.

I lowered my forehead to the top of her scalp and breathed in and out slowly and deeply. I had to do better. Every time I faltered, I brought her down with me.

'Some of your hair has changed colour, did you know?' Lacefirm said.

I raised my head to see her sitting on a branch above and slightly to the left of my shelter, peering down at me. 'No. What colour is it?'

'Some of it's grey and some of it's white, on the top of your head and above your eyes. Will that happen to me when I'm a teenager too?'

I thought of QMC61, who had been more than thirty years older than I. His coat had been solid brown. I shrugged. 'I don't know. We'll have to see, won't we?'

————

Benevolence was as good as his assertion that he would stay beyond detection by our kin as we slowly made our way west. I was always at the front of the long line of kindred who only followed in my footsteps because they were more frightened of having to survive in our original forest without me, and I never saw him, so those following in my wake had no chance of doing so.

The closest he came to being discovered was when, on the sixth morning of crossing the plains and becoming ever more tired of tripping through the long-stemmed plants and being wet, Ash asked irritably, 'Where's Laceheart? This is the fourth morning in a row he hasn't been with the rest of you. I don't see him behind us, and I can't sense him.'

I immediately withdrew my sixth sense from where Laceheart was astride Ben and moving faster than any of us could have dreamed possible, some distance ahead. I directed all of my other senses to Ash and drew my other four youngsters' attention with me so they couldn't give away Laceheart's location either. The four of them trudged on beside me in silence, but I sensed Lacehope's concern, Lacefirm's interest, Lacekeen's readiness to back up whatever I said, and Lacebold's anticipation of interjecting at the slightest opportunity.

'He went on ahead before dawn,' I said. 'He likes to spend time getting to know the new plants and animals he comes across without worrying he'll get left behind. He's already discovered three new plants that can heal.'

It was true; when Ben stopped to eat, that was exactly what Laceheart did. I implicitly trusted the big, brown horse who had more knowledge and experience of the ways of our new world than I could fathom, and knew he wouldn't leave Laceheart if there were any chance predators would reach him before we did. It was easier to let him be where his heart led him than to insist he walk with us and risk any of those behind us picking up on where his mind tended to be.

'You think that's safe?' Ash said.

'Definitely,' Lacekeen said.

'Not really,' Lacebold argued.

'Not for most of us,' I said, 'but Laceheart has a way of

integrating with everything that surrounds us, and feeling his way around. He won't let himself get into danger.'

'You have a lot of trust in an eight-year-old youngling,' Ash said.

'I trust all five of them. They each have their strengths and they need to learn how to use them. I won't always be here to guide them.' I felt something settle within my stomach and knew, without knowing how, that I had spoken the truth. Not only that, but I had spoken it as if it were mine rather than just a regurgitation of something Ben had told me.

'You'll be here for a long time yet though,' Lacehope said. She took hold of my hand and squeezed it, desperate for me to agree with her. Her touch infused me with a surge of energy that I realised I needed. She thrummed with life, as if there was so much of it left for her to live, it could barely be contained moment by moment. All the other younglings were the same, I realised, and the babies were even more vibrant. By contrast, I and the other adults felt flat. Tired.

'I'll be here for a while yet.' I squeezed Lacehope's hand back and smiled down at her, sensing Lacebold and Lacefirm observing me as keenly with their eyes as with their sixth sense, even as Lacekeen nodded encouragingly to Lacehope.

As soon as Ash diverted his attention to one of his younglings, I looked into the distance while throwing my attention back to where Ben was practically flying above the tall, narrow-leafed plants that continually trapped and tripped the rest of us, while Laceheart sat easily upon his back.

When we reached our new forest four days later, Laceheart was waiting for us by one of the nearest trees, and Ben, as always, was out of sight and mind of most of our number. The younglings all sprang for the trees with an energy that was incomprehensible to those of us who had worked so hard to keep up their spirits and nurture the babies as we travelled across plains that were as inhospitable to us as the forests were nurturing. While the rain had kept cool those of us with thicker skin, it had sapped our spirits as much as had the wet, tacky plants and soft, sticky earth that had hindered our progress. It was all we could do to identify the trees that sang to each of us in welcome, climb to a comfortable height, settle the babies, and sleep.

Chapter Twenty

Let it be recorded for the Histories that on this day, the Third Monday of July, Eighth year of the Eighth Decade of The New, I, Jinna Lace, have been given the honour of becoming Keeper of The Histories in Plainsview. I am finding it strange to be forming letters on paper, using a pen sung from metal, and ink made from plant sap, when I have only ever before caused them to form on a screen with the tap of my fingers. My hand aches at the end of every day, but Keeper Dace Kildare is a patient teacher and assures me he is happy with his choice of Keeper to replace him so he can retire. I will ensure that his confidence in me is not misplaced.

Histories of The New, Keeper Jinna Lace

WE SETTLED QUICKLY in our new home, largely thanks to my younglings. Lacekeen found vines that were much finer than those we had used to weave our shelters in our previous forest, and could be woven tightly enough to exclude even the heaviest rain.

Laceheart followed the conduit provided by the forests to others far, far away, where birds wove hanging nests with an entrance hole halfway down and soft bedding for their young in the lower half. Lacefirm and Lacehope took Lacekeen's vines and wove the first nest that emulated that of the weaver birds Laceheart had found, only for Lacebold to argue that hanging it from a branch like the birds did would leave it swinging in the wind and possibly even dropping to the ground under the weight of the larger families. I suggested fixing it to a lower branch as well as to one above it, which Lacekeen and Lacefirm immediately made preparations to do.

Within just a few weeks, all families and individuals, under the tutelage of my younglings, had shelters that protected them from the rain when it came. We found new plants that our previous forest hadn't offered, both medicinal and nutritional. Wise as we had become to the effort required in fetching enough water to sate our community each day and having settled by a stream of fresh water as a result, we enjoyed the sound of it bubbling through the middle of our new settlement as much as we appreciated its convenience. Hunting was once again easy and plentiful as the forest's inhabitants recognised our role in its ongoing success, and nourished us as we in turn pruned the forest to its benefit.

We began to thrive again, and I thanked the forests repeatedly in my mind for insisting so firmly that we made the difficult, exhausting two-week journey across the plains. I tried – and repeatedly failed – to convey the importance of tackling that which was difficult in order to make life better, to the other kindred communities. I bombarded their leaders with a sense of my community's contentment, but even as their communities struggled more and more by the day, they blocked out the forests' guidance to leave one and move to another, in the same way as had I.

If you won't trust the forests about this, you should at least trust me, I told Moffat one morning. *I'm telling you, you can't delay moving much longer. You're exhausting the forest and that means both it and you all will starve. Autumn will be here soon and your shelters aren't robust enough. Even if you stay, you'll need to make new ones like ours, but there's no point putting effort into that when you need to leave.*

This is our home, he told me, repeating the same thing he had, over and over, during our last few conversations. He no longer had the energy to conjure up reasons to stay, when really there was only one – fear.

My exasperation at my failure to convince the other leaders to take their communities onward, both in distance and in life, drove me to leave my shelter and head out to where I knew Benevolence waited for me. As I swung through the trees, feeling a little stiff and shocked at the loss of power in my limbs after weeks of focusing all my efforts on pleading with the other kindred leaders, my eagerness to see him increased. I wondered why I hadn't made the effort before.

My question only increased in size and strength when I saw him at the edge of the forest, head down and eating plants, as he spent so much of his time doing. His coat absorbed the sun's rays before churning them back out an almost impossibly rich, red-brown colour. The black hair along the top of his neck and sprouting from his hind end glistened as nothing that was black should have been able to. As expected knowing how diligent Laceheart was in caring for his friend, a swarm of tiny flying predators hung in the air a short distance from him. I felt their desire for his blood holding them there despite the repellent my youngling always made sure coated the horse sufficiently to keep them at bay. His body was as toned as mine was not, due to the daily runs he undertook with Laceheart astride him. As he moved slowly from plant to plant, selecting very precisely those his body needed in any given moment, I felt at peace.

I had communicated with him several times over the past weeks, each time begging him to tell me how to convince the kindred leaders to listen to me, and he had told me the same each time. But even as I sensed he would only do the same now that I was with him in body, I felt none of the frustration that had been plaguing me.

I dropped from the outermost of the forest's trees and sat at its base, content merely to watch the horse who was a vision of everything I was not. I thought over the response to my pleas for help that he had given, over and over.

The answer to all of your difficulties is the same. I have already provided it. When you can accept it then the survival of your kind will be assured.

I sat very still, watching the prey animal who had chosen to be separate from his herd and in the presence of a formidable predator, yet was utterly serene. I scented the dusty earthiness of his coat. I listened to the steady, rhythmic grinding of his teeth. I tasted the tiny fragments he released from the tops of the plants he disturbed as he moved between them. I felt the thud of his feet on the ground beneath me as he moved. Now that I was before him, he filled all of my senses instead of merely my sixth, and I found myself considering his advice in a way I hadn't been able to before. I had to accept something he'd already told me.

He'd advised that I had to listen to the forest even when it was difficult, and I'd done so. He'd warned that the shelters we'd built previously weren't sufficient, and thanks to my younglings, that issue had been rectified, within our community at least. I moved on to the next thing he'd told me… and stopped, immediately back-tracking to the advice I had accepted. But where I had taken refuge there, in the part of my mind where it felt safe, over the previous weeks, Ben's peaceful presence prevented me from doing so now.

I eased out of it, towards the counsel I had been avoiding, and for the first time acknowledged the fact he had highlighted – that my community, and all the other kindred communities, were completely dependent upon me. Aside from my younglings, not one member of my community would do anything I hadn't instructed them to do; if I hadn't left our previous forest, they would all still be there. And short of physically visiting every forest that housed kindred still clinging to the exhausted remnants of their once vibrant homes, and leading them away, none of them would leave for the forests that called to them either. I had taken to chewing the bark of the tree that had offered its blossom in spring to help me with my constant sense of overwhelm, but even that wouldn't sustain me if I undertook such a task, and my own community, including my younglings, might well fail in the meantime.

As Ben had told me weeks before, the situation wasn't sustainable. The kindred had to learn to make decisions for themselves. My stomach, which had been roiling as I thought of trying to fix everything by myself, settled and felt stable. Strong. It was the truth. I had done what I could for the kindred in other communities, and it was time to leave them to their own devices while I focused on leading my own.

My stomach began to feel unsettled again at the thought; the other adults brought their questions and concerns to me daily – hourly sometimes. Should they feed their babies more now? Should they allow their younglings to do what they had seen other younglings doing? Was there a better way of storing water? Their queries were endless and exhausting. Those posed to me by my younglings were less so, but when I thought about it, they still demonstrated a lack of confidence to make decisions without my confirmation.

I sensed the answer – I couldn't help it while Benevolence was so close – and tried to push it away. My stomach roiled so much it hurt. The more I resisted accepting that which Ben had told me on more than one occasion, the more it tore at me until finally, I could resist it no longer.

I thought of Laceheart, who was at the centre of my turmoil. He would be the beginning. If he could be alone with the forest until he found all of himself and not just the parts that the forest, Benevolence and I had already brought out of him, then, interconnected as we all were, he would lay down the pattern for others to do the same and they would no longer be so dependent upon me.

My stomach settled comfortably with the truth, even as my mind now churned with its implications. I didn't have a favourite among my younglings, but in the same way that Lacehope inspired me to be as brave as she had to be in order to get through every day, Lacekeen inspired me to keep helping others even when I didn't feel like it, Lacefirm reminded me what it was to be determined in every task I undertook, and Lacebold brought out an attitude within me of taking no nonsense from those I led, it was Laceheart with whom I felt the greatest affinity and who inspired me the most. It was he whom I would find hardest to let go, even if only for a short while, for he was my heart.

You will not be letting him go. You will be setting him free, Benevolence informed me, lifting his head from the plants and holding my gaze with his own. *The situation is now urgent.*

He turned nine years old just last week, I protested weakly. *Nine.*

I have been in my body for six turns of the seasons.

But you're an adult of your species. He's a youngling of mine.

Ben made his way over to me and breathed his words into my mind as well as my face. *There will not always be such a great need for younglings to find themselves at such a young age. But it is always the case that when there is need there will be those who can fulfil it however unlikely the match may appear to be. You are one such. Strong Of Heart is another and he is not alone.*

You're another. I knew in my stomach that my assertion was as true as everything he had told me. *You call him Strong Of Heart, and I know he is. Will it be enough though?*

That is up to him to find out. You should not reach for him while he is absent. If he is truly to discover his own strength, you must not help him in any way.

But he's never hunted before! He knows which plants to eat and which will heal him if necessary, but he's never hunted prey.

While you continue to hunt for him he never will. Doing so is part of who he is. He has ridden in your mind with you when you have hunted. He must find that part within himself as much as the rest that will remain dormant if he does not spend time alone with the forest.

I felt as if I would gag, yet strangely, my stomach felt strong and settled by the truth Benevolence had imparted to me.

Express that which is on your mind or you will strangle yourself with it, the horse advised. He lowered his head so that he breathed into my lap while looking into my eyes with one of his large brown ones. It seemed to get even bigger as I focused on it, drawing me into what seemed like an impossible depth. From there, it was easy to say the words out loud.

'I'm more terrified of losing him than I've ever been of anything else. I love him.' The tightness in my throat loosened and my chest relaxed. Warmth burst from me and found Laceheart napping in the shelter he shared with Lacebold. I sensed the part of him that was always awake, and the parts that had been shut down by his early years. The forest was constantly reaching for those parts, attempting to tease them out of him, but I stood in his way. 'I will encourage him to do what he must for his and all our sakes. I will advise him to be alone with the forest and find himself.'

It was done. I had spoken the words that opened the way for the forest to reach for the youngling of my heart even more strongly. He woke and looked around himself. Then he nodded once to himself and left Lacebold dozing in their shelter, without looking back.

Chapter Twenty-One

Let it be recorded for the Histories that on this day, the Fourth Wednesday of August, Eighth Year of the Eighth Decade of The New, Alan Nixon of Rockwood was tugged by a horse at the age of thirty-one. He is the first from our village to receive the honour of being called to join the ranks of the Horse-Bonded whom we have all come to respect and admire, and will carry the love and pride of the whole village with him when he leaves on the morrow.

Histories of The New, Keeper Milicent Butler

BENEVOLENCE RETURNED to the spot where he had been eating. I sensed that his mission to educate me had been accomplished and our conversation was therefore over. He nibbled at a few plants and then continued to walk away from me while chewing them. I climbed the tree against whose trunk I had been resting, and was just about to leap to a branch of a nearby one when I paused where I was. Ben was still moving away from me, and I sensed he had no intention of stopping.

I turned to watch him. The long hair growing from his rear end swung from side to side in time with his long, unhurried strides. His feet thudded on the soft ground as the tall plants seemed to part willingly before him. He appeared exactly the same, yet he felt different – in the few minutes since I had last looked at him, his essence had changed.

Panic shot through my heart and my stomach lurched. I dropped back down to the ground and bounded after him. *Where are you going? WHY are you going?*

Your question ill fits your capabilities. He didn't stop or look back.

Laceheart had gone and now Benevolence was leaving too. His reply was in no way adequate to calm either the pace or intensity of my heart's thudding.

I flattened the plants that stood in my way in order to draw level with him. *You think you've done everything you can to help us, but you haven't. Laceheart may not need you now, but I do. I can't always see the way forward unless I'm with you – that's why you came to me, to help me, like you did just now.*

You may consider my departure confirmation of your ability to decide the way forward at any time of your choosing. Benevolence continued on his calm, unhurried way.

I bounded forward in front of him and spun to face him, stretching my hands to the ground and balancing on my knuckles. Then I stood up straight so that, tall as he was, I looked down into his eyes.

Please don't go. Not yet.

He blinked unhurriedly, his long eyelashes sweeping his cheek each time before revealing his eyes once more. *I have called to the soul of another. There can be no retreat now that I have woken him to our bond.*

Pain added to my panic. *Your… bond?*

He blinked again and watched me as I frowned. I sensed it, the bond to which he had referred; it was a thread like no other I had sensed before. Where some of those connecting me to others – Charlotte Lace and my younglings in particular – had a strong sense of possibility about them, this one was practically aflame with it, and now that it had been ignited, changes had begun in the horse who stood patiently before me.

I followed the thread; I couldn't help it. I had to know who was more important to Benevolence than my kindred and me. I found a human on the other end. Except he wasn't on the other end. He was as much with Benevolence as the big brown horse was with him, though he didn't seem to know it yet. He was busy tearing around, telling all the other humans he met that he was being tugged by a horse, and yet other than feeling restless and drawn to move in a certain direction – Ben's direction – he couldn't sense anything about the horse at all.

He wouldn't stop tearing around until he had found the horse in whose way I stood. I knew it as surely as if I were him, which, at that moment, I truly wished I were. And Benevolence wouldn't stop moving towards him until they met and their thread could settle into a steady smouldering of the potential it carried.

My shoulders sagged, not just with the resignation and exhaustion that accompanied my acceptance that I would have to let Ben go, but with the heavy weight of sole responsibility that settled upon them.

There will come a time when your kind will stand tall. Benevolence stared into my eyes as he had before when he had something of import to tell me. *I leave in order to ensure it.*

He couldn't tell untruths like humans could. Even so, I

couldn't help but question him. *Your leaving will help us in some way?*

I will share a bond with a human in order to help all three of our species move closer to balance.

I couldn't begin to fathom what he meant, but I sensed the import he gave the concept to which he had referred. Balance was everything to him. It was far more than my ability to be stable as I ran along a branch. It was calmness and strength. Confidence and intelligence. Wisdom and compassion. It was everything he was… my stomach twinged, telling me that wasn't quite true. It was everything he knew how to be, but wasn't entirely – not quite yet. In order for him to move closer to it and take us all with him, he needed to be with the male human whose name was Alan Nixon.

I stepped out of his way. He reached towards me and blew gently into the crook of my neck. Then he walked past me and off to live the rest of his life without looking back.

Chapter Twenty-Two

Let it be recorded for the Histories that on this day, the Second Monday of September, Eighth Year of the Eighth Decade of The New, the last of us who arrived in Plainsview from The City Of Power has been provided with a beautiful new home. None of us have quite come to terms with how different life is here, and we grieve for those who we wish were living it alongside us. I would record the names of the fallen kindred, for they should never be forgotten. The list begins with my mother, Charlotte Lace…

Histories of The New, Keeper Jinna Lace

MY REMAINING four younglings began hunting soon after Laceheart's departure, often bringing back plants – both edible and medicinal – as well as meat from their forays. Their increasing confidence, hunting ability and plant knowledge had Laceheart's stamp all over them, and as my younglings embraced his knowledge and experiences, I held well back from them, every

single touch of Laceheart's success burning my mind with pain
and worry about where it would lead Lacebold, Lacefirm,
Lacekeen and Lacehope.

When I checked in with the other kindred communities, I
sensed most of their leaders now considering leaving and striking
out for new forests as I had urged them so many times;
Laceheart's enthusiasm for his findself mission, his curiosity
about everything the forests had yet to teach him, and his
determination to feed and water himself so that he could learn
everything there was to learn, was reaching them all too. None of
us were immune to the pattern he was laying down for us all to
follow, such was his wholehearted dedication.

I knew I should have been proud and relieved to see and sense
the effect he was having on my kin, but every second of relief I
allowed myself to feel was quickly followed by an avalanche of
grief at his absence, and concern for what may yet befall the nine-
year-old youngling. So, I distracted myself from my desperation to
reach for him by sitting in my shelter and following
Benevolence's journey across the countryside instead.

He much preferred the open plains to the forests in which we
felt safer; he had space to move at speed when he chose, there was
a plethora of the plants his body needed, and he was unconcerned
by the distances he had to travel between water sources since his
long, powerful legs made little of them. He wasn't safe though.
The only predators that could really trouble him lived mostly on
the plains too, and they could run faster than he, I discovered to
my horror when he was chased by a couple of them early one
afternoon.

I felt the terror that spurred his enormous heart to pump
greater volumes of blood around his body at ever greater speed,
and his legs to take even longer and more frequent strides. I
sensed his ears swivelling backward as he listened to, as well as

sensed, the approach of the cats whose genes I carried. Then I shared his relief as their gaining on him slowed and eventually halted. As fast as they were, they didn't have his stamina, and that made him stronger in the end. It also bolstered me, and I found myself exiting my shelter and visiting all the others as I hadn't in several weeks.

I visited the shelter shared by Hob and her younglings first. Of the younglings, there was no sign – my sixth sense found them out hunting with Ash and one of his younglings, Laceheart's influence having now extended further than his siblings – but Hob was sitting on a branch, weaving vines in a way I didn't recognise.

She smiled at me, then her eyes widened slightly. As she looked back down at her weaving, I sensed the source of her discomfort.

'I know, I've gone whiter. Lacebold told me,' I said, noticing with surprise – it was a while since I had used my voice – that it was more of a strain to speak; my throat felt thicker and tighter. 'What are you doing?'

I knew the answer as soon as I asked, and Hob sensed the fact, but she replied anyway, relieved at the diversion I had provided from my appearance. 'I'm weaving a basket. Lacefirm showed me how.'

'Lacefirm?' I coughed and rubbed my throat. She hadn't mentioned it to me. Now that I came to think of it, I hadn't been to the shelter she shared with Lacekeen and Lacehope for some time; it was my younglings who had been checking on me.

'Yes, she and Lacekeen are teaching anyone who wants to learn. I started weaving them when my younglings started hunting, and they like helping me when they're not doing that or throwing themselves around in the trees with other younglings.' She pointed to eight completed baskets stacked against the wall of her shelter. 'I made those for anyone who wants them. The handles are difficult to get right. I'm hoping your younglings will find a thicker, stronger vine we can use instead of having to twist the thinner ones together.'

Her eyes were bright but they dulled when I said, 'Or you could look for a vine that might suit?'

There was a hard edge to the sense I had of her, and to her voice as she replied. 'I could. I should.'

'But you won't,' I said and sensed the hard edge of her fear increase. 'You're safe in the forest, you know that, or you wouldn't let your younglings play and hunt in it.'

I knew it wasn't that. I knew her panic came not from fear of harm to herself, but from the emptiness, the sense of overwhelm that accompanied free will after having lived through nineteen years of being completely controlled. I understood it, but I wanted her to remain open to Laceheart's continuing influence on the collective mind of which we were all a part, and from which she retreated whenever she was left wondering what to do.

'I'll make sure you have a constant supply of the relevant tree essence that'll help you listen to your sixth sense when you're struggling to,' I told her, trying to remember whether we had much stored or would need to make more; my younglings and I were using the bark of some trees and the leaves of others to make the essences now that the trees weren't in blossom, which was harder work and a longer production process because of the increased steeping times necessary.

Hob nodded but didn't answer. She wouldn't go searching for vines, tree essence or no. She would wait until my younglings found what she needed and told her how to use it. The same was true for all the adults I visited that afternoon. Without exception, they were doing everything the way I or my younglings had told them. By the time I returned to my shelter, I had depleted the brief surge in stamina I had felt as a result of Benevolence's triumph, and felt exhausted again.

There was a rustling above me and then outside my shelter, and Lacehope appeared, as she always did when I was struggling. She no longer came for reassurance that I was alright though; the past week had seen her snuggling up to me in order to provide comfort rather than because she needed it for herself. She would be the last of my younglings to follow the path Laceheart had set and embark on her findself, but she had set foot on that path which, the following morning, Lacebold informed me he would be taking.

I shook my head firmly as he told me of his plans to leave once he had broken his fast. He pretended not to notice as he handed me the meat ration he had brought. It wasn't lost on me how rare it was for him to try to soften the blow of something he said, and it surprised me that his brow was pinched with concern, presumably about the possibility of me attempting to stop him from leaving.

Lacefirm hurried into my shelter and handed me one of the small wooden vessels she had taken to making. It was full to the brim with what I instantly sensed was the tree essence I had suggested Hob take in order to allow her sixth sense and the forest to guide her when her courage failed. Lacefirm stared into my eyes with the vibrant green ones now possessed by all the younglings who were coming more and more into their own as the days passed.

'This will help,' she told me matter-of-factly, as if I had no idea what it was and should take it on trust.

As soon as I had swallowed it, the forest burst into my awareness along with Lacebold's frustration at sensing what Laceheart was achieving without him, and his readiness to test himself in the same way.

But he isn't Laceheart, a small voice nagged at me – too small for Lacebold to sense, but loud enough to give me pause again.

He doesn't need to be. Lacefirm surprised me with her perceptiveness; there had been a time when only Laceheart would have picked up on my thought. She bored her next thought into me with her stare. *There's enough of Laceheart in the four of us that we all know what we have to do. I'll be going after Lacebold once Lacehope's okay with it, and Lacekeen will go shortly after me, but Lacehope will need the four of us pulling her to do it by going on ahead of her, and you pushing her from behind. You can do that for her, Lace.*

I wanted to shake my head, to order her to cease her planning and to forbid Lacebold to leave, but she drew on the collective experience of the kindred as she continued to stare at me, reminding me that if our race were to survive, those of us most open to the forest needed to show the rest the way.

I didn't want to accept it. I turned to the distraction upon which I had come to rely whenever I needed to escape from the decisions I had to make, and found Benevolence slaking his thirst from a wide, fast-flowing river.

He didn't acknowledge me; his attention was focused on his body's needs and on reaching the human who would be his partner in life. All my reaching for him did was remind me of an observation he had made while urging me to get out of Laceheart's way. *It is always the case that when there is need there will be those who can fulfil it however unlikely the match may appear to be. You are one such. Strong Of Heart is another and he is not alone.*

I lifted my eyes to Lacebold's and nodded. I couldn't speak, so instead thought to him, *Go and find yourself. I'm proud of you, Lacebold.*

He nodded back, turned and left my shelter. When Lacehope

arrived to nestle into my side once more, Lacefirm left, telling me she would be back later with my lunch.

Lacehope pulled gently at the fur coating my arms. 'It's going white to match your face,' she murmured.

My voice was hoarse as I replied, 'I know'.

Chapter Twenty-Three

Dearest Isabel,

I write with exciting news! Rockwood has produced a Horse-Bonded! You won't believe who it is though – Alan Nixon, of all people! The village already feels lighter for his absence, I can tell you. Maybe he was chosen because he isn't married and the only family he has won't miss him, there's certainly no love lost between him and his brother. Regardless, his selection by a horse is something we're all proud of, and we held a farewell ceremony just like the one you told me was held for Yasmin. A Quest Ceremony, his father called it when he invited the rest of us to take part. Imagine that, being invited to participate when it was me who told him how to hold the ceremony? I should have been invited to organise it, but that's neither here nor there. We all did exactly as you described, and it was lovely to have another reason to celebrate, even if the object of the celebrations was as hard faced as ever. Hopefully, he'll come back to Rockwood soon though, I'm dying to meet the horse brave enough to want to share a bond with him. Your father's toe

*is no less sore, in fact, it's going black. Hurry home, darling, we
miss and need you.*

 All our love, Mum

MY BODY FELT STRANGE. I seemed to have four legs instead of
two, and they were moving in a fast, three-time gait across the flat
plain. My ears were much longer than normal and pointing
forward towards the human who was still some distance away but
moving steadily towards me, even as my awareness extended in
all directions and dimensions, alert for anything worthy of my
attention. There was nothing of enough significance to divert me
from my course, as was to be expected; I was always going to
meet the human with whose soul I had made an agreement.

Benevolence. I stirred just long enough within my dream to
realise that I rode within the horse's mind, then fell eagerly back
into it.

The nearer I got to the human, the less weary I felt, despite the
distance I had travelled with so little rest due to being alone.
When I had rested near the forest, Strong Of Heart watched over
me so I could sleep, and I watched over him while he gathered his
herbs. It was right that we had parted ways, but I missed his
companionship and was keen to rest alongside one who could take
a turn at monitoring our surroundings once more.

I slowed my pace as I approached a tall hill that rose steeply in
front of me, yet, looking at it through the eyes of Hard Around
The Outside as he approached it from the other side, dropped far
more shallowly towards him. My nostrils flared as I scented water
nearby. The herbs growing around it would be sweet and moist,
and easier to chew than the dry, mature herbs that had made up
most of my nourishment over the past weeks. I would remain on
this side of the hill and nourish my body while Hard Around The

Outside completed his journey to find me. He was hot and thirsty and would appreciate the coolness and freshness of the water as much as I.

I stirred again as I shifted from Benvolence's mind to that of the human on which he was focused, this time settling into a lighter, less restful sleep.

The sun burned down on the top of my head, and I cursed myself for having lost my hat. I stumbled up the hill that, while not steep, seemed to go on forever, punishing me with each rock that protruded enough to trip me but not enough to be visible above the tall growing grasses that seemed to wrap around my legs on purpose. Sweat soaked my shirt and shorts, ran down my temples and dripped from my sunburnt nose as I finally topped the hill and saw him grazing far below. It had to be him; though he appeared only as a brown dot amid the green of the grass he was grazing, I knew he wasn't a deer or one of those cursed wild cats I'd had to shoot at three times in order to ward them off during my weeks of travelling. I knew in my heart it was him, and even if I hadn't, the pull he had been exerting upon me that kept me trying to find him when I was hot, thirsty, tired and scared, had finally ceased. It was definitely him.

The human's focus on Benevolence provided me with a conduit down which I slipped gratefully back to the horse's mind.

Hard Around The Outside looked down at me as I selected the best of the delicious herbs that surrounded me. He wasn't as content as I felt, but he could be once he reached the water. His impatience would ensure he reached it and me very soon, as surely as it would ensure a difficult descent down the hill.

I continued to graze, barely flicking an ear when the shout reached me that confirmed my sense that Hard Around The Outside had lost his footing and was tumbling down the hill. The shouting continued for some time after he regained his footing, and I was glad of the distance that still parted us; he would learn that my ears were sensitive to the slightest sound, and I had no desire to be subjected to the volume he was capable of producing.

When he reached the bottom of the hill, I saw him with my eyes, as opposed to my soul, for the first time. His energy and demeanour were incongruent with the sense I had of the human he would become. I responded to both without thought and rapidly increased the distance between the two of us. By the time I spun to face him, he had come to a standstill. He put his hands on his hips and looked down at the ground, shaking his head and radiating disappointment and frustration.

My eyes shot open and I sat up, looking around myself, initially confused to find myself in my shelter. Then I remembered; I had unwittingly reached for Benevolence during my afternoon snooze, and through him, had experienced his coming together with Alan Nixon! I reached for him again and found him still regarding the human he perceived as Hard Around The Outside, who now stood staring back at him, his hands still on his hips.

Ben didn't move other than to turn his head away, towards the source of a faint and distant sound, which he decided was not of concern.

'You can't even look at me?' Alan Nixon said. He shrugged out of the straps of the bag on his back and hurled it to the ground. 'Look at the state of me. You pulled me away from my village and across the frigging countryside, through wild cat territory and woods that were so dark I bumped into the trees, around lakes and across rivers, and all in this never-ending, sodding heat. I'm hungry, thirsty, sunburnt and tired, and now I've finally found you, you look like you haven't bothered to move an inch since you tugged me, yet you act like I'm the one giving you a hard time?'

There is water here. You may quench your thirst and cool

yourself. Then you should rest. I will ensure you are safe and undisturbed.

I stood up in my shelter in fruitless protest. Benevolence was going to allow Alan Nixon to rest when he himself needed to so badly? Despite the man's complaining, he was far better rested than the horse. He had climbed high enough in the trees each night to be out of reach of the large, heavy wild cats, tied himself to the trunks of his hosts and slept soundly. Ben had snatched a few minutes of sleep here and there, otherwise dozing when he could, with one ear alert for danger. And he was actually moaning about Ben inviting him to share a bond and receive his wisdom and companionship?

Alan Nixon put both hands up to his head and held it, his eyes wide in disbelief. 'You just spoke to me in my head. I heard that's what happens when a horse bonds with a person, but I didn't believe it. How are you doing it?'

You found the courage to leave your old life behind by listening to the voice of your soul. Listen to it again now and you will find your way past your anger and frustration to me. Your mind will be better able to concentrate once your body has rehydrated.

'Rehydrated? How do you even know about the functioning of my body, let alone a word for it?'

It is your mind that chooses the words it requires in order to understand my counsel. I know much without being cognisant of all I know for it is unnecessary.

Alan Nixon scratched his head. 'You know a lot without knowing you know it? That makes no sense at all.'

Your mind attempts to fit the information it receives into the constraints of your previous experiences. Merely accept without judgement that which I convey to you and in time your understanding will increase.

'I doubt it. Where's the water, anyway?'

I couldn't believe it. Benevolence had left me and my kin for this human? I had expected more. I had supposed he would have chosen one who would at least be glad of his company and be open to learning from him, as Laceheart and I had been.

A pang went through my heart as I thought of my distant youngling, and it was all I could do not to reach for him. I threw myself back to Benevolence and his chosen human instead.

————

Alan Nixon was indeed Hard Around The Outside. It was days before he could reduce his need to fit his relationship with Benevolence into the framework defining his relationships with his human friends, and use his mind to communicate instead of speaking out loud. It was weeks before he began to realise that everything Ben told him was the truth and had a purpose – his ability to argue far outstripped Lacebold's. I admired, yet was frustrated by, Benevolence's patience, though I shouldn't have been surprised given the name I had chosen for him. It was almost a month before the human began to follow his horse's advice and accept, mostly, what he was told without arguing or railing at his failure to understand straight away.

I found it painful to follow the very slow progress of their relationship, yet less so than spending time being present in my own life, which now contained only Lacehope, and her for not much longer. The pull of my other four younglings upon her was strong, and I knew that as soon as I encouraged her to leave and be alone with the forest, she would go. In the meantime, she cared for me as if I were aged and incapable, which, in truth, I felt.

I was relieved that my younglings' strengthening of the pattern to make one's own decisions had now drawn all the other communities to move to the forests that called to them; to a one further south than those in which they had first settled. I was exhausted by the knowledge that I would soon have to uproot my own community again and also travel further south, as I was increasingly being guided to; the weather was rapidly cooling and the warmer forests beckoned to us. There would be decision after decision to make on the journey, and once we reached our destination, and my community would still look to me to make them – the pattern was strengthening but not strong. Each time I thought of the journey ahead, and travelling it without any of my younglings, I hurled myself back to Benevolence and his chosen human.

They were heading for a place where Alan Nixon would apparently be able to learn from other humans who were bonded to horses, including someone called "He Who Is Mettle". When I found the latter through Ben's thought of him, I sensed a human who was far more the type of human with whom I had expected Ben to bond and with whom I wished he had bonded; it would have made his leaving so much easier to understand. I only hoped that Alan Nixon would indeed learn from the other bonded humans to the same extent that he was resistant to his horse's advice.

It was only when their destination came into sight that Alan Nixon finally thought to ask Benevolence what name he should use for him when they were among other people and horses. I had long since become used to being shocked and disappointed by him.

You should sit down, Benevolence told him.

I've spent most of the day sitting down, waiting for you to finish eating, Alan Nixon replied. *Can you just tell me while we carry on walking? We're nearly there.*

Ben stopped walking and looked at him in the same way he had looked at me when it was important I heeded him.

Alan Nixon sighed. *Fine.* He exaggerated the effort it took to shake his almost empty bag off his shoulder, squash some grass down with his foot, and sit on the ground.

Ben rested a hind leg. *I will reveal all that I am to you. You may choose the name that best suits what you sense in me.*

As my attention went to Alan Nixon for his reply, I was drawn along with him into Benevolence's essence.

I was relieved that I too happened to be sitting down, for that which I had perceived with my sixth sense when naming Benevolence was but a fraction of who he was. A small part of me registered how much more limited was my sixth sense than I could ever have supposed, while the remainder bathed in the soul of the horse who had committed the rest of his life to the human by his side, and would have him know him for who he truly was.

Alan Nixon was equally stunned as the two of us explored the immense sense of age, knowledge, experience and love that were Benevolence; it was as if they were what held the components of his body together and made him healthy and powerful.

Benevolent. Your name is Benevolent, Alan Nixon told Ben.

The thought occurred to me, reluctantly, that maybe the human and I weren't so different after all.

Chapter Twenty-Four

NOTICE TO ALL AT THE GATHERING
from Overseer Lacinda Rooney

Since our numbers have swelled so much recently, I no longer have the time to find you all individually to give you your share of the chores for the week. Instead, I will put up a rota on this newly erected noticeboard – thank you to Carpenter Paul Nolan for crafting it at short notice for me – each Sunday morning. I trust you will all remember to check it when you come to the dining hall to break your fasts, and attend to the chores assigned to you. Thank you for your understanding and co-operation.

WHEN THE TREES of the forest we called home started dropping their leaves and withdrawing into themselves in readiness for Winter, I could put off moving my community further south no longer. The forest that had been calling to us was far away, but I had no choice other than to make the journey.

I was more tired than I could ever remember having been before, partly because of continuing to be asked to solve each additional problem that arose with any member of my community, but mostly from the effort of not reaching for my younglings. I was finding leaving Lacehope to her findself the most difficult. She had been gone for nearly three weeks, and despite my hope that she might, she had neither reached for me to ask for help, nor returned. She was the least likely to cope with being alone in whichever forest had attracted her, and as a result, she was the one I knew it was most important not to interrupt lest I make it harder for her to stay away, so I was devoting a huge amount of energy to restraining myself.

Whenever the urge to reach for any of my family became too much and I needed a diversion lest I let myself and them down, I continued to reach for Benevolence instead. He was my source of patience when my kin came to me with yet another hurdle they knew how to negotiate but couldn't bring themselves to without first checking with me; my source of compassion that enabled me to continue caring for all members of my community when all I wanted to do was turn in on myself; my source of strength when I woke up on the morning we were to leave our home without the will to face the day. Benevolence was a continuing reminder of Charlotte Lace and whom I wanted to be.

When I reached the edge of the forest and lowered myself from the lowest branch of the last tree, the almost threadbare blanket that was tied to my back and full of hunted and gathered food banged against me and made me wince. It was all I could do to take my first step onto the plain area that stretched as far as my eyes could see, but take that step I did. Then another, and another, and another, until my feet moved of their own accord. My kin followed obediently, the adults in single file behind me, placing their feet almost exactly where I had mine through grass that was now brown and fibrous where it had been green and lush. Some carried babies, others called to the younglings who bounded exuberantly around us, happy to be moving on to somewhere new.

Each glance out of the corner of my eye at the younglings who had shared a dormitory with mine made my heart ache a little more. I stumbled often and found that Ash's hand was always ready behind me, grabbing either my arm or the fur on my back to prevent me from falling. To begin with, he did so without comment. During the afternoon of our second day on the trail, he kept hold of my arm after I had righted myself and drew level with me.

'I can feel how tired you are, yet you're well fed and watered, and you rested well last night,' he said. 'We have a long way to go. How can I help you to lead us there?'

My heart felt as if it sank even lower in my chest than where it had been resting uncomfortably. I wanted to rail at him, to tell him he could help me by figuring something out for himself and acting on it for once, regardless of whether it was right or wrong, then learning from it and improving on it if necessary until he found a way to help me by himself. My younglings were showing him the way with their continual strengthening of the pattern of self-sufficiency, and I knew most of my kin could feel it, yet the adults resisted it as much as the younglings were invigorated by it.

So I shook my head and, too tired to strain to use my voice, replied, *I don't know*, as I trudged onward.

I reached for Benevolence and found him carrying Alan Nixon on his back. He was walking in a circle around the human whom I recognised to be He Who Is Mettle. The old male stood with composure and strength, yet I perceived that neither was as fervent as they had been. Part of his mind was always somewhere else, just like mine. I followed it and found him reaching, no, yearning, for a thread that was as fine as the one connecting

Charlotte Lace and me. I felt my way back along it to him and found the part of his mind that reached for that which was denied him. It was full of memories of a horse with large, almost black eyes and white fur with grey outlines of circles on it, like pebbles. I sensed all that the man and horse had been to one another, and everything the pair of them had been to all the other humans who had escaped the cities in the hope of living a better life. Without the two of them, the human communities would have failed.

They were like my younglings and me; they had carried the weight of responsibility for their race, but unlike us so far, they had succeeded in helping it to thrive. Even now that the man, Jonus Blair, was without his horse, he continued to help those chosen by horses to continue his work, including, in this case, instructing Alan Nixon how to ride Ben.

My mouth curled up into a smile that made my cheeks ache with its unusualness. Laceheart had needed no such instruction, he had sat astride Ben as if they were two halves of the same whole. This human was bouncing all over the place, causing Ben no end of discomfort, which I could sense he was happy to tolerate. There was clearly a point to it that he could see and I couldn't.

'Don't worry, you'll get the hang of it,' Jonus Blair said to his student. 'You're trying to force yourself into the right position instead of relaxing into it. You need to trust Benevolent more. Move with him and just make suggestions to him with your body if you'd like him to alter course or speed, instead of trying to take charge of every move he makes.'

'I haven't been in charge from the moment he tugged me,' Alan Nixon retorted.

'So, give up trying to be,' Jonus Blair said. 'Has Benevolent ever put you in any danger or caused you any harm?'

Alan Nixon sighed. 'No, I suppose not. Not directly, anyway.'

'Has he taught you things that you could never have learnt any other way?'

Alan Nixon glared at him and then said with tight lips, 'I guess.'

'So then, why do you resist him? How you feel when you're not on his back affects your ability to ride when you are, and it stands out a mile.' He held his hands out in front of him. 'Make no mistake, I'm not judging you. All of us here have discovered the same thing, and all of us have had to get over ourselves in order to ride well enough to have our horses carry us to the villages so we can keep helping them to move forward.'

Alan Nixon leant forward and swung a leg over Ben's back before sliding to the ground. He put a hand to Ben's neck and stroked him. 'I'm not used to trusting anyone.'

My heart softened a little towards him as I sensed him swallowing down the emotion that threatened to erupt out of him. Ben turned his head and nuzzled Alan Nixon's chest, and something began to swirl there; the hurt and anger that Alan Nixon had suppressed since being taunted by his peers during his school years would remain buried no longer. Alan Nixon stepped away from him, but Benevolence followed, still nuzzling the human's chest.

Alan Nixon made a choking sound and leant against his horse as if his legs would give way.

Jonus Blair moved to his side and said, 'We're finished for today. Go and spend some time with Benevolent.' He slapped Alan Nixon on the shoulder a few times with a wrinkled, bony hand and then left him.

When Ben walked slowly to the gate of the field, Alan Nixon went with him, still leaning against his horse. They sauntered past lots of other fields – some with horses grazing in them, some with smaller animals I'd never seen before, and others covered in a single type of plant. I scented water through Ben's nose, and it wasn't long before I heard it with his ears. When I saw it tumbling past in front of the pair, I felt Alan Nixon let go of everything he had been holding in. Ben continued walking so that he drew the human with him to stand immediately before the wild, turbulent river, knowing it would help to draw out some of the poison from Alan Nixon that his frequent nuzzles kept moving in order that the pain of being different – of not being attracted to females – couldn't remain static and settle back down where it could continue to harm him.

When Alan Nixon was spent, he sank to the ground, panting. He reached out a hand and gently grasped Ben's leg, needing the security of a physical connection with his horse now that some of that which had made up his personality had fled. There was a lot more to release, but the pain and suffering he had let go had left small perforations in the hard exterior he had erected around himself. I wondered how much longer Ben would refer to him as Hard Around The Outside.

I tripped again and gasped as Ash's grip on my arm yanked me away from the peaceful companionship of human and horse resting together by the river, to the cold rain that now lashed down on me and my kin as we traversed the never-ending plain area that was interspersed only by the odd tree or clump of bushes.

We had walked into the rain, I realised as the ground became soft beneath my feet. I turned around when Ash released me, intending to thank him for keeping me on my feet again. The sight of all the adults continuing to walk in my footsteps, so that those further back were slipping and having to slow down, exasperated me, and the energy I had gained from sitting in Benevolence's mind dissipated.

Then I thought of Jonus Blair. He was tired by life too, now that he no longer had his horse by his side, yet he continued to hold himself together and help those who couldn't see a way forward like he could.

I remembered his composure. I reached for him and felt the strength that had amassed within him during the years he'd had his horse at his side. Mettle – the name he had chosen for his horse – was the first word that entered Jonus Blair's mind when he woke, and the last before he went to sleep. I sensed again all they had been to one another and found that it was the horse who had referred to Jonus Blair as "He Who Is Mettle". So, he had somehow become that which he had seen in his horse when he named him. Courage and determination were who he was.

I had chosen the name "Benevolence" for the horse whose life had briefly touched mine; compassion, generosity, unselfishness. That was who he was. Alan Nixon chose "Benevolent". Compassionate, generous, unselfish. That was who he would be by the time Ben left him.

I reached for Benevolence and through him, all the other bonded horses. I absorbed the names given to them by their humans and when I reached for those humans, I sensed the changes that had been elicited within them as a result, not only of their bonds with their horses, but the names they had chosen for them.

I began to understand what the horses were doing; they were waking up The Way Of The Horse in the humans they had chosen. They were prodding it and making it swirl around within them as Ben had done when he nuzzled Alan Nixon's chest, and as he had done when he found me. But the humans weren't aware of what was happening; they felt themselves changing, but they didn't know why.

I was part human. In fact, I was mostly human, although my handlers had always gone to great lengths to reinforce the idea that I was much less than they. But I was more, I realised. Ben had spent so little time with me because that was all the time I had needed in order to open to The Way Of The Horse enough to contribute to the survival of my race. The humans were as closed to everything around them as even the least sensitive of my kind were open, and that meant they needed to share their lives with horses as we did not.

Jonus Blair entered my mind again. He had suffered at the hands of the people of his city almost as much as had I. He had learnt what he needed to from Mettle and was carrying it through the rest of his life, even though Mettle was gone. I may not have had much time with Benevolence, but I'd had what I needed. If Jonus Blair could carry on, then so could I.

I found the eighty-seven-year-old male strolling along a stony path, pausing often to greet the horses standing in fields on either side who stretched their necks over wooden barriers in order to touch him with their noses. They knew exactly who he was and what he had done, and they celebrated him though he didn't know it.

He also never knew that he saved me from giving up, that day. It was down to him and the strength I could feel from him that instead of sinking to the ground and remaining there until the rain beat the life out of me, I called to those following in my footsteps to move out into a horizontal line behind me so that each trod their own path rather than wallowing in mine. It was down to He Who Is Mettle that I remembered the compassion of which I was capable and led my kin onward to the forest that would shelter them through the winter.

Chapter Twenty-Five

NOTICE TO ALL AT THE GATHERING
from Overseer Lacinda Rooney

It seems that more than twenty of our number disappeared from The Gathering overnight without a word of warning to me. Although it is only Wednesday, I have made emergency changes to the rota and can only hope that everyone affected sees this notice in time to ensure there are sufficient numbers in the kitchen to enable meals to be prepared on time. I respectfully request that if any more of you are planning to leave during the next few weeks, you give me adequate notice so I can reallocate your chores without everything descending into chaos. Thank you for your understanding and co-operation.

WHEN WE CAUGHT sight of the dark line on the horizon that confirmed to my eyes what my sixth sense already knew – we would reach our new home by nightfall – the younglings bounced around with an increased exuberance that picked up the rest of us, so that we all moved towards the forest that lay ahead with greater energy and purpose.

We adults were beyond exhausted when we reached the trees, but I wouldn't let anyone so much as touch any of them until we had negotiated our way deep into the forest, where there was a small but deep pool of fresh water fed by a stream trickling over a narrow bed of rocks. There, I instructed my kin to settle in whichever tree called to them, eat and then rest. Though the night air lacked the warmth that had carried from the summer into the days of autumn, it was dry and the weaving of shelters could wait until the following morning.

It was strange to encounter different trees from those that had sheltered us further north – some we recognised, but many sang different songs from those to which we were accustomed, and it took a little while to sift through them and recognise which sang the loudest to each of us.

I was drawn to one that seemed to reach out to me with its branches and wrap itself around me as I climbed to its strongest branch and nestled as snuggly against its trunk as my younglings always had against me. I let out a deep sigh and slept deeply for the first time since leaving our old forest.

As when we had arrived at our last forest, our new home embraced us wholeheartedly, enabling us to settle within it easily and well. We were relieved beyond measure to enjoy the constant shelter of ever-leafed trees, and the safety they offered after only brief interludes of relief amongst weeks of trudging across increasingly wet and bewilderingly open ground. The vines that grew up their trunks were plentiful and suitable for weaving our new homes, which eased somewhat the frustration and weariness we all felt at having to weave new ones for a third time. The hunting was bountiful and the water full of vitality as a result of the long, gushing journey it had taken on its way to us.

I felt invigorated by our new forest, almost sufficiently to distract me from the fact that I was forced to weave my shelter without the chatter of my younglings reaching me from the branches above, but not quite. I consoled myself by weaving a shelter large enough to accommodate all six of us. I threw myself into my effort to such an extent that for several weeks, I neither reached for Benevolence or Jonus Blair, nor yearned to reach for my younglings; I focused on making a shelter which they would be happy to call home, for I felt certain they would return to me before the winter weather arrived.

It was Lacebold who was the first to touch my mind in order to find my location. I had been with Benevolence as he carried Alan Nixon during one of his riding lessons with Jonus Blair, and rejoicing with him at the progress his rider had made so that he was no longer so much of a burden to his horse. The instant I was aware of Lacebold, however, I withdrew wholly to my own mind and my sense of my beloved youngling.

Lacebold! A part of me that had been missing slotted back into place even as I almost fell out of my tree at the difference I could sense within my youngling. His desire to be strong in character, which had always tended to surface as being argumentative, had been realised as a result of him having softened. It seemed he had been tempered by a sense of respect for the many forests and their components, which had provided for him when he allowed them to guide him, and shown him the consequences of doing the opposite.

My heart sank as I sensed he had been severely ill due to eating something against which the forest had warned him, but lifted again as I learnt that he had allowed Laceheart's influence on the pattern, of which we were all a part, to help him relax into sensing the remedy that the forest offered up to heal him.

I followed the thread linking Lacebold and Laceheart without meaning to… and found that as Lacebold had absorbed some of that which was Laceheart, so the reverse was true; where Laceheart had tended to allow himself to drift off to everything he could sense, he now retained an even stronger sense of himself than Benevolence had helped him to achieve. He was anchored at a central point within himself, from which he extended his sixth sense to everything around him. As a result, he excelled at deciding what to do or where to go rather than being pulled from one activity or location to the next with little conscious thought.

He was aware of my contact with his mind, and though he didn't push me away, he didn't engage with me either; he wasn't ready to come home like Lacebold.

I nearly am, Lacebold thought to me, *but not yet. There's something I want to do first.* He couldn't hide his intention from me.

Lacebold, no, I told him firmly. *Ben told me we should leave the humans to themselves.*

I WILL leave them to themselves. I just want to see what the humans living outside the cities are like, I won't let any of them see me.

You can sense them. Let the forest guide you to them and then see through their eyes and hear through their ears. You don't have to use your own.

I've already done that. They're not like the humans who reared us. They don't hurt each other, they like each other, and they say things that make their mouths smile and open while they make a noise we never make. When they're doing it, they feel happy, only it's more than happy. I don't understand it. I need to watch them properly. Lots of them all at once. I want to be able to feel like they do.

I knew he wouldn't rest while his confusion lingered, and, intensely nurtured by my tree as I was, I knew I had to let him do as he wanted. I gave him a warning, however. *Stay in the forest. Watch the humans from the trees and make sure they don't see you. Ben never told me anything that wasn't important, so you should heed his advice and leave them alone.*

I'll stay in the forest, Lacebold assured me. *I'm heading to one right next to a group of shelters made from stone. They call it a "village". There's a big rock nearby, so they call the village "Rockwood". We should have a name for the new village you've made for us to get through the winter. Winterwood. That's what we should call it.*

Well, do what you must and then hurry home to Winterwood, then. Hopefully, the others will do likewise. I didn't ask him the question to which I was sure he knew the answer. He proved me right and didn't leave me to suffer.

They won't be too much longer, he told me. *Laceheart could have come home ages ago, but he wanted to explore a forest a lot further away. He's on his way to meet Lacefirm, Lacekeen and Lacehope, and they'll all come to find you together. It was meant to be a surprise for you, but I don't like those. See you soon, Lace.*

He withdrew from me, leaving me with lingering feelings of worry, wonder and pride. He had been gone a matter of months, yet had changed so much; I felt old and inert by comparison. I couldn't wait to see my other four younglings and get to know the characters they had all become.

I lived through the next few days feeling more buoyant than I had since Lacehope had left to go on her findself. I woke with the dawn and joined the hunters who had continued to feed our community without me when I had lacked the energy. The thrill of the chase combined with the satisfaction of fulfilling my agreement with my prey to energise me, and I began to feel alive again instead of merely existing.

I took shares of the meat I caught to the families who needed it and sensed their relief that I seemed to be more like my former self.

'Your younglings are coming back,' Hob said with a knowing smile as I handed her family's share of meat to her.

I smiled. 'Not yet, but soon.' I could barely hear my voice and coughed with the effort of speaking.

'Do you think they'll recognise you?' one of her younglings asked me.

'Hobworth, didn't I ask you to fetch Hobkind back for his breakfast?' Hob said quickly. 'Go and help him carry the vines he's been gathering, and hurry back.'

I held a hand up to Hobworth as she got to her feet and made for the entrance to their shelter. *Did you recognise me?*

She stopped in front of me. *Yes, but they haven't seen you for ages. Your coat is much whiter now.*

Well, maybe it'll go browner once I have my family back with me, I replied. *Do as Hob said, now.*

Once she had gone, Hob said, 'I'm sorry.'

There's no need. She only said what everyone else is thinking.

'I don't mean for what she said,' Hob replied. 'I mean for what we've all done to you. We know why your coat is turning white and your throat is thickening faster than the rest of ours. You're ageing quicker than the rest of us because we're such a burden to you. We all try our best not to be, but we just can't seem to… to…'

I know. I'm beginning to think that making decisions isn't your role in all this. It's the younglings who'll take our community forward, we just have to find the courage to let them do it.

'Do what?' Hob asked, though the stirring I sensed in her stomach told me she already knew.

Find the parts of themselves that they've been forced to bury, like my younglings have. Unlike most of us adults, they have nothing buried so deeply within them that it can't be uncovered with the forests' help.

No. Hob had never been so definite about anything, and she surprised herself as well as me.

I understand your objection; the fear my suggestion caused you is familiar to me. You must encourage your younglings to find themselves though, Hob. They'll probably want to when mine return so changed from who they were when they left, but they won't do it unless you encourage them to. Let the idea sit with you and... Lacebold.

Hob picked up from me the shock that Lacebold had unwittingly broadcast with such force, it blasted down the thread joining him and me and almost knocked me off my feet. Hob's long, narrow pupils dilated as I'm sure did mine, as we sensed my youngling's situation.

A human had seen him. Through his eyes, I saw her running away from where he perched on the low branch from which he had been observing her while she gathered herbs growing at the edge of the forest below him. I heard her screams and felt her terror.

'There are enforcers in the woods!' she yelled as she reached her village. 'They must have been released from the cities before they perished. Run! Hide!'

Two men ran to meet her. One wrapped his arms around her and held her close. The other put his hands on his hips. His breaths were shallow and came quickly as he said, 'I'm not running like my ancestors did.' He looked towards the trees. Towards Lacebold. He gasped when he spotted my youngling and took a step backward, his hands falling to his sides. Then he returned them to his hips, stuck out his chest and moved his feet further apart. He didn't take his eyes from Lacebold as he said, 'We should stand and fight.'

I was out of Hob's shelter and swinging through the trees towards my youngling before either of us had time to draw another breath.

Chapter Twenty-Six

Let it be recorded for the Histories that on this day, the Second Monday of November, Eighth year of the Eighth Decade of The New, we are no longer safe in Rockwood. The cities may have perished, but some of their inhabitants clearly did not. An Enforcer observes us from the trees, and we have to assume it isn't alone. We are divided in how to respond to the threat. Some have barricaded themselves within their homes, hoping that by the time they venture back out, everything will be as before. Others are packing their belongings and intending to flee the village, though where they will go hasn't been made clear. Many have been preparing to defend the village, while one or two are speaking of taking the fight to the forest. We are all stunned and horrified at the reversal of our situation – we thought we were safer than ever before, but it seems we have never been in more peril.

Histories of The New, Keeper Milicent Butler

I FELT STRONGER than I had in months as I powered through the trees, completely at one with the forest that guided me, so that I flowed from branch to branch as effortlessly as the water that trickled over its bed of stones to the pool at the centre of Winterwood.

Lacebold, flee, I told him. *LACEBOLD!*

He didn't move. He was shamed and fascinated in equal measure by the views he could hear being exchanged by members of the rapidly swelling crowd in Rockwood. Many of them were pointing directly at him as they spoke words carrying their fear and revulsion. Some humans joined the crowd, heard what was being said and tore back to their homes, slamming doors behind them and rushing to close their windows. Others hurried to gather implements they intended to use as weapons.

Lacebold, I'm on my way. Leave there now and come to me, they mean you harm.

Some of them do, he agreed. *They hate me, they think I'm...* He struggled to repeat the word so many of them had used to describe him, but finally managed it. *They think I'm an abomination. Something that should never have been created yet alone allowed to live.* I felt his hurt, his shame and his anger. *They've heard what we look like from stories told by the humans who got out before there were enough enforcers to stop them, but they don't know I'm a youngling. They think I'm here to kill them or make them serve me.*

You're as big as their teenagers and you're above them, so you'll look even bigger. They don't know you're on your own, but they will if you stay there. Leave, Lacebold. Please, leave.

But we're invincible, that's what we were told in our lessons. We were made to be hard for humans to hurt or kill, so we could kill them first. We couldn't hurt our handlers because our control programs protected them, but they don't work anymore, so we can hurt anyone we want to and they can't hurt us back.

Lacebold, no! Listen to the forest. Does it tell you that humans are prey? I swung between the branches with increased urgency.

There was a pause as Lacebold considered. It stretched out as he became distracted from the forest by the discussion that was continuing between the humans.

Get out of sight while you're thinking about it, I told him. *The longer you remain visible, the more scared they'll get and the more likely they'll be to attack you. Lacebold, Ben told me not to interfere with humans and this is obviously why. Please, please get out of sight.*

My panic subsided a little as I sensed my youngling finally doing as I had begged. Yet he wasn't obeying me due to being scared. His time in the forest had given him confidence in his ability to survive practically anything, and though he was hurt and angry at the humans' reaction to him, he was still fascinated by them and their wild emotions that leapt around all over the place, seemingly without limit. He wanted to observe them from a greater distance – as I had asked him to do in the first place – and see what happened next. He wanted to understand. All that was left for me to do was try to get to him as quickly as possible.

———

The days that followed were both arduous and torturous. I stopped only to drink, gather plants to eat when I was weak with hunger – there was no time to hunt – or sleep for short periods before nightmares, involving all the awful things that might happen to Lacebold if the humans were to catch him, woke me. When I ran out of trees through which to swing, I was forced to race across open ground. The only way I could do that for long periods at any kind of speed was to leap forward onto my knuckles, on which I braced myself while positioning my legs underneath my body ready for my next leap.

All the while, a small part of me scanned my surroundings for any sign of a threat and ensured I avoided human settlements, while the rest was with Lacebold as he hunted, gathered, and stubbornly continued to observe the humans.

We were both fascinated to witness rocks floating to their village from some distance away and landing in precise formation to form walls across either end of the stone road that bisected the village, while several humans hummed a strange, almost tuneless tune. They were singing the rocks into place! I wondered whether we could do it and focused my attention on sensing exactly how they were doing it.

When they had finished singing the walls into existence, rocks continued to float to the village, now landing in piles behind the newly erected walls, ready to hurl at those whose attack the humans were convinced was coming.

I found myself thinking of Charlotte Lace and all she and the other human kindred had done in order that these humans, and we kindred of the new way of life, could live past the horrors of the old way. I knew I owed it to her and to Benevolence to ensure that Lacebold didn't put all of that at risk and provoke enough fear in the humans that they reverted to behaving in the same way as those who had persecuted their ancestors. It occurred to me to wonder, however, why the humans weren't listening to their sixth sense where my youngling was concerned. All the humans who had left the cities were those who had trusted their feeling that there was a better way to live, and trusted the human kindred to help them leave and find that better way. They had listened to their inner sense when frightened almost witless before, so why weren't they doing it now?

I reached out to those guarding the wall of rock at the end of the village nearer to the forest. One was a twenty-seven-year-old female who went by the name of Kayla Bowler, and the other a forty-year-old-female called Romona Salt.

'What if we don't have enough rocks here to kill them all? We don't even know how many there are,' Kayla Bowler said.

'If we run out,' Romona Salt replied, 'we'll use the rocks from the walls. It was a waste of time building them anyway; by all accounts, enforcers were bred to climb buildings taller than trees, so a shoulder-high wall isn't going to keep them out. I told everyone that, but would they listen? No. So you and I and the other Rock-Singers had to waste our time and energy singing walls into existence that may as well be made of paper.'

The two of them were sensitive; they could sense the rocks they wanted to move without seeing them, and could make a pathway to those rocks with their voices, along which they sent willpower for the rocks to reposition themselves. If they were to try, I was sure they could sense who Lacebold was and what he was about. But they didn't have the human kindreds' courage to bolster them as did the humans who escaped the cities. Where Charlotte Lace and her kind had blasted through any fear that would have prevented them from helping people and enforcers alike, these people allowed their fear to stand between them and their sixth sense, to the extent that they were at risk of behaving like those from whom their ancestors had been so desperate to escape.

I was shocked to realise that the humans whose ancestors had been so severely oppressed could easily become oppressors themselves; in the absence of the strengthening, supportive influence of the human kindred, they could well abandon The Way Of The Horse.

I thought of Benevolence... and suddenly felt calmer. The

humans of the new way of life would rediscover that which simmered deep inside them because horses, and the humans they had chosen, would ensure it.

I reached for the horse who had become my strength and sanity whenever either were failing me. I found him running at top speed with Alan Nixon sitting almost easily on his back and with as great a sense of purpose as that which was driving me. He didn't know where he was going exactly, but he didn't falter as he followed his rider's sense of the place for which they were heading – Alan Nixon's home village of Rockwood.

I resolved to eat, drink and rest even less than I had been, and despite my body's protests, propelled myself across the plain at even greater speed.

Chapter Twenty-Seven

My Isabel,

Enforcers are in the trees of Rockwood! Lots of them! Your father and I have packed what we can carry on our backs and plan to flee the village for Jonustown. We know we may be struck down on the way, but we have to try to reach you so that if the end of The New is coming, at least the three of us can face it together. I'm leaving this note so that if we don't make it, and, by chance, you happen to survive and come here, you'll know that our final thoughts were of you.

All our love, Mum

LACEBOLD WAS asleep in his shelter when I sensed a young adult male, whom I had been monitoring during the hours it had taken him to build up to his intended task, finally taking it upon himself to see what exactly was going on in the trees that stood so close to his village. He sneaked out of the village at dawn, armed with the weapon with which he was an expert at bringing down not only prey animals, but, I found as I searched his thoughts further with my sixth sense, the large cats to whom we kindred were related.

He crept towards the forest with the practised stealth of a hunter as I loped, on sore feet and shredded knuckles, across the vast area of sand punctuated only by rocks and stones that had been frustrating and exhausting me over the past few days. I barely noticed the cold rain that lashed down upon me, or the gusty wind that threw me off balance every time it blasted into my left side, such was my effort to wake Lacebold, who rested peacefully in the shelter he had woven for himself in his preferred tree. It was doing an excellent job of keeping the wind and rain from him, but was also giving him a false sense of security when he was so close to those who were so terrified of him. He had hunted and gathered food for himself, the leftovers of which were dotted around the base of his tree, acting as a beacon for the human searching for him, who I sensed was called Max Wilder.

I felt the hunter's heart racing as if it were my own as he stood at the base of Lacebold's tree, looking up to the shelter that, while so much a part of the forest, was a strange sight to his eyes. He looked around at the surrounding trees and could see no other shelters. He crept away as silently as he had arrived, searching a wider area for any sign of other enforcers. When he found none, his jubilation pierced my heart. He had tracked down his prey and now he would wait to enact the kill that would make him a hero to everyone in the village.

He slunk back to Lacebold's tree and settled down between a bush and another tree to wait for his prey to either arrive or depart the shelter – he thought Lacebold was probably inside but he wasn't absolutely sure – with a slender, pointed weapon sitting ready against the string from which he intended to propel it at my youngling's eye at the first opportunity.

LACEBOLD! LACEBOLD! I screamed his name over and over in my mind as I reached for him, desperate to wake him and warn him of his peril, but he was so deeply immersed in his dreaming, I couldn't make him aware of me.

He was dreaming that he was standing in the village of Rockwood. There were no walls at either end of the street, and the humans had welcomed him almost as warmly as all the forests he had visited. Like them, he was smiling with an open mouth while making the same noise they were all making; one that began deep down in his stomach. He felt as happy, as joyful as they, but only because he was absorbing their emotions from them and expressing them as his own, not because he understood why they were all laughing, as they called it.

He was desperate to understand so that he could recreate the sensation for himself, but whenever he tried, the cruel cackling of his handlers, sounding so similar to, yet feeling so different from, the laughter of the villagers, echoed within his mind and something inside him shut down. He was convinced that if he could just be around humans more, he would get it; he would absorb from them the ability to spontaneously laugh a joyful laugh, and they would stop seeing him as being unworthy of existence.

I didn't understand the humans' laughter either. As I explored Lacebold's mind for his observations of it in the absence of being able to do anything else, I discovered that these humans of the new way of life laughed when someone made up a story that didn't appear to have any other purpose than just that – making others laugh. They also did it if someone tripped and hurt their toe, and so did the human in question. They did it when one of their so-called Rock-Singers misplaced a rock and it wobbled and fell from the wall they were erecting. Parents did it when their children said something unexpected... the list went on, and the more Lacebold had added to it, the more confused he had become.

I understood his need to remain near Rockwood and scrutinise the humans who had the final piece he felt was missing from his findself, but I also cursed it, and I cursed the villagers of Rockwood for lacking the courage of those who had ensured their survival. Had Charlotte Lace been at Rockwood, she would have helped Lacebold, not hurt or hunted him.

I tried again to rouse him. *LACEBOLD! WAKE UP!* I threw all of myself behind my mental shout, but still to no avail. In desperation, I reached for the tree in which he slept; maybe I could cause it to sway, somehow, and wake him?

The tree welcomed the touch of my mind, but instead of succumbing to my will, it drew me into the dream within which it existed along with Lacebold. All of a sudden, I was standing with him and the villagers on the stone street of Rockwood as he relived a conversation he had witnessed using his sixth sense, while observing those involved from the safety of the forest.

'I took my eyes off her for all of about two minutes,' an adult female said, 'and in that time, she completely undressed herself and drew all over herself and the kitchen table with a piece of charcoal.'

Everyone laughed, including Lacebold and me. It was the strangest sensation, but I liked it. Like Lacebold though, I still didn't understand it.

'Why are we laughing?' I asked.

All the humans were instantly quiet, their faces devoid of expression, their bodies motionless; they didn't even appear to be breathing.

Lacebold turned to me. *Lace? What are you doing here?*

You're dreaming, Lacebold. While you sleep, there's a human hunter waiting for you at the base of a nearby tree. He plans to shoot you in the eye as you leave your shelter, and as far as I can ascertain, he's capable of doing so. You have to stay where you are until I reach you.

Lacebold scowled. Then he stopped. *If I'm dreaming, then I'm dreaming this too. The humans are scared of me and they think I'm one of many enforcers in the forest. None of them will dare to try and find out.* He turned back to the villagers, who became animated once more and continued their conversation.

I took hold of Lacebold's arm. *If you think you're dreaming I'm here, then cast me out of your dream.*

What? No. Why would I do that?

For once, don't argue, Lacebold. DO IT. Dismiss me and continue dreaming as you were. Immediately, something closed around my mind and squeezed it so that I could only view Lacebold's dream from a distance and through what appeared to be a small viewing hole. I pushed back against the hole, widened it and squeezed back through so that I was standing beside Lacebold once more. *You can't dismiss me because I'm not part of your dream, I've invaded it in order to tell you that you're in danger.*

I was relieved to see circles of white appearing around the vibrant green of Lacebold's eyes as they widened in shock. Then the dream was no more and my knuckles were bleeding as I loped across a bed of stones towards a wide, fast-flowing river. Almost everything within me wanted to stop; to find a way around or over the water that didn't involve my being immersed in it, but the part that shot to Lacebold as his eyes finally opened and he sensed the nearby presence of Max Wilder, ensured that I plunged into the river with no thought other than to reach the other side and continue on my way to my youngling.

The shock of immersing myself in cold water quickly became secondary to that of losing contact with the stones beneath my feet and being diverted from my course by the river. To begin with, I fought it as I would anyone who attacked me. I lashed out with my arms, I sliced at it with my talons and I roared as loudly as my tight, thickened throat would allow. But the river was a foe like no other. It simply absorbed my attack while draining what remained of my voice, my strength and my body heat, and continued on its way regardless.

At last, I had met a force of will stronger than that which resided within me. At last, I knew what it felt like to be prey instead of predator. At last, I succumbed, taking my sorrow at failing Lacebold with me.

Chapter Twenty-Eight

Let it be recorded for the Histories that on this day, the Second Friday of November, Eighth Year of the Decade of The New, the first villagers have left Rockwood – yet they did not leave in flight. A most reckless young man, who goes by the name of Max Wilder and has for some time been set on proving his masculinity and hunting prowess to the amusement of those older than he, led a group of his equally reckless peers to hunt what he tried and failed to convince the rest of us is a lone enforcer. We do not expect to see any of them again and already mourn their losses. What will become of the rest of us, only time will tell.

Histories of The New, Keeper Milicent Butler

SOMETHING WAS DIGGING into the left side of my face. My nose twitched as smoke drifted past it, carrying with it a scent that made saliva pour from the left side of my mouth. I shivered with cold, yet my back was warm. I tried to move but couldn't. I tried to open my eyes instead and couldn't do that either. I let go of trying to hold on to the sensations that had woken me and drifted into the dark, heavy fog that welcomed me back into its grasp.

When I woke a second time, my back wasn't as warm as before but I no longer shivered. Smoke stung the lining of my nostrils and then was taken by the breeze that gusted at my back and carried a different scent.

Benevolence.

I sat up very suddenly and took hold of my head in my hands as it spun nauseatingly. A sharp intake of breath nearby made me open my eyes. Alan Nixon sat across a small but fierce fire from me and was in the process of turning his body slightly to the side and drawing his legs up in front of him, ready to bolt at the slightest provocation.

I turned my head slowly, not trusting myself to remain conscious if I moved any part of my body too quickly, to where a familiar sound emanated. Relief flooded me as my eyes confirmed that which my nose, ears and sixth sense had already told me; Benevolence stood eating a short distance away.

The sun was as high in the sky as it would reach that day, yet its rays were weak and oblique; they hadn't been responsible for the warmth at my back that had kept me alive. An area of flattened plants beside me smelt of the horse whose presence I was struggling to reconcile with my own on the bank of the river that had overpowered me.

You warmed me when I would have died of cold, I observed to Benevolence.

In the same instant, Alan Nixon asked him, *Can we go now, Ben? She's awake and clearly okay. Shouldn't we hurry up and leave before she attacks one of us? Both of us?*

I turned back to the human, and he shuffled backward on his

rear end, his heart almost leaping out of his chest with the strength and rapidity of its beating.

'Before I attack?' I croaked. 'You are not prey and your horse is my friend. It is the adult male human called Max Wilder whom you should fear; he hunts my youngling for no reason other than that he doesn't understand him and hasn't tried.' Pain and fear stabbed at me as I remembered I had been on my way to protect Lacebold, and by now had surely failed him.

'Max? What do you know about...'

I took my attention away from Alan Nixon's voice as I reached for Lacebold while dreading what I would find.

He is unharmed. Benevolence interrupted my reaching, bringing me back to my immediate surroundings. *That is not to say he will remain so should we linger. Replenish yourself with the food Hard Around The Outside has prepared for you. Then we will go to your youngling.*

I managed to stand on wobbling legs and look at the brown horse who stood eating so peacefully in circumstances that were anything but. *We? How did I come to be here with the two of you? The last thing I remember was drowning while freezing to death.*

We were aware of your plight. We diverted from our path in order to pull you from the river. The remainder of your life awaits you.

I turned back to where Alan Nixon also now stood. He shifted his weight as if he would run from me. I saw that some of his clothes were arranged on some large, flat stones that surrounded his fire.

'You and Ben pulled me from the river?' I met his eyes, and he shrank back from me, making himself smaller and, I sensed, desperately trying to maintain control of his bladder. I rubbed my throat in the hope it would release more of my voice when I spoke. My effort was in vain. 'You have nothing to fear from me,'

I croaked. 'As I have already told you, you are not prey. I am grateful to you. You and Benevolence have given me a second chance to save my youngling.'

'His name is Benevolent, but you were close. How did you know that?'

'It is a name I gave him too. He helped me before he began helping you.'

Alan Nixon looked past me to Ben. *You already knew this… this enforcer? You… helped her? Why? How?*

Ben helped me to see how to ensure the survival of my kin. He couldn't hear me. Exasperated, I repeated myself out loud.

'That's the second time you've answered me like you can hear my thoughts as Ben can,' Alan Nixon replied. His shoulders sagged. 'You can hear my thoughts. You know how I feel too, like he does?'

I nodded. 'You fear me. You think I'm an enforcer who's come to kill you and your people, or make you serve me, but I and my kind are as much refugees as your ancestors were.' My throat constricted and I began to cough – and couldn't stop. I had more to tell him, but my throat wouldn't allow it.

You choke on everything you weren't permitted to say in your former life, Benevolence observed. *You could heal yourself but doing so will take much time and attention.*

I don't have either, I told him as I bent double while continuing to cough. *I have to get to Lacebold.*

A shaking hand appeared by my face, holding a beaker of water. Alan Nixon dropped it as I reached for it, and quickly stepped back. 'Sorry. I'll try again,' he said.

When next he offered me water, it was in a bowl that I could grasp without scoring his hand with my talons. I drank the lot and my coughing subsided.

Ben, can you tell him what Lacebold was doing at Rockwood, so he can tell his fellow humans that my youngling meant no harm? I asked the horse who continued to eat as if I hadn't almost choked to death right by him.

It will change nothing, Benevolence replied. *We will ensure that humans do not hunt your kind but just as you and your kind carry the shame of your ancestors, so they carry the fear of theirs. Both will take time to release.*

'How are you alive?' Alan Nixon asked me. 'How did you and however many other enforcers there are...' He shuddered. 'How did you all survive when the cities perished?'

'Only those of us who were...' I coughed again until Alan Nixon handed me another bowl of water. I swallowed some and then said, 'Only those of us who were underground survived. The humans and those of us who were aboveground are all gone.' I coughed again until I retched. I spat out a globule of blood and then drank more water.

Alan Nixon managed to lift his eyes to look into mine. 'So it's just...' He swallowed. 'It's just us humans in the villages, and... and... you and your... kind who are left?'

I nodded and held out my hands. 'Food, please,' I whispered. 'Then I have to rescue my youngling from your hunters.'

I couldn't bring myself to sit back down when Alan Nixon handed me a full bowl of what he said was rabbit stew, because I didn't trust myself to get back up. As I tipped small amounts of warm stew into my mouth at a time, barely chewing it before swallowing so that an almost constant stream soothed my throat, I reached for Lacebold.

The extreme distress that was driving him through the trees at a rate that could challenge me at my best was a combination of fear, anger and humiliation – but as Ben had told me, he was at least alive and unharmed. His recent experience was at the forefront of his mind, driving him as far away as possible from those who, Max Wilder had assured him as he fled, would hunt him down.

Lacebold had remained in his shelter for some time after he awoke, searching Max Wilder's mind and confirming for himself everything I had told him. He recoiled from the human's mind as he sensed the full extent of fear and loathing the human felt towards him as he sat with his eyes and weapon trained on the entrance to Lacebold's shelter. The fear, my youngling understood – he was, after all, created to be feared. The loathing was more difficult for him to comprehend. He examined himself, trying to find what it was that was so repulsive about him... and discovering, somewhere deep within, a sense of familiarity with the emotion it elicited within him; the shame of our ancestors was what Ben had called it. He couldn't stand it, and he wouldn't remain near this human – or any other humans – any longer.

Lacebold had surprised Max Wilder with the speed and agility of his exit from his shelter. He burst out backwards so that his eyes faced away from the human's weapon, grabbed the vine across the top of the entrance and swung himself from there to a nearby branch. Heart pounding, he climbed high into the tree, thankful that, like those that had called to me, it had kept its leaves and gave him cover. Even so, several of the sharp, metal-tipped weapons whistled past him.

'Did I get you, Abomination?' Max Wilder shouted. 'Did I? No? Well I will. I'm as good a tracker as I am a hunter, and I and my friends will hunt you down. Go on, flee. Leave me a trail of leaves and twigs to tell me where you've gone. There's nowhere you can hide that I won't find you. Enforcers stopped my grandfather from leaving the city. He was supposed to leave the day after my pregnant grandmother squeezed out with her life intact. She waited and waited for him, but he never came. There was only one thing that would have stopped him, and one of them is right above me, cowering in a tree. Breathe while you can, Enforcer.' His voice trailed off as Lacebold fled, a trail of twigs and leaves fluttering to the forest floor behind him, just as Max Wilder had predicted.

I began to breathe away the rage that erupted throughout my body – old habits died hard. My legs trembled, my stomach turned over, my heart fluttered and my mouth lifted into a snarl as I breathed to get my body back within parameters that no longer existed.

Movement in my peripheral vision caused me to turn my head towards Alan Nixon, who was moving at speed towards Benevolence. I remembered I wasn't in the city. I wasn't under the control of any program or handler. I could feel rage, and what was more, I could act on it. I threw my empty bowl to the ground, looked towards the pale blue autumn sky and roared despite the pain it caused my throat and the blood that sprayed from my mouth.

I leapt in the direction of my youngling and his hunter, noting as I did so that Ben and Alan Nixon had pulled me out of the river on the far side from that which I had entered. Nothing now stood in my way except for the plain across which I bounded as if my life depended on it, the forest for which Lacebold was now heading having just exited the one by Rockwood, and the plain before him.

He was far ahead of Max Wilder and the others whom the hunter had roused and incited to follow him, but now that he was out of his element and loping awkwardly across theirs, they were bound to catch up.

I'm coming, Lacebold, just keep going towards the trees. You're fit and strong, you can do it. Reach the forest and I'll meet you there.

Lacebold was too scared to answer me.

We're coming too, Lacefirm told him. *We're heading towards the same forest now.*

Lacefirm, no! Head for Winterwood. Lacebold and I will see you there.

They think Lacebold is on his own. It was Lacekeen who made her thoughts known now. *They need to see there are six of us, then they might leave us all alone.*

Please, both of you, take Lacehope and Laceheart with you to Winterwood, I pleaded.

They won't take me anywhere. I could barely believe the thought was Lacehope's. *Laceheart and I will stay with the rest of you. We are kin.*

Laceheart was my last chance. *Laceheart? You know Ben's feelings about this. Please, turn around with the others.*

He wanted us to leave the humans alone, but they know about us now, Laceheart replied calmly. Firmly. *He wanted me and the others to find ourselves and we have. We don't need to ask you what to do now, we can decide for ourselves. Lacebold needs us and so do you. We're coming.*

I increased my pace further, ignoring the splutters of blood that exited my mouth with every outward breath. Lacebold was not only in mortal danger, but he was taking it to my other four younglings. I had to reach him before they did.

Chapter Twenty-Nine

Let it be recorded for the Histories that on this day, the Second Friday of November, Eighth Year of the Decade of The New, Herald June brought news to Plainsview of an enforcer being sighted in the trees near Rockwood. Despite the Heralds all having sworn to tell nothing but the truth, the news has been met with universal disbelief. Though as a Keeper of the Histories, I understand it isn't my role to comment on my recordings, on this occasion, I feel it necessary because of my recent first-hand knowledge and experience of enforcers. The enforcer building in my city was built twelve floors deep into the ground, so it is conceivable that the enforcers occupying the lower levels survived the blasts that killed everyone else. Having witnessed the strength of the poor creatures with my own eyes, it is further conceivable that they could have cleared a way for themselves up and out of the ground. If it weren't for my role as a Keeper binding me here, I would be inclined to head for the location of the sighting with the aim of helping any surviving enforcers in any way possible, for I do not believe they are a danger to us. As it is, the sight of more than twenty horses carrying Horse-Bonded at speed past Plainsview this morning gives me hope the enforcers will receive any help they need.

Histories of The New, Keeper Jinna Lace

BY THE TIME I could make out in the distance the forest for which Lacebold and I were both aiming, blood was spraying from my mouth with every outward breath and almost choking me with every inward one. I was slowing rapidly.

A rhythmic thumping on the ground behind me preceded Benevolence drawing level with me and pausing so that Alan Nixon could dismount. The human landed heavily beside me and stumbled, grabbing the seat he had strapped to Ben, in order to remain on his feet.

'Benevolent will carry you. Get on his back,' he panted.

I shook my head. I was too heavy for Ben to carry, and I didn't think I could leap onto his back anyway. I would make it to the forest on my own two feet, and I would save my younglings before I died, however many humans I had to take with me.

Ben positioned himself in front of me, forcing me to stagger to a stop. *Your solution is not one that will be helpful to any of the individuals concerned,* he told me as I stood swaying in the chilly autumn air. *Hard Around The Outside and I will educate the humans. You will take your young back to your community where you are all needed.*

I won't make it. I'll stop the humans and then I'd be grateful if you and Alan Nixon would ensure my younglings reach Winterwood. Laceheart will listen to you, and the others will listen to him once I'm gone.

You are not expiring, Benevolence told me. *You are merely failing to heal after releasing some of that which you were forced to swallow. Strong Of Heart can help you but you must reach him first. Should you insist on attempting such on your own feet you will fail. Find the strength to climb onto my back. Hard Around The Outside and I will take you to your younglings and prevent that which would set all three of our species on a path away from that which approaches balance.*

I'm twice the weight of Alan Nixon.

I have the strength to carry two of him. He didn't just mean physically, either. I could sense the total lack of doubt Benevolence had in himself, and the potency that confidence gave him.

What about Alan Nixon? Will he be able to keep up?

He will doubt it at times. He will learn to think differently.

The thought of Alan Nixon struggling while Ben carried me was almost as strong a motivation for me to do as he instructed, as the thought of taking my younglings to safety and living to see them flourish.

I won't fit on his seat, I observed.

Hard Around The Outside will remove it, Ben replied as Alan Nixon frowned, then moved to do exactly that. He lowered the seat to rest against a nearby rock and covered it with plants. Then he stood at Ben's head and the two of them looked expectantly at me, one with pinched, scared, blue eyes, the other with deep, knowing, brown ones.

I wasted no more time. I thought of my younglings, gathered all of the little strength I had left, and leapt at Benevolence. I sensed his heart rate increase at the sight of a predator launching herself at him, but it steadied immediately and when I landed on his back, he shifted beneath me in order to help me find my balance.

He was warm against my legs and backside, and far more stable than the many branches upon which I had balanced with ease. When he moved forward, however, though I managed to go with him, I was forced to grasp hold of handfuls of his long neck hair in order to keep my place; balancing on my backside differed greatly from doing so on my feet when my side-facing toes worked in concert with the fingers of my hands to stabilise me. The thought occurred to me that I might fall from Ben's back if he increased his speed, and I might be better struggling onward on my own two feet after all.

You doubt your balance to the same extent that Hard Around The Outside doubts his stamina, Benevolence informed me. *Doubt presents an opportunity to learn and strengthen.*

I don't have the capacity to do either.

It is at such a time that you have the greatest capacity to do both. Ben picked up speed so that Alan Nixon had to run to stay beside him, and I had to grip hold of him with my legs as well as my hands in order to remain in position.

You have to let your body follow his like we do when we stand on branches that are moving in the wind. Balancing on his back is easy then. Laceheart's thought was wistful and a balm to my soul. He drew me into his memories of riding Benevolence and I was chagrined to discover how harmonious his experience had been; a total contrast to the very bouncy, uncomfortable one I was having. *Close your eyes,* Laceheart told me. *That's what I did, then Ben could help me. Try it.*

I had nothing to lose. If it didn't work, I would fall as I was on my way to doing anyway. If it did, I would enable Benevolence to get me to my younglings quicker. I closed my eyes – and everything seemed to slow down. I left my world of haste, fear and discomfort, and entered that which consisted only of touch, feel and awareness.

It was peaceful. The essences of all living things moved around one another, sometimes bumping into one another, sometimes merging, sometimes becoming entwined and then separating, but always moving in the same general direction – always being gently drawn that way, I realised. When there were collisions, the gentle energy of the horses teased apart the essences in question and drew them back into the gentle stream that would take them where they had been heading. The destination called to me, and to Alan Nixon, though he couldn't hear it.

I wanted to go to it. I wanted to find it. I relaxed and allowed my body to respond to Ben's in the way Laceheart had advised. Immediately, he drew me along with him in the stream more quickly, more easily.

When I opened my eyes, I was balancing on Ben's back without needing to grip him with my hands and legs. I sensed he was closer to the balance for which we were all heading than I, and I was closer than Alan Nixon, but all three of us were heading very definitely and inextricably in that direction.

The humans of the new way of life were colliding with my younglings though, and trying to hold them back. I wouldn't allow it. I would stop them.

Immediately, I began bouncing on Ben's back again. I sighed and closed my eyes. I felt for the stream along which Benevolence was drawing me, and relaxed. This time, I kept my eyes closed; the only way I could maintain my balance was to keep the world out. I swallowed and was relieved to find doing so a little easier. The bleeding in my throat had slowed, and it felt less tight. I attempted deeper breaths and achieved them despite my body's efforts to move with Ben's.

I can't keep up. Alan Nixon's desperate communication to Ben invaded my peace. *I can't get my breath, we need to stop.*

I sensed that the reason he couldn't regulate his breathing was because his chest was tight with worry he wouldn't be able to – he needed to relax as had I. I couldn't tell him though. I couldn't bear to use my voice and risk irritating my throat just as it seemed to be calming down. I realised I didn't need to; Benevolence would tell him. He had to. He couldn't allow Alan Nixon to slow us down.

Ben maintained his speed and direction without comment to either of us.

Benevolence, tell Alan Nixon what he needs to know in order to carry on. I know you won't leave him behind, so we can't let him stop. Ben! Tell him, before he stops. We don't have time to get him moving again.

The horse, who was now breathing hard and sweating due to the exertion involved in carrying me, ignored my demand. It occurred to me that I was working the least hard of the three of us, so I was in the best position to help if I could only speak.

I closed my eyes, joined Ben and Laceheart's world again, and felt around for the solution that Ben's silence assured me must be there. I reached for the horse labouring beneath me, then through him to his bonded human in the same way I had used the connection between the forests to reach those sheltering within them.

Alan Nixon, it is I, Lace, who now touches your mind. I opened my eyes and looked down at him, hoping he would read from my eyes the truth of my thought. He looked up at me with scared eyes while holding his side and gasping. *We can't stop and we don't need to,* I continued. *You can breathe well enough to carry on running if you stop doubting yourself and relax.*

His eyes narrowed, squeezing out the fear they had contained so that his intense dislike of his current situation, and of me and my part in it, could take its place. *I take advice from Benevolent, not you. Never from you, especially not right now.*

That WAS Ben's advice. He gave it to me and it worked, so I'm passing it on to you. We can't stop. We have to reach my younglings before your friends do.

Do you really think I care what happens to your younglings after what your kind did to mine in the cities? I'm just trying to stay with my horse.

Trust him, then. If he really thought you needed him to stop, he would. Look at him. He labours in order to carry my weight, yet he does not think of stopping. He knows he has set a pace that you and he can maintain, and that is what carries him forward.

You dare to tell me what my horse knows and what I should do about it?

Only because you're too hard around the outside to see it for yourself. That's what he calls you, you know. Hard Around The Outside. You're harsh and stubborn when you don't need to be. You don't have to hold everyone away from you and assume they mean you harm. Alan Nixon, don't stop – DON'T! I reached down and grabbed him by the back of his coat in order to keep him upright as he stumbled, glad that my arms were so much longer than my legs, enabling me to reach him. *Relax, like this.* Without thinking, I drew him into the world of essences. *Stop fighting and allow yourself to be pulled along with Benevolence and me,* I told him, dragging him alongside us now.

Still, the horse beneath me didn't stop. As I felt his courage, his determination, his absolute knowledge that he could keep going, so did Alan Nixon. He lightened in my hand and then stumbled as he managed to get his legs moving again. I held fast to him until he was running beside me. He glanced up, a look of amazement in his eyes, which hardened when he took in the sight of me. I understood. Like me, he was finding it as difficult to transfer the experience he had felt to the real, physical world. He had done it enough to be able to run though, and that was all that mattered for now.

I turned my attention back to Laceheart. *You have learnt so much – become so much – during your findself. Thank you for your help.*

He ignored my gratitude with an ease that reminded me of Benevolence, telling me instead, *I have herbs that will heal your throat.*

That can wait. As can you. Don't go to Lacebold, Laceheart. When you and the others get to the forest, climb a tree and wait for me and Lacebold to come to you.

Lacekeen surprised me by arguing with me again. *We might be able to get to him before you do though. He's tired. They're chasing him across the plain and even though he was a long way in front of them when he left the forest, they're catching up with him, and he knows it.*

We should definitely try to reach him before they do, Lacehope agreed, surprising me even more.

Don't worry about us, Lace, Lacefirm told me. *We'll save Lacebold.*

No! You may have learnt a lot, all of you, and you may be able to survive on your own, but you're nine years old and you will not risk being attacked by humans! Do as I tell you and let me protect Lacebold.

My panic caused me to bounce on Ben's back again, and I winced as I felt the extra burden it caused him. I closed my eyes, not daring to reach for Lacebold to find out his current situation in case I caused Ben a problem again and slowed him from getting me to my youngling.

It was only when we reached the trees with Ben slathered in white foam, Alan Nixon wet with sweat, and me slightly recovered after having been carried for the past hour or so, that I allowed myself to reach for any of my younglings.

Laceheart, Lacekeen, Lacehope and Lacefirm had continued to ignore my instructions and were now swinging through the trees towards the far edge of the forest from where Ben stood under a tree so that I could leap up into its branches. Lacebold was terrified and exhausted but still gambolling awkwardly across the plain towards us all. Sixteen humans – all much younger than Alan Nixon and, as hunters, a great deal fitter – were running easily behind him. Every now and then, a few of them stopped to fire their weapons, all of which had so far landed short of Lacebold but were rapidly getting closer. Soon they would be within range of him and not long after that, my other four younglings towards whom he was leading them.

Humans. They had created us. Threatened us. Frightened us. Beaten us. Caused us pain every single day of our lives until we were free of them. I had expected the humans of the new way of life to be different, but they were exactly the same as those of the old.

I forgot all about Benevolence and Alan Nixon as I powered my way from tree to tree, my eyes now well and truly open. I immersed myself fully in the forest and searched for the threads that would take me to those of the humans I would kill first. Benevolence pulled at me to heed him, but, full of rage at the humans who dared to threaten my youngling for no reason other than existing, I snatched myself away from him. I didn't want to be reminded of his earlier counsel. For the first time in my life, I wanted to kill humans. I wanted to wipe the planet clear of them so they could never hurt any of my kin again.

Chapter Thirty

Let it be recorded for the Histories that on this day, the Second Saturday of November, Eighth Year of the Eighth Decade of The New, the headstrong young hunters of Rockwood have, as expected, failed to return from their pursuit of what they believed to be a lone Enforcer. Their failure to return confirms the belief held by the rest of us that their quarry is far from alone. Seven families have now fled the village in the hope of being able to say their last goodbyes to relatives in other villages before we are all killed. The rest of us live each minute wondering if it is our last.

Histories of The New, Keeper Milicent Butler

I SEARCHED and searched for the threads that would confirm my conviction that today was the day I would willingly spill human blood. By the time I had swung my way across most of the forest and was almost on top of the four younglings tiredly swinging through the trees ahead of me, I was frustrated. I had ignored the threads that were thrumming with the most urgency, each time sensing the prey animal that scurried away in relief as they sensed the presence of the one destined to seal their fate.

So then, fate didn't really exist, I told myself. If I could ignore the pull of a thread connecting me to one with whom I had an agreement, then I could interact with someone else with whom I had no such arrangement. I could create my own fate as I went along. I ignored the sick feeling in my stomach and what I knew it meant, and swung with even more determination despite the blood spraying from my mouth now that I was exerting myself so hard again.

I sensed Lacefirm, Lacekeen, Laceheart and Lacehope over to my right and overtook them, my rage and determination to save Lacebold continuing to give me greater power and speed than their youth and health were giving them.

Lace, no, stop! Lacekeen's thought was desperate as she sensed my presence and intention.

We still need you, Lace. Lacehope's reminder of that which Benevolence had told me almost swayed me from my course.

Then Lacebold's terror swamped me as the sharp metal tip of a weapon bounced off his shoulder. His skin was almost as tough as mine and saved him from serious injury, but the force of the impact sent him sprawling onto his front.

I roared and then choked on the resulting blood even as the sound of my fury erupted out of the trees. I sensed the humans pulling up short as it reached their ears. The cowards. When they thought they outnumbered Lacebold by sixteen to one, they were full of bloodlust. As soon as they heard evidence to the contrary, their hearts raced almost as hard and fast as his.

LACEBOLD, GET UP! My mental shout was full of panic, which added to his own and spurred him to push himself up onto his feet and knuckles, grimacing at the pain in his bruised shoulder. *Get moving. You have to get to the trees before any of them decide to risk coming after you again. And DON'T look back, your face is the only part of you that's vulnerable to their weapons. Put all your focus on moving forward. I'm nearly with you.*

I sensed the humans' frustration when their quarry began to stumble away from them and knew that, fuelled as they were by a frenzy I had seen in humans before when they were afraid but urging one another to feel a sense of bravado, and with no sign of whoever had emitted the sound that had made them pause their hunt, it wouldn't be long before one of them would provoke the others into chasing my youngling once more.

The sound of wood splitting reached me; my other younglings were panicking too and increasing their efforts to reach Lacebold. Their panic had edged between them and the guidance that was always available to them from the trees, and their selection of safe branches between which to swing was less accurate as a result. As a consequence of knowing it, so became mine.

The branch for which I reached wasn't strong enough to take my weight, let alone be used as a pivoting point in order to swing to another, I realised in the instant that it became too late to change direction towards another. There was a loud crack as the branch split, dropping me much lower than I had planned to be in order to swing to the next. I flailed around with both arms, frantically trying to reach another branch that would save me or at least slow my fall. There were none; not only had my branch selection been misguided but also my choice of tree. There was another crack, and the branch sheared from the trunk completely.

A few seconds could last a long time, I discovered as I plummeted to the ground. I had time to wonder whether I would die and if so, how much of a mess my body would be for my younglings to find if any of them even survived the next hour. I considered the range of injuries I could sustain from which I might live but be rendered unable to reach Lacebold in time to protect him. I decided I would rather die. I even had time to grasp the irony of my situation; having scaled high rise apartment blocks with minimal foot and handholds and hands that were often slick with blood, I was falling from a tree that was less than a tenth of their height.

Close your eyes. I couldn't identify whether the thought came from Laceheart or Benevolence; they felt so similar to me now. Either way, they were just in time. I closed my eyes and remembered my place in the stream of essences, a good many of which were currently colliding with mine. It didn't matter. None of the details did; the outcome was inevitable. I relaxed.

I landed on my feet and felt the soft forest floor welcoming me and allowing me to bend my legs more slowly than I would otherwise have managed, minimising the impact through them. My bloodied knuckles were likewise welcomed as I tilted forward onto them, and though I gritted my teeth at the dead leaves and earth pressing into their open sores, I was able to stand and relieve them within seconds.

I stood in silence, my eyes wide open once more and, as a result, feeling nowhere near as sanguine as I had been on landing. I was unable to comprehend that I had landed from the height I just had without injury aside from a mild, jabbing pain in my left ankle, even though I remembered exactly how it had happened.

There was movement through the trees, and my heart both leapt and sank at the sight of Lacehope, Lacekeen, Laceheart and Lacefirm swinging to lower branches, heading for me. All I could think to do in order to keep them safe was stumble to the nearest tree that – unlike the one from which I had fallen – had others in close proximity, and try to reach the edge of the forest before them.

I felt their upset as they sensed my intention, and, as I hurried away from them, their horror at the sight of me. Their shock carried with it the image of me they had seen.

I looked truly frightful. My gait was stilted and uneven due to exhaustion and the mild ankle sprain I had just sustained, and blood dribbled down my fangs and chin.

I ignored their concern; I couldn't spare the time to reassure them that I would be alright and I didn't know that doing so would be honest. I put them out of my mind. The only way to keep all five of my younglings safe was to focus on reaching Lacebold.

He was now a long stone's throw from the trees, and staggering as if he would collapse at any moment. The precious time I had wasted by falling, recovering and having to climb back into the trees had given the humans time to rediscover the frenzy of fear and insanity that had driven them to run across the plain brandishing weapons and shrieking in a disturbing – and deeply disappointing – imitation of those in the cities. Max Wilder howled, brandished his weapon above his head as he ran. The rest followed him eagerly, and they were all closing in on Lacebold.

I cared nothing for the stream of blood that I left hanging in the air in my wake, or for the racking cough that left me gasping for breath as surely as did my exertion. I found the energy I needed to swing to the trees that lined the edge of the forest, and once there, descended rapidly but carefully so that I landed as lightly as possible on my injured ankle. Then I threw myself across the short distance of plain to my youngling.

I reached him as another weapon – an arrow, I sensed they called it – came arcing through the air towards him. He fell into my arms and I swung him around so that the arrow thudded into my back before dropping to the ground.

A burning sensation erupted in my stomach and spread upward to my throat so that I could not prevent myself from roaring again and covering Lacebold in blood. I set him down, turned around and faced our attackers. I didn't see humans of the new way of life. I just saw humans. They had created me and my kind for their own ends. They had beaten us, tortured us, controlled us and forced us to do things that hurt us deep inside. Just when we thought we were free of them, they hunted and attacked us. They would feel the full effect of my revenge now that I was free to exact it.

Make your way to the trees and stay there with the others, I ordered Lacebold, who lay shaking and cowering in the grass. They would shoot no more arrows at him, for I would give them a more urgent target, one who came at them so that they had no option but to abandon all thoughts of their original quarry. I wouldn't allow their weapons to slow me down or hold me back. I would reach them and then I would kill them all.

I dropped to my knuckles and sprang forward, feeling an enormous rush of satisfaction at the horror I sensed exploding out of the humans – but it wasn't just because of me. I saw through their eyes the sight I posed as I practically flew across the ground towards them, red droplets spraying from my hands and mouth as if I had already just killed in the most savage of ways, my fangs bared and my eyes focused on those I would slay... followed by four more versions of me who, while smaller, bore expressions that were every bit as savage.

Seven of the humans turned and ran. Five more dithered and then followed them. The remaining four, including Max Wilder, stood their ground. They raised curved pieces of wood whose ends were joined by string, and pulled arrows back against the strings.

I turned to my younglings. *Turn your backs and make yourselves smaller. The arrows will hurt if they hit, but they'll bounce off you.*

They obeyed me just in time. Arrows soared over Lacekeen's

and Lacehope's heads, but the arrow aimed at Laceheart's face had been fired by a poorer marksman and hit him at the base of his neck as he ducked. Max Wilder's arrow skimmed the back of my head as I did likewise.

I felt the remaining hunters' renewed horror as the five of us turned back around to face them, unharmed. They stretched their arms backward, over their shoulders, for fresh arrows, but they couldn't get their shaking hands under control in order to pull the arrows back against the strings of their bowed wood launchers.

Fresh rage exploded out of me from where it had been buried for so long, and I hurled myself towards the humans again, enjoying the scent of their terror as they dropped their weapons and ran.

Chapter Thirty-One

NOTICE TO ALL AT THE GATHERING
from Overseer Lacinda Rooney

So many Horse-Bonded have now left for the villages that my
rota is a nonsense. Patience counsels me to reconstruct a new
one for the second time this week, but I don't see the point when
in a few days' time, there'll probably be only her and me left
here. If anyone wants to take over the role of Overseer, be my
flaming guest.

I WAS INJURED, exhausted, suffering from blood loss, and out of
my element as much as the humans were in theirs as I pursued
them back across the plain. The thought of the humans who had so
disappointed and enraged me escaping to hunt another day,
however, or even worse, my younglings overtaking me and
putting themselves in harm's way, more than made up the
difference.

As I gained on the runners at the back of the group, I attempted to hone in on the one I would kill first. Max Wilder had been the last to turn and run, yet had overtaken several of his kin – he would be the third to die. Of the two females who trailed the others, I should instinctively have known who to bring down first... yet I couldn't seem to grasp who my target should be even though I knew I would barely have to break stride in order to take down either, or even both of them. It felt as though part of me was snagging on the part intent on killing, and I almost tripped physically as a result. I pressed onward despite it, yet its influence took hold and became bigger. I slowed, then sped back up at the sight of my prey widening the gap I had shortened. I decided to take them both down together, one with either hand, then there would be no one between Max Wilder and me.

Yet still, a part of me pulled back on the rest.

The threads you follow are not those that connect predator and prey. Benevolence's observation folded itself around my rage, directing it away from those in front of me.

I slowed my pace again and when my blood stopped pounding through my ears, I heard the horse's approach as well as felt it. There was a shout from behind me, and the hunters within earshot stopped and turned around. They stumbled backward as I continued to advance towards them, albeit at a hobble, but when Benevolence overtook me with Alan Nixon balancing easily on his horse's bare back, they stopped and shouted breathlessly to those still running away behind them.

Benevolence halted between me and the humans. Alan Nixon shouted for the hunters to gather together, but when his message reached those furthest away, I sensed their reluctance to come back and stand with their fellow humans; they preferred to have their friends acting as a buffer that would slow me down long enough for them to escape, should I resume my pursuit.

Alan Nixon glanced at me and my four younglings, who now stood two on either side of me, panting. Then he turned back to the hunters. 'Villagers of Rockwood,' he called loudly, yet not loudly enough for the furthest humans to be able to hear him. Tentatively, they edged closer, their heads turned sideways as they tried to catch his words so that they needed approach no closer than was absolutely necessary. 'Explain why you pursued Bold By Nature with the intention of killing him.'

Benevolence gazed at me so that I couldn't talk myself out of my knowledge that Alan Nixon's question had originated with his horse. The hunters all looked at Max Wilder. He glanced around at them, then turned back to Alan Nixon. He heaved several deep breaths in and out to slow his panting, spread his feet apart and put his hands on his hips. 'Ex-villager of Rockwood, explain how you hold sway over those dangerous abominations. Maybe if we can tame them too, we can have them ploughing our fields instead of threatening us from the trees.' He cackled as he turned, nodding, to his friends. A few of them smiled weakly and nodded back, but the rest looked ready to run again.

'It's true, I was a villager of Rockwood,' Alan Nixon said, almost spitting his words out. I sensed Benevolence redirecting the human's thoughts to those he had counselled him to speak, and he paused for a moment and took hold of himself before continuing, 'Now I am bonded to Benevolent.' His voice softened as he spoke his horse's name. 'He would have you answer his question.'

No one spoke.

I sank to the ground and hands clasped hold of both of mine – Lacehope's on one side and Lacefirm's on the other. Laceheart appeared in front of me and opened a container woven from, and secured to his waist with, the most delicate of vines. He handed me the leaves of a herb that was unfamiliar to me, and the dried petals of another. *These will help your throat and calm you down so you can heal. You won't need to run anymore.* His thought rang with his absolute confidence that he spoke the truth now that Benevolence had arrived. *Lacekeen has gone back to Lacebold with herbs that will ease his bruising and give him back his energy.* He drew the leaves of a herb I recognised from his container and stuffed them into his own mouth. *I could use some help too.* He rubbed the back of his neck where the arrow had hit him and I turned an anger-filled gaze back to the humans who still could not – or in Max Wilder's case, would not – answer Ben's question. I could make him.

Lacefirm and Lacehope pulled back on my hands. *No.* Their thought was echoed by that of Benevolence. Now that he had somehow dispersed my rage, I had little energy with which to either argue or defy him.

The silence persisted for long enough that the humans gained a measure of confidence that my younglings and I were indeed, as Max Wilder had surmised, under the sway of the bonded horse and human. They grouped around the one who had incited them to hunt, and I sensed the confidence it gave him, and his increasing need to maintain his assumed position as their leader by acting in some way.

Benevolence and Alan Nixon waited for a reply from the hunters with apparently endless patience, although I sensed that their state of being had little to do with the human and everything to do with the horse.

I grimaced at the amount of blood I swallowed along with Laceheart's herbs, but obediently ate a sizeable amount of them, which he calmly handed to me as if we were back in the safety of our community rather than out on the plain and vulnerable, with only a man and horse between us and those who had tried to murder us.

'What if we don't want to answer his question?' Max Wilder volunteered finally.

Then they will be the undoing of all that their ancestors achieved and the instigators of a return to insanity.

Alan Nixon was unable to pass on Benevolence's counsel with anywhere near the gravitas with which he had received it, yet still many of the hunters gasped. Some put their bare, perfectly formed hands over their mouths while others shook their heads upon sagging shoulders. Only Max Wilder pretended to be unaffected.

'Why don't you ask those sad attempts at being human why they threatened our village?' he asked Alan Nixon, oblivious to the fact that the pain he caused us with his words was far worse than that which he had caused with his arrows.

At Ben's request and for Max Wilder's benefit, Alan Nixon turned to me and said, 'Benevolent requests that you answer Max's question.'

'My youngling is nine years old and was never a threat to you.' I coughed and then swallowed the resulting blood from my throat, surprised that it already felt looser and I felt able to continue speaking, albeit with a significant croak. 'He was curious. He was raised by humans who tortured and threatened him, and he wanted to learn about the humans of the new way of life, particularly why you laugh. He discovered instead that you're no different from those who raised him.' I coughed again, and this time spat out a mouthful of blood.

'I'll speak for her from now on,' Lacehope said quickly and loudly. 'She needs to get better before she talks again.' She squeezed my hand with a level of self-assurance that was more in line with my age and experience than her own. *Tell me what else you want to say.*

I have said it all, but thank you, Lacehope.

I turned my attention back to the humans and was surprised by the misery I could feel emanating from them. They couldn't look at me or my kin without shuddering, but it seemed my words had left them as ashamed of their actions as their words had caused us to feel about our bodies – all but Max Wilder who desperately clung to his cause and the status he believed it gave him.

'And we've discovered that you're no different from the enforcers who persecuted our ancestors,' he replied. 'If it hadn't been for Alan and his horse, we'd all be dead by now.' He turned to Alan Nixon. 'I can't believe you're standing up for them after what happened to my grandfather. You know the only reason he didn't get out of the city was because their lot killed him.'

Alan Nixon stiffened on Ben's back, but his horse stood as placidly as ever. It took some time for the human to succumb to his horse's influence and relax again. When he did, he said to Max Wilder, 'Your question has been answered satisfactorily. It is your turn to provide an answer. Explain why you pursued Bold By Nature with the intention of killing him.'

'BECAUSE HE THREATENED US!' Max Wilder shouted.

'How did he do that?' Alan Nixon asked, just about managing, at Ben's request, to keep his voice calm when he wanted to shout. He bit the inside of his cheek to stop himself from adding any words beyond Ben's question.

'BY SITTING IN A TREE AND STARING AT US.'

'He just watched you? He did nothing else?' Alan Nixon asked.

'NO!' Max Wilder frowned. 'But how were we supposed to know he wasn't going to attack us when he's an enforcer, like in the stories our grandparents told us? That's what they did – they attacked and killed humans who disobeyed or resisted the city governors. How were we supposed to know he was just curious?'

'How did your ancestors know it was worth risking their lives in order to leave the city where they were born? They didn't know what was out here any more than you knew what Bold By Nature's intentions were, and they were every bit as scared as you were,' Alan Nixon replied.

'I wasn't scared,' Max Wilder said. 'I just wanted to protect my village.'

'Answer Benevolent's question, please,' Alan Nixon insisted. 'How did your grandparents know that there was a better way of life waiting for them out here than what they were enduring within the city walls?'

'Intuition,' another hunter called out. 'They trusted their intuition.'

'Benevolent invites you to find the courage to do the same.'

The big, brown horse walked calmly and slowly backward so that he no longer stood between me and my younglings, and the humans.

Alan Nixon continued, 'Look at those you see as enforcers with the reassurance of knowing that Benevolent assures your safety. Trust your intuition to tell you of their intentions. Not your fear.'

It was strange to see the expressions change on the faces of those who stared at my kin and me as we stared back. To a one, they studied my younglings – who had just been joined by Lacekeen and a largely recovered Lacebold – first. Their frowns disappeared as their eyes flickered briefly to me and they gained a sense of how young the five smaller kindred were in comparison. Then their jaws tightened as they sensed a glimmer of the younglings' strength and self-assurance. When they turned their attention back to me, I couldn't help glaring my resentment back at them, and their jaws dropped even as their eyebrows shot upward.

All of them except for Max Wilder shrank backward. He pointed at me. 'That one hates us and wants us dead.'

He wasn't completely correct, but he wasn't far wrong.

Lacehope spoke. 'She resents you for frightening Lacebold and hurting some of us. She's disappointed that you're so like the humans we left behind when she hoped for so much more. She wishes you had even half the courage of the kindred who died so you could live.'

'Courage?' Max Wilder's voice was so high-pitched it was almost a shriek. 'We've been frightened by stories of enforcers since we were children, but we alone of everyone in Rockwood found the COURAGE to come out fighting instead of cowering behind useless walls like everyone else.'

'YOU DIDN'T NEED TO FIGHT!' I couldn't stop myself from shouting.

The fresh spray of blood that accompanied my words prompted Lacehope to speak the rest of my reply for me. 'The kindred of our city never fought us even though we killed their fellow humans. It didn't matter how bad things were, how frightening, they always had the COURAGE,' she shouted, echoing the mental emphasis I put on the word, 'to follow what their sixth sense – their intuition, as you call it – led them to do. If you think fighting and killing anything that scares you makes you brave, then you don't have the faintest idea of what courage is.'

Alan Nixon's eyes flicked between Lacehope and me as she spoke my words, and I felt his surprise as he compared her to a nine-year-old human. His grandmother had told him we were bred to mature much more quickly than humans, but he found Lacehope's confidence and bearing almost as disconcerting as did the hunters. They shifted about on their feet, as uncomfortable with their sense and sight of her as with the message she had spoken for me.

I felt desperation growing within Max Wilder as he sensed the support of his followers falling away from him; he had revelled in leading them, in having them obey his every word as the bravest and most skilled hunter. Without any of that, he would revert to just being a good hunter. He hadn't shown aptitude for herbalism or any of the singing skills that led to others in his village being respected – revered, even – and everyone knew it was rare for more than one person from a village to be chosen by a horse. Unbelievably, as far as Max Wilder was concerned, it was Alan Nixon, the grumpy baker, who had been chosen when Max Wilder would have been a far better choice.

His fear extends far beyond merely the threat to his life, Benevolence agreed. *And of the humans of the new way of life he is not unusual. You see now.*

Why we need to leave them alone? Yes, I think we're all clear about that. The humans need to develop courage before they can cope with being near us.

It is not just the humans who will benefit from time to mature and evolve in the absence of provocation. So too will your kind require time to recover from your history so that you may venture in a different direction from that for which you were created. The humans indeed chose to act out of fear rather than according to their inner guidance but so did you.

I was protecting my younglings!

They were safely behind you when you pursued the humans with the intention of killing them.

I was spared from the need to respond to Benevolence's uncomfortable observation by Max Wilder. He ground his jaws together as I sensed him step away from the truth Lacehope had spoken, to the lie that gave him comfort. He squared his shoulders and stuck out his chest, followed by his chin. 'I know what courage is. It's standing up for your family and friends, even when they don't appreciate it, and getting rid of any threat to them so they can sleep at night.' He pointed at my younglings and me with a sweep of his arm, and walked towards us. 'None of you should be here. You should never have been created, but since you were, you should have perished with the cities. You're not human and you're not animal, you're not even enforcers anymore because there's nothing for you to enforce. You're just woeful.' He shook his head as he stopped by Benevolence's muzzle.

Alan Nixon leant forward and swung a leg over Benevolence's back. Once he was on the ground, he moved to stand in front of Max Wilder so their noses almost touched. 'And you're a silly little boy who wants to run back to his mother for approval she won't give you, because you're a being a tool. I don't care what you think of them,' he said, flicking his head sideways towards us, 'but when Benevolent gives you counsel, you act on it. Grow up and find the courage to follow your inner voice, which sure as hell isn't telling you to behave as you are. If you can't do that, then go back to Rockwood and leave the woeful... I mean... them... alone. You're never to hunt them again. Do you understand? Ben tells me they SHOULD be here – that they, and only they, will be able to give humans the help they'll need in the future, but until that time, they should be left ALONE.'

Max Wilder stuck his chin out so that it touched Alan Nixon's. 'And if I don't?'

Alan Nixon butted his forehead suddenly and violently to Max Wilder's, and the younger man sat down very suddenly on the ground. In the next instant, Benevolence was standing between them, shielding his bonded human from Max Wilder's influence so that Alan Nixon could remember the part of himself that resonated with his horse. He looked up to the sky in frustration with himself.

I'm sorry, Ben, he told his horse. *He's always been a little upstart and old habits die hard.*

Yet they will die given time, Benevolence answered. I sensed his response was also for me.

The Way Of The Horse lives in us all, I agreed. Then I added, *None of us could have survived without it, yet we ignore it at will.*

Proving my point, Max Wilder got to his feet, side-stepped Benevolence, and punched Alan Nixon in the face. His disregard for Ben's presence and advice was as incendiary to me as it had been to Alan Nixon; it wasn't just the horse we both loved whom he had dismissed, but Charlotte Lace and everyone else who had followed The Way Of The Horse regardless of the consequences. I flew at Max Wilder.

Chapter Thirty-Two

Let it further be recorded for the Histories that on this day, the Second Saturday of November, Eighth Year of the Eighth Decade of The New, more than forty Horse-Bonded and their horses passed by our village at speed. When we heard them coming, we thought our hopes had been answered and they were here to protect us, yet they galloped straight past us all without word or glance in our direction as we stood gathered in welcome. While the sight of them lifted our hearts, their apparent single-mindedness and unprecedented number have only confirmed the magnitude of the peril in which we have found ourselves, leaving us feeling more desperate than ever.

Histories of The New, Keeper Milicent Butler

MAX WILDER THOUGHT he was safe; he thought the presence of the horse he had ignored would ensure it. And it should have. Yet his attitude and behaviour were infectious, I realised far too late. When I looked back on what happened, I consoled myself with the fact that Alan Nixon had succumbed to them too, despite being Benevolence's bonded human and far more under his influence than I. Even so, Charlotte Lace would have been horrified at my behaviour and therefore, on reflection, so was I.

Fortunately for me, after my talons had shredded the neck of Max Wilder's shirt and coat and scored the pale, delicate skin that lay underneath, and I had raised my other hand with the intention of slicing through the artery in his neck that I was so well-trained to target, I became distracted by tremors in the ground beneath my feet, which rapidly increased in magnitude and were soon audible. I looked into the distance, to where a gigantic dust cloud hung over the plain. Its source was immediately obvious to my sixth sense as soon as I focused upon it, which wasn't easy over Max Wilder's shrieking.

The horses were a spectacular sight as they tore towards us side by side, I guessed so that the humans on their backs wouldn't be blinded by dust as would have occurred had they been following one another. Their long neck hair almost appeared to float above them, obscuring the riders I could sense bending low on their horses' backs so as to provide as little resistance to the air as possible. They rode with the same sense of urgency as that which drove their horses to carry them at such speed, and as I stood next to Benevolence on trembling legs, clutching Max Wilder and with Alan Nixon sitting dazedly at my feet, the world seemed to swim and tumble around me.

The dormitory in which I and my younglings had been raised shimmered before me, only to be replaced by my cell. Different handlers came and went, collecting and depositing me before and after my kills at such speed that weeks, no months, passed before me in an instant. Then Charlotte Lace was before me, talking calmly to those who would intimidate her, smiling at me, supporting me and radiating everything I wanted to be but still, despite all my efforts, was not. My younglings swam around me, their scared faces transforming into happy, confident ones even though in reality they stood nearby, paralysed with horror at the sight before them. Max Wilder's hurtful words came back to me, his face contorted and snarling in front of mine though in fact, it ran with tears as he struggled in my grasp and begged for his life.

I couldn't seem to pull myself out of the waking nightmare that the horses' desperate race across the plain had evoked within me... because I knew it was I who was the cause of their urgency. It was I who would determine the way forward for us all – who could send us all into a spiral from which it would take many generations to pull back. It was I who had caused so many bonded horses to unite in order to prevent it.

Benevolence was next to swirl around before me even though, in fact, he stood by my side. Both versions of him were patient and loving as he waited for me to choose wisely regarding the man who squirmed and squealed in my grasp. Yet he and the horses who rushed to his aid knew that his influence alone wasn't enough to ensure I would.

It was, however, enough to draw me out of myself so that I swirled around with the rest of my past and looked back to see who I really was. It was enough to help me admit to myself what I had been denying; I wanted to kill Max Wilder. Not because it was necessary to protect my younglings or anyone else, but because I wanted to hurl all my rage into the act. I wanted to expel everything I felt about the violence and cruelty of humans through my hands and talons, and see it soak into the ground along with the hunter's blood.

I raised the hand that had dropped to my side, and prepared, with relish, to slit his throat. The hooves of countless horses beat even harder and faster on the ground, drawing my attention away from the blackest part of my nature, to their increasing desperation. They wrapped themselves around me and held me stationary even as I held Max Wilder above the ground, urine dripping from his legs as he kicked them in mid-air. The horses weren't afraid of me or what I would do, but intensely loyal to a cause that had been in place since the beginning of time. And they were powerful. Try as I might, I couldn't break their hold on me. As they got close enough for their dust cloud to obscure the gentle warmth of the autumn sun, I found myself relaxing even as they tightened their hold further – for it was infused throughout with Benevolence.

Fine, brown dust wafted gently past me, carried on the light wind that preceded the horses and their Horse-Bonded. I coughed as I breathed it in, spraying blood over Max Wilder who now hung limply from my hand. I lowered him to the ground but maintained my hold on the torn collars of his shirt and coat.

No one spoke; I sensed my younglings' fear, and that of the hunters and Alan Nixon, that if they did, they might break the spell that was holding me.

The horses galloped around us in a mass of hooves, neck hair and sweat, forming a circle around me, my younglings, Alan Nixon, Max Wilder and Benvolence, and separating us from the rest of the hunters. Max Wilder didn't try to run when I finally let go of the shreds of clothing from which I had suspended him.

The horses came to a stop, all of them facing the centre of the circle they had formed and blowing hard, their sides heaving and their nostrils flaring red. It wasn't until the dust had cleared that I noticed their riders sitting in silence upon – and sweating and breathing as hard as – their horses as they took in the sight with which we presented them.

It was some time before anyone moved. Laceheart was first. He walked slowly, carefully, to the nearest horse, on an arc rather than a direct line to her, his body turned slightly away as he got closer. The horse didn't move, but her rider stiffened initially, then relaxed and gave a slight nod of surprise and approval as his horse accepted Laceheart's approach without concern. Once in front of them, he stood still and did nothing, still turned slightly away from the horse. I could feel him exploring her as an individual now that he was close enough to separate her from the rest within his mind. The horse reached towards him and gently rested her muzzle on my youngling's shoulder.

It was a beautiful sight and so at odds with the scene in which I had been recently engaged that I felt the need to step away from Max Wilder – to leave the world I had so nearly entered, and root myself in the one that Laceheart and the horse were sharing; the one that offered potential rather than just a rehash of the same story that had been lived and re-lived, over and over again. I blinked at my realisation and was suddenly awash with sorrow.

Lacekeen and Lacehope wrapped their arms around my torso.

It's okay, Lace, Lacehope assured me. *You didn't do it. You didn't go through with it.*

Her words were no comfort. I hadn't gone through with it because more than fifty horses had run themselves to exhaustion in order to join with Benevolence and stop me. I sank to the ground beside Max Wilder, who flinched and scrambled away from me.

'She won't hurt you now,' Alan Nixon said to him, his voice firm but not unkind, despite the strange angle of his nose and the rapidly forming bruises around both of his eyes. 'According to Benevolent, she's sorrowful. So should you be.'

I sensed Max Wilder's intention to defend his actions as he opened his mouth. He shut it again without issue as the horses standing in a circle around us all moved closer, tightening their circle so that even one as witless as the twenty-six-year-old, urine-drenched male, who was still too weak with fear to recover enough strength in his legs to get up, could feel its effect. Stripped bare of his fear and aggression, Max Wilder seemed to shrink to half his size, so that his clothes almost appeared to be too big, though neither he nor they had altered. He began to cry.

The horses standing between us and the rest of his group turned away and made a larger circle that now included the remaining hunters. A young female walked tentatively to Max Wilder, crouched down beside him, and pulled him to her. She wrinkled her nose at the smell emanating from him, but didn't stop comforting him.

I knew what I had to do. It was only because of strength borrowed from fifty-seven horses that I trusted myself to do it.

I got to my feet and walked the few steps to where the shamed and beaten hunter sat sobbing. I held my hands out in front of myself as so many humans had done to me while begging for their lives; the gesture had never prevented me from completing my assignments but I hoped it would confirm the sense I was attempting to convey to Max Wilder, while the horses still had hold of both of us, that I no longer meant him any harm.

'I will take measures to educate my kind as to the necessity of staying away from yours,' I told him, my voice the faintest of whispers and my swallowing frequent so that I expelled no more blood. 'I require your assurance that you'll support those bonded to horses in their efforts to ensure that if, by chance, any human should catch sight of one of us, they will allow us to leave unmolested and unpursued. You and I have proven what Benevolence tried to tell me; our races have much healing to do before we can be trusted in one another's presence.'

He glanced up at me and then quickly looked back down at the ground, unable to bear the sight of my gaze upon him. He gave the briefest of nods.

'You should speak your agreement so that all here, including yourself, can hear it,' Alan Nixon said. 'That's Benevolent's advice,' he added.

Max Wilder bit his lip and then said, still looking at the ground, 'If the woeful leave us alone, we'll leave them alone.'

I turned and hobbled wearily away from him.

Chapter Thirty-Three

Let it be recorded for the Histories on this day, the Second Sunday of November, Eighth Year of the Eighth Decade of The New, that late last night, our Hunters returned to us accompanied by four Horse-Bonded, including our own Alan Nixon with his Bond-Partner, Benevolent! It seems that Hunter Wilder was correct, and it was indeed a single Enforcer who scared us all witless. Not only that, but the Enforcers are not such any more, and are to be known as "Woeful" on account of the fact that they are as much refugees from the perished cities as the rest of us. We have been told in no uncertain terms by the Horse-Bonded that no human is ever to hunt a Woeful again. Should we happen to see one, we can be sure that they will be as keen to avoid us as we are them, and will retreat so that we may do the same. The feeling in Rockwood is largely one of relief, tempered with trepidation for what lies ahead.

Histories of The New, Keeper Milicent Butler

MY YOUNGLINGS and I retreated to the forest without looking back at the humans, but I was aware of Laceheart looking back at the horses now and then as they watched us leave. I wondered whether we would ever see Benevolence again and doubted it. He had done what he could to educate me, in order to prevent the situation that had just occurred. More horses and their bonded humans had come to his and Alan Nixon's aid when I defied him, and together they had succeeded. Humans and kindred would avoid one another so that we didn't risk pulling our races back to the old way of life. Benevolence had done what he set out to do, and I wouldn't blame him if he never wanted to see any of us again.

My younglings and I remained in the forest for almost a week, resting and in my case recovering, thanks to Laceheart's ministrations.

'The humans sing each other better,' he told me apologetically one day after I managed, for the first time since the confrontation with the hunters, to use my voice without blood erupting from my throat, and thank him out loud for his help. 'Three of those hunters can do it. I searched their memories while they were watching you and Max Wilder, and I know how they do it, but my voice won't work like theirs; I can't make the sounds they do. I'm not human enough.'

'They sing to rocks to make them move when they're building walls and houses too,' Lacebold said. 'I tried to copy the sounds they were making when they were building their walls to keep me out, but I couldn't do it either. It's like you said; we're not made that way.'

'I don't think we should try to do what the humans do,' I said. 'We can do plenty of things they can't. Where they are deaf and blind to so much of the world around them, we hear and see. We should focus on that and on taking our guidance from the forests.'

All five younglings nodded thoughtfully.

'When we get back to Winterwood,' I continued, 'I'd like all of you to spend time with the other younglings. Talk to them of your time alone with the forests, and encourage them to go off and find themselves when they're ready. They're unlikely to be for some time, but we have to hold the thought between us that they will be at some stage. That way, they'll pick up the sense that it's not in question whether they'll go, but inevitable. Benevolence was careful to make sure I understood that the survival of our race depends on it.'

I was pleased that they took it upon themselves not to wait for our return to our community before doing as I had asked. Where they had held themselves mentally apart from their peers while they were alone with the forests, they now reached out to all of those sensitive enough to be aware of them and regaled them with stories of their travels and everything they had learnt.

By the time we arrived back in Winterwood several weeks later, many of the younglings waited for us at the edge of the forest. Most of them had persuaded adults to accompany them as had been my rule when I left, but a few had defied me and come without. My heart lifted. They would be the first to leave on their findself, and sooner than I had originally thought.

Ash and Hob left the trees in which they had perched to watch our approach, bringing their younglings out onto the plain with them, to welcome us.

We are relieved to have you back with us, Hob told me.

I noticed the white hair that now dotted her forehead and Ash's cheeks. Though they had made no decisions without checking first with me, acting on those decisions or causing others to act on them had been as much of a strain for them as it was for me.

I am relieved to be back, was my only reply. I didn't need to tell them what had happened, for they knew. Just like when we had been in our cells in the enforcer building, our mutual knowing of each other's difficulties was a source of togetherness and comfort that continued to take the edge off the hardships we endured.

My mind flicked to Alan Nixon, knowing that he gained the same comfort from his bond with Benevolence. I was surprised to find them, not back at the home they shared with other bonded horses and humans, but at a village even further from it than was Rockwood. I was even more surprised to sense Alan Nixon sitting astride his horse, talking passionately about us "woeful" and how we were as much victims of the old way of life – "the old" as he had taken to calling it, as everyone who had escaped the cities before we were created. He was very careful to emphasise Ben's counsel that if any of the villagers ever spotted any of us, they should return to their village immediately so that we could be left to go on our way in peace and without provocation. Why he was using Max Wilder's name for us, I didn't understand until I realised that while Max Wilder had meant it as an insult, Alan Nixon genuinely saw us that way; sad and worthy of pity and compassion. He had changed as a result of Ben's influence, but he was still, as I had told my younglings, blind and deaf to much of what was before him.

We were best off well away from humans, I realised all over again. And I would ensure, if it were the last thing I did, that all the leaders of the other communities understood that and obeyed the agreement I had made to leave the humans to themselves.

But what if they don't leave us alone? A leader from one of the furthest communities from mine asked me when I reached for her and told her what had happened. *Can we trust them not to come after us if they see any of us and get scared, like they did with your youngling?*

We can trust the horses who are bonded to humans to ensure they don't, I replied, my thought strong with certainty. *That brings me to the other stipulation I will make. You must ensure that none of your community ever hunt horses who are bonded to humans. Never. Without them, all of us will return to the old way of life. ALL OF US. Do you understand?*

There was no way she couldn't – the feelings and memories I associated with my order made sure of it. She was thoughtful for a while as she explored everything I had imparted to her. When I felt her grasp of what was at stake overshadowing her reluctance to have her community's hunting limited, I let her be. No more instruction was necessary for now.

Not all the community leaders were as sensitive and astute as she, and it was months before I felt confident that they had all understood and accepted the way forward I had unequivocally laid out for them.

My younglings took good care of me during that time, making sure I was fed and watered when I forgot to ask for rations for myself, spending time with me every day so that I had the company of those who didn't need me to tell them what to do at every step of our new way of life, and, in Laceheart's and increasingly Lacekeen's cases, bringing me plant essences and herbs they thought I needed for mental and sometimes physical support.

'Ashhelp has gone on his findself,' Lacebold announced to me proudly one morning. 'Ash was upset and Lacefirm and I didn't want Ashhelp to be put off from going at the last minute, so we went with him to the edge of the forest.'

I smiled at him. He would always be more strong-willed than all the other younglings put together, but he employed a level of thoughtfulness that rendered his actions appropriate to the situation in question, and the other members of our community –

even the adults – usually heeded him as a result. They went to Laceheart when they needed medication to help their bodies or minds, and took what he gave them – herbs, plant essences and advice – as if he were a sage of adult years. Lacehope too was seen as a source of wisdom, Lacekeen as one who could always provide encouragement and motivation, and Lacefirm as one who could easily settle disputes.

During my occasional forays out of my shelter, I saw and felt the reactions of my kin to my appearance, and knew I was still ageing at a fast and visibly obvious rate – I could see it in the ever-whitening colour of my coat and I could feel it in the weariness that I increasingly couldn't shake, despite Laceheart's care. It was therefore as much of a relief as it was unbelievable to me, whenever I gave myself leave from my own work to think about it, that five nine-year-olds had essentially become the leaders of our community.

When the winter weather set in, it was Lacefirm and Lacekeen who discovered that the dense, soft, furry plants that grew low to the ground in damp spots were perfect for plugging the tiny gaps between the woven vines of our shelters to keep out the cold. It was Lacebold who encouraged our hunters to store excess meat in ice that he chipped from the edge of our water pool, so that we had food on days when we were all better off staying inside. It was Lacehope who kept everyone's spirits up on those darkest, coldest days, and it was Laceheart who visited every shelter on a regular basis, checking their inhabitants, dispensing his remedies and either answering their questions himself or sending along whichever of my younglings he thought better suited to do so.

When spring arrived, bringing warmth, blossoms, easier hunting and the prospect of gathering plants for food again, my younglings, far from being exhausted like the rest of us, had an extra level of vibrancy about them. It was they who organised us all to travel back north before the heat in the south became uncomfortable for us adults, and they who kept everyone together behind me while I pretended – as they insisted I did for the sake of morale – that it was I who still led them when in fact, I could barely put one foot in front of the other or follow one thought with the next.

When they turned ten years old, I couldn't help thinking that the humans were so much poorer for remaining apart from us; they may have been able to use their voices in ways we couldn't, but my younglings were proving just how much the kindred could achieve when we used the abilities at our disposal.

There would be a time in the future when we, humans and horses would help one another. That was what Benevolence had told me. I often wondered how far in the future that would be, but eventually decided it didn't matter. I only hoped that the descendants of my younglings would be there to witness it.

Chapter Thirty-Four

NOTICE TO ALL AT THE GATHERING
from Overseer Kennet Bloom

Hi everyone, I'm new here, so I might make a mess of this, but I gather no one else wanted to take on the role of Overseer, so here I am. Conviction helps me to knuckle down and get on with things when he isn't confusing me, so if you'll bear with me, I'll get to grips with the role as soon as I can. Could any new Horse-Bonded register with me as soon as possible after arrival, please? I gather there is a steady stream of us, and it's important to get everyone onto the chore rota as soon as possible so that the roles vacated by all those off travelling between the villages are filled as soon as possible. Many thanks!

I HAVE MANAGED to hang on until my younglings are twelve. I've been a burden to them during the last two years, I know I have, though they will never admit it. I acknowledge that my reasons for hanging on to the life that is now very definitely slipping away from me have been selfish – I have longed to see the proof that my race will survive; that where we were created, one by one, by humans, future kindred can and will be conceived and born naturally.

My younglings have now reached adolescence, and their vitality has increased a hundredfold. I sense the males watching the females and vice versa, as none in my generation ever have – our control programs sapped any desire we felt by associating it with pain and anxiety, and the association persisted – but as yet, there are no naturally-born babies or even pregnancies.

Laceheart is adamant that some of the younglings' bodies will venture down the pathway towards reproduction and that they will succeed, but I can't hang on any longer in order to witness it. When my kin travel south for the winter on the morrow, I will remain here, in the forest that was the first to nurture us and to which we have returned every year since. It feels right that my body should give back a tiny amount of what it took from the forest to which we all owe so much, and that I should burden my community no longer by attempting to travel with them.

I'm not looking forward to telling my younglings my decision, however. Lacebold and Lacefirm will argue with me about it. Lacehope and Lacekeen will try to persuade me I am wrong. Only Laceheart will remain silent; only he will turn to the forest and his awareness of everything to which he is connected, and know I am right. He always has the final say if there is any disagreement between the five of them, since they all accept that he is most closely attuned to the forest, but the time that will elapse between them discovering my decision and leading our community south without me will be uncomfortable.

I am proud that any one of them could take on the mantle alone and manage it better than I ever did. They aren't weighed down like I was by the responsibility and decisions that need to be made on a daily basis, and I've never quite been able to pinpoint exactly why.

They were raised with love.

Benevolence? I hardly dare to hope it's him. We've had no contact since the day I came to within a hair's breadth of killing Max Wilder, and I haven't dared even to reach for him since I discovered the mission upon which he and Alan Nixon embarked to prevent humans from hunting us; I knew I would be too tempted to seek him out and break the agreement he and his human were promoting.

We are here.

Here?

Everyone, a horse and a human are approaching our village, Laceheart broadcasts urgently. *No one is to threaten or harm them in any way. All of you who can sense my message, tell it to any of your neighbours who can't use mindspeak, straight away.*

The horse, I can just about manage, Hob replies, *but no human should be here.* Her thought pulses with hostility. *We leave them alone and they leave us alone. That's the agreement.*

They're here for me, I announce, *and they're welcome. Both of them. Obey Laceheart, all of you.* I can't seem to put much energy behind my thought to my community, and sense the surprise of those who pick it up and realise not only how weak I am but how long it's been since I've given any kind of instruction.

Those who are strong in their sixth sense move from reaching for me to doing so for Benevolence and Alan Nixon. They try to understand the bonded pair's reason for seeking us out when, to any other human, even a bonded one, it would be tantamount to suicide. Benevolence doesn't attempt to hide it from them, and Alan Nixon doesn't have the ability to do so.

I sense the gasps and cries I can't hear, and grimace at those I can, including those of all my younglings except Laceheart. Even he will find it difficult to leave me though – he will need the extra strength that only Benevolence can give him.

The horse affects him as soon as Laceheart reaches for him, and I feel him nodding to himself as he finishes skinning one of the rabbits he killed earlier in the day, though he's biting his bottom lip to stop it trembling. He puts the meat to one side to bring to me, and goes to meet the friend he has missed so much.

The rest of my younglings come crashing down through the branches to my shelter, all thoughts of Benevolence and Alan Nixon forgotten.

'We're not leaving you here,' Lacebold says whilst still in mid-air. He lands just inside the doorway of the shelter Lacekeen wove for me when we arrived back here months ago, and hurries to the side in order to make space for Lacehope. He only just gets clear in time for her to land and similarly make room for Lacefirm, who shakes both her head and a finger at me as she makes way for Lacekeen.

I look up at my beautiful younglings and smile faintly. I don't attempt to speak, for the thickening in my throat has long since prevented it. *I'm proud of you all. I know the four of you and Laceheart will do a better job than I ever managed of leading our kin until, like me, you are too old and weary to continue.*

'You're not old, you're twenty-three!' Lacekeen says. 'None of the other adults are giving up and you shouldn't either.'

It is true they will outlive me, but they will not live to see nearly as many years as your generation will. Our past has enough of a hold upon us that each move away from it has taken its toll – especially on me, as is obvious.

Saving us has killed you, Lacefirm observes sadly.

The problems that have arisen and the decisions I have taken have all used far more of my energy than I would have liked, but I regret none of them and I certainly don't regret saving you. The five of you, who you are and what you've become, have made my life worth living. Now I need you to make me proud one last time, and leave me here.

We aren't leaving you to die alone, Lacebold protests.

I won't be alone; Benevolence will be with me. Now, carry on making your preparations to leave. Our kindred need you, as do all of those in the other communities. Their leaders are all adults and so haven't even attempted the findself you've all achieved. Of their younglings who have left to attempt theirs, none have yet returned. The adult leaders will need your strength and insights until their younglings come back to them, as they hopefully will.

It has been several years since any of my younglings have demonstrated their youth, but the way they cling to me, all four of them at once – one on either side and one each on my front and back – reminds me how quickly they have been forced to grow up and how young in years they still are. I hate myself for not having the strength to be there for them in the years to come, and feel sad that I'll never know whether any of them will be parents by blood instead of by adoption as I have been.

You can know. Laceheart has found Benevolence and the strength he needs to do as he knows he must. As has happened before when they've been in close proximity, I can't tell whether the thought that was whispered, so gently yet so confidently, into my mind originated with the horse or my youngling. It matters not; they are as inseparable as the horses are from one another, and that is a good thing.

I can see the future? How? I ask.

They take hold of me and lead me gently to the threads

extending from all five of my younglings to those with whom they will share a connection physically at some point in their lives. There are so many of them and I don't have the mental capacity to search them all for the information I want – no, need.

Here. They guide me to a thread that, unlike many we pass on the way, is insubstantial – yet not in the way of those whose lives have expired. Where those of Lacehope's human handlers, and the prey animals she has killed, are the thinnest of threads that hold echoes of the past, this one, while as thin, holds a promise for the future.

My heart beats more strongly. *Lacehope will have a daughter.* I have the faintest sense of her, though at the moment, "she" isn't a female kindred but the idea of one waiting to happen. *Thank you.*

There has been no hiding my brief exploratory journey from my other four younglings, and they all pull apart from me slightly, Lacekeen, Lacefirm and Lacebold all looking at Lacehope with wonder in their eyes, and compassion as they sense her concern at venturing even further into the unknown; none of our kind have ever been pregnant, given birth or had to nurture a baby from our own bodies before.

We'll all help you, Lacefirm tells her, *and if anything happens that the three of us can't fix, Laceheart will know what to do. You won't be alone. And then there's whoever you choose as the father... you've already chosen.* She smiles. *Hobkind is a good choice.*

I can't help wishing I could be here to be a part of the future upon which they will embark in my absence – but then just as quickly, the energy required to wish such a thing fades. This will be their future, their time to continue creating a new world for the kindred.

But you'll always be part of it, Lacehope tells me. I'll name her after you and the human you loved. My daughter will be called *Lacespirit.*

I smile. *Lacespirit.* As I repeat the name, I feel the thread between her and mother-to-be become a little more substantial. She won't be too long waiting to be born into this world.

All young born to our kind should carry the names forward of the human kindred who died making sure of their existence, Lacebold decides suddenly. *It shouldn't be just us, it should be something our race takes forward forever.* He moves from where he has been snuggled against my back, to sit in front of me and takes my hands in his. *The name you chose will live on forever, I'll make sure of it. I love you, Lace.*

I love you all too. I reach out to Laceheart and draw him into the mental embrace within which I am already holding his siblings. *Make haste now in your preparations to leave, knowing you have made me happier than I ever thought possible.*

The four with me get to their feet obediently if reluctantly, bend to embrace me and then leave, the three females exiting my shelter first.

Lacebold?

He turns in the entrance and looks back at me.

You were right to be curious about the humans' ability to laugh, so don't ever regret what happened as a result; if it hadn't come to pass, we never would have learnt how important it is to avoid them. Make sure, won't you, that every youngling in every community understands that before going on their findself? And that hunting bonded horses is forbidden? You, above all others, know that both of those things are as important for the continued survival of our kind as the findself, and you above all others have the strength to ensure the rules are obeyed.

I feel the slight weight lift that he has been carrying within his mind, and he almost smiles. *I will ensure the rules are obeyed.*

I nod faintly, feeling even weaker now that the last of my concerns has been addressed. Then I turn my attention inward and use all of my remaining will to keep my body going just a little longer.

Chapter Thirty-Five

Let it be recorded for the Histories that on this day, the Second Wednesday of October, Tenth Year of the Eighth Decade of The New, a Woeful was sighted in the forest closest to Plainsview, and moved on without challenge or being challenged. Five hours later, Paul Nolan of the Horse-Bonded arrived in the village with his horse, Steadfast, and announced their intention to remain until any lingering fear and upset has passed.

Histories of The New, Keeper Jinna Lace

I WAKE WITH THE DAWN, knowing it is my last. Having tried so very hard to stay alive up until this point, it feels strange to realise that I feel almost as much joy as I do sadness at the thought of dying, and even stranger to discover that I feel absolutely no fear. The presence of Benevolence will not allow it.

I use the last of my strength to get onto my hands and knees, crawl outside my shelter to the low, wide branch on which the middle part of it rests, and climb down the trunk of the tree that has nurtured me during my visits to this particular forest. My talons are blunt where I have neglected to sharpen them, and when they fail to maintain a hold on the dark brown bark of the tree, my arms don't have the strength to drive them in deeper.

There is a rustle beneath me as I fall the short distance to the ground… and I land on something warm and solid. Benevolence shifts closer to the tree trunk so that, sitting sideways on his back as I now am, I can regain my hold on it and support myself as I slide from his back to the soft, welcoming floor of the forest.

Thank you.

Make haste to present yourself in a way that will help them to leave you. They come. While Benevolence is addressing me, he ensures that Alan Nixon receives the message too.

The human gets to his feet and brushes dirt and fallen leaves from his clothes. He folds his blanket, spreads the remains of the fire that helped to keep him warm as he and Benevolence held vigil beneath my shelter all night, and moves to stand by my side even as my legs give way and I sit down with my back against the tree trunk. Ben stands on my other side so that when my younglings arrive at my shelter to find it empty, sense where I am and drop easily to the floor around us, we present a united front.

Benevolence doesn't give them an opportunity to change their minds about leaving me. He takes a step forward, his movement combining with his calm, compassionate presence to ensure he has their full attention. *We will remain with your parent. At no time will she be alone. Leave now so that you do not cause her to try to stay beyond her time.*

Laceheart nods immediately and sinks to his knees in front of me. Tears spill over his lower eyelids and cling to the short, fine hairs of his face until they are too many and form a stream that drips from his chin. He blinks repeatedly so that he can stare into my eyes, willing me to know everything he feels for me. Then he gets to his feet and makes way for Lacekeen, who holds me tightly before moving quickly aside, desperate not to make the situation harder for me. Lacefirm is next. She wipes her face and touches her wet fingers to my cheeks so that her tears blend with mine. Then she touches her lips followed by mine, like humans do. When she stands and moves away, Lacehope throws herself into my lap and sobs openly, but like Lacekeen, doesn't linger any longer than is necessary for me to feel her love and her grief.

Lacebold waits until last. When he crouches in front of me, his eyes and cheeks are dry. He feels no less than the others, but I sense his determination to show me that my confidence in his strength is well placed. He will give the others the support they need and when they have moved past their sadness, he will allow them to support him in return. I manage to lift the corners of my mouth and move my head forward very slightly to acknowledge the effort I know it is taking him. He nods back and moves away.

'Right,' he says to the others. 'We'll get everyone together and be on our way. No one is to bother Lace. No one,' he adds firmly. 'She needs us to leave. Now. Come on.'

Their footfalls are heavier than normal as they move to nearby trees, and their ascent into the rapidly thinning canopy is laboured.

Over the next hour, the sounds of protests reach my ears, and desperate pleas for me to override my younglings' orders to leave me in peace bombard my mind. Benevolence and Laceheart stand between my mind and all of theirs, filtering out the pain and allowing only the love my kin feel for me to reach me as my body weakens. I am prouder than ever of my younglings that they reach for me not at all.

Then there is silence, apart from the tapping of orange and brown leaves as they knock into branches on their way to the ground; the calls of the birds who continue to welcome in the new day; and the whistling of my short, rapid breaths as I struggle to force them past the thickening in my throat.

Alan Nixon, who has stood before me since my younglings left, with the brave intention of barring the way from any of my kin fearful enough at the news of my impending death to defy their new leaders' instructions, now sits down beside me. Benevolence, who stood all night in a dozing watch lest I woke and felt anything other than calm about my impending departure, lies down at my feet. He lowers his nose amongst the leaves and breathes out a long, deep breath so that those which are nearest flutter where they have come to rest.

Thank you. For coming. For making this easier on my younglings. For everything, I tell Benevolence. I don't have the strength to reach Alan Nixon through him, but sense that Ben has ensured my thought reaches them both.

'I'm sorry,' Alan Nixon says out loud. 'I just wanted to say that on behalf of all humans, because when it might have made a difference, none of us did.'

I am sorry too. I should have found the strength and courage to choose differently. My younglings will make better decisions than I did, and hopefully the next generation will do better still until the day comes when our races can come together in peace.

A heaviness I wasn't aware I possessed lifts from me, and I feel grateful to the human for allowing me to shed it. He nods when his horse enables him to sense my response, then he is silent.

The forest seems to be getting darker even though the sun has risen higher and its rays are reaching me with greater intensity. Benevolence fills my awareness, and I willingly follow where he leads. The world recedes from me until I view it only through a mere pinprick of light in the distance... and then not at all.

Where I was weak, suddenly I feel strong again – but this is a different type of strength. It is not finite and subject to the supply of food, water and acceptable circumstances, but more the total absence of fear, pain and weakness. I cannot see, yet I know Charlotte Lace is before me and she's smiling. She holds her hands out to me and I take them without concern that I will score her flesh, for none of my worldly concerns have any relevance anymore.

I panic as I realise that Benevolence is no longer with me. Then I realise that while the horse has returned his focus to the world I have left, he is always with me, for benevolence is all there is.

Epilogue

IT HAS BEEN five years since Lace left us and we all still miss her. I often think I see her in my peripheral vision, and sometimes I believe for a moment that I've caught her scent. Both phenomena are just echoes of the past though, unlike her influence, which continues to reach far beyond our community to all others, and is as strong as when she left. A lot of that is due to Lacebold and his promise to her, which he puts all his energy into upholding. Lacefirm does a good job of making sure he gets plenty of rest so that he doesn't age as quickly as did Lace.

We all feel the weight of the responsibility we took from our parent and mentor though, and we are ageing at a faster rate than our peers. Lacehope worries that she won't be around long enough to support Lacespirit until she is ready to go on her findself, but I have no concerns; the forest will continue to nurture all of us as surely as the horses and their human partners continue to protect us from the rest of the humans.

I've never witnessed them racing to villages whose occupants have caught sight of careless – and very occasionally disobedient

– younglings; I always sense the threat to one of my kind rippling through their forest to mine, then sense it abating under the influence of the horse and bonded human in question. It has been difficult at times to refrain from reaching out to the offending youngling to offer advice, or indeed from racing to the scene in order to provide protection as Lace attempted to do for Lacebold, but I know the importance of doing neither. When I forget, both the forest and Lacekeen are there to remind me.

It's happening again? she asks, my restlessness rousing her early from sleep beside me.

It's one of Hoyle's younglings, I reply. *She's been struggling to hunt enough recently and gave in to the temptation of stalking a human who was gathering herbs in her forest, to see if he had any food she could steal while he wasn't looking. Benevolence and Alan Nixon are visiting a nearby village and will be on their way to calm the villagers frightened by Hoyledeed at first light.*

I know you miss him, Laceheart. She reaches out in the darkness and takes my hand. *You can reach for Benevolence any time you want though, like Lace used to.*

I shake my head firmly as I lie beside her. *If I touch his mind, I can't help but affect his essence and, as a consequence, his bond with Alan Nixon. Benevolence must be free from interference if he is to wake The Way Of The Horse within the man whose influence on the son of his brother will carry through to the human who can mend the rift between our races. We must focus on helping Lacehope and Hobkind to ensure that Lacespirit acknowledges The Way Of The Horse within herself, so that it carries through to the kindred who will be the equal of the human for whom the horses all wait.*

Did the forest whisper the names of this human and this kindred to you, like it did when Taylorfix and Smithson asked you to name their baby? Lacekeen asks.

It did. Much time will pass before the world is ready for Amarilla Nixon and Lacejoy. When they make their entrance, it will be because the horses of the new dawn have called for them. Until then, the bonded horses of each generation will ensure our races avoid one another while supporting the humans' progress as the forests support ours.

The horses will be united in keeping us apart, Lacekeen observes.

I nod into the darkness. *And when the horses unite, the outcome is always certain.*

Books by Lynn Mann

The Horses Know Trilogy
The Horses Know
The Horses Rejoice
The Horses Return

Sequels to The Horses Know Trilogy
Horses Forever
The Forgotten Horses
The Way Of The Horse

Origins of The Horses Know Trilogy
The Horses Unite

Prequels to The Horses Know Trilogy
In Search Of Peace (Adam's story)
The Strength Of Oak (Rowena's story)
A Reason To Be Noble (Quinta's story)

Companion Stories to The Horses Know Trilogy
From A Spark Comes A Flame (Novella)
Tales Of The Horse-Bonded (Short Story Collection)

Tales Of The Horse-Bonded will take you on a journey into the lives of some of your favourite characters from *The Horses Know Trilogy*. The book is available for purchase in paperback and hardback, but is also available to download for free. To find out more, visit www.lynnmann.co.uk.

A regularly updated book list can be found at
www.lynnmann.co.uk/booklist
(The QR code below allows quick access!)

Did you enjoy The Horses Unite?
I'd be extremely grateful if you could spare a few minutes
to leave a review where you purchased your copy.
Reviews really do help my books to reach a wider audience,
which means that I can keep on writing!
Thank you very much.

———

I love to hear from you!
Get in touch and receive news of future releases at the following:

www.lynnmann.co.uk

www.facebook.com/lynnmann.author

Acknowledgments

None of my books would have reached publication without the help and support of my sister, and the same is true for this one to an even greater extent since the story of how the Enforcers became the Woeful was her idea. Thank you, Fern Sherry, for the idea, and for pushing me out of my comfort zone.

Thanks, as always, to my editorial team, of which Fern is a part along with Leonard Palmer, Caroline Macintosh and Cindy Nye. All of their help and advice has been as crucial and as appreciated as always.

Amanda Horan has created all of my book covers for me, and it's always an exciting part of the process as I love to see aspects of my stories brought to life by her talent. This is the first time, however, that seeing a cover for the first time has made me gasp! I'm very grateful to Amanda for producing a cover that is far more powerful than I could have envisaged.

Lastly, huge thanks to my wonderful husband for coming up with the title for the book. I had one in mind but it proved to be for the book that is likely to follow this one, and once it was in my head, I couldn't seem to move past it. I gave Darren a very brief synopsis of the story, and he came out with the perfect title, just like that! There was talk of him charging me for its use, but that seems to have died down for now so I'm hoping he's forgotten…

Printed in Great Britain
by Amazon